HOW IRELAND VOTED

THE IRISH GENERAL ELECTION 1987

Edited by
Michael Laver, Peter Mair & Richard Sinnott

POOLBEG

A Paperback Original
First published 1987 by
Poolbeg Press Ltd.
Knocksedan House
Swords, Co. Dublin, Ireland

in association with
PSAI Press
Social Sciences Research Centre
University College Galway

©PSAI Press, 1987

ISBN 905169 93 X

All rights reserved. No part of this publication may be reproduced or transmitted in any form or by any means, electronic or mechanical, including photocopy, recording, or any information storage or retrieval system, without permission in writing from the publisher. The book is sold subject to the condition that it shall not, by way of trade or otherwise, be lent, re-sold or otherwise circulated without the publisher's prior consent in any form of binding or cover other than that in which it is published and without a similar condition being imposed upon the subsequent purchaser.

Cover design by Stephen Hope
Maps by Michael and Conor Laver

Text origination by the
Centre for the Study of Irish Elections
University College Galway

Printed by
The Guernsey Press Co. Ltd, Guernsey, Channel Islands

CONTENTS

Acknowledgements

Introduction   1

1. The road to 1987   *Tom Garvin*   4

2. The campaign   *Brian Girvin*   9

3. Policy competition   *Peter Mair*   30

4. Campaign strategies: the selling of the parties   *David Farrell*   48

5. The Outcome   *Michael Gallagher*   63

6. Patterns of party support   99
     A Social class   *Richard Sinnott*   101
     B Issues, attitudes and party policy   *Michael Laver*   113
     C Leadership factors   *Michael Marsh*   127

7. The road from 1987: government formation and institutional inertia   *Brian Farrell*   141

8. The election in context: historical and European perspectives   *John Coakley*   153

Notes on Chapters   173

Appendix: Results and maps   180

Notes on contributors

ACKNOWLEDGEMENTS

This volume has been made possible by the collaboration of many people. The authors of the chapters, of course, deserve great praise for delivering high quality analyses to a very tight schedule. Philip MacDermott of Poolbeg had the interest in Irish politics and the enthusiasm for publishing that enabled these chapters to be published at all. Jack Jones and Aine O' Donoghue of the Market Research Bureau of Ireland were immensely co-operative, both in allowing Laver and Sinnott to poke their noses into the framing of survey questions in the first place and in making available their raw survey data for reanalysis.

The Centre for the Study of Irish Elections (CSIE) at Galway prepared the camera-ready copy, with the help of a grant from UCG's Presidential Committee on Research. Support from the Nuffield Foundation assisted the participation of Peter Mair in the project. Anne Byrne of the CSIE oversaw the entire production process, from copy editing to laser printing, with a fine attention to detail, while Michael Cuddy let us use his laser printer. Kay Donohue of UCG's Department of Political Science and Sociology and Mary Silke of the CSIE, both consummate keyboard artistes, input the original text.

If any one of these people had failed us, there would have been no book. But none did and for this we offer them our sincere thanks. Any blame, and there is probably plenty, rests firmly on the shoulders of the editors.

INTRODUCTION

The Irish general election of February 1987 inspires superlatives, as John Coakley argues in the final chapter of this book. A watershed election by any standards, it was the most volatile contest in postwar Irish history. Fianna Fáil recorded its lowest popular vote since 1961. For the fourth time in succession it failed to achieve an overall Dáil majority. Fine Gael, the main challenger to Fianna Fáil for the past fifty years, recorded its lowest popular vote since 1957. Labour, always on the margins of Irish politics was already one of the smallest social democratic parties in Western Europe. It recorded its lowest vote since 1933. The new Progressive Democrats, touting themselves as mould breakers *par excellence*, picked up almost 12% of the vote and, with fewer candidates, came within an ace of matching the record set by Clann na Poblachta in 1948, the last mould breakers in Irish politics. The Irish party system, long seen as among the most stable in Western Europe, now seems in disarray.

The February election has also provoked a striking new ideological clarity in Irish party politics, as Peter Mair argues in his chapter on the party programmes. Notwithstanding Labour's decline, there are clear signs of the emergence of a more vibrant and articulate left. The Workers' Party, for example, consolidated its achievement in the local elections of 1985 and again outpolled Labour in Dublin. Jim Kemmy of the Democratic Socialist Party regained his Limerick seat and the independent left wing TD Tony Gregory was also reelected. The left also appears to have made gains within the Labour Party itself, with the election of Emmet Stagg in Kildare and Michael D. Higgins in Galway. This shift has been mirrored on the other side of the political spectrum by the success of the Progressive Democrats, whose unabashed appeal to the middle class represents the most unequivocally conservative position seen in Irish politics for decades.

Both Fianna Fáil and Fine Gael face evident difficulties in their attempt to hold the centre of this increasingly polarised polity. In his chapter on the 1987 campaign, Brian Girvin charts the breakdown in relations between Fine Gael and Labour, and the rightward drift of the former as it attempted to head off the challenge of the Progressive Democrats. The problems facing Fianna Fáil are also significant and, though lying outside the scope of this book, are easily seen in the party's conversion to the politics of retrenchment during its first months of office. As Tom Garvin suggests, this new 'beggar-my-neighbour' approach to austerity poses an obvious challenge to the traditional catchall strategies which have long been a feature of modern Irish politics. The potential for catchall politics is further reduced by what appears to be an emerging class alignment of voting patterns, discussed by Michael Laver, Richard Sinnott and Michael Marsh in their analysis of the surveys preceding the February election. While party loyalties still seem strong enough to overwhelm both policy preferences and feelings about the party leaders, it is clear that all voters are no longer accessible to all parties. Fianna Fáil support is skewed quite heavily towards the petty bourgeoisie and the working class. Fine Gael and, in particular, Progressive Democrat support is skewed towards the bourgeoisie. Since the continuing economic recession is likely to accentuate the impact of economic self-interest on voting behaviour, these emerging electoral ghettos are likely to increase in importance.

All of this underlines the increasingly competitive nature of modern Irish politics and reinforces the significance of the February election. More intense party competition is clearly apparent at the electoral level, as Michael Gallagher demonstrates below in his analysis of voting patterns. It is also evident in the parties' campaign strategies, as David M. Farrell shows. Finally, as Brian Farrell suggests, governance itself is becoming more competitive, with government formation and survival now more finely balanced than at any point in the past thirty years.

For these and for many other reasons, the 1987 election merits close assessment, and it was felt that a first step in this process could usefully be undertaken by the Political Studies Association of Ireland (PSAI) through this volume of essays. These chart the background to the election (Garvin), the campaign itself (Girvin), as well as the policies (Mair) and marketing strategies (D. Farrell) of the parties. There are chapters analysing the actual results (Gallagher) and the evidence of the opinion surveys on the class basis of party support (Sinnott), the issues and the attitudes of the voters (Laver), and the impact of leadership factors (Marsh). Finally, there are chapters assessing both the process of government formation (B. Farrell) and the wider context of the election (Coakley).

The PSAI was formed in 1982 with the intention of promoting the study of politics in Ireland and of Irish politics generally. The Association now has a membership of around 140, mainly drawn from departments of politics and the other social sciences in Irish universities, as well as from universities in Britain, Australia, the United States and continental Europe. It publishes a bi-annual newsletter and, since 1986, has published a yearbook, *Irish Political Studies*, which includes articles, reports, book reviews, data and a comprehensive bibliography on politics in both Northern Ireland and the Republic. The formation of the PSAI and the success of the yearbook reflect a growing interest in Irish politics both at home and abroad. Political scientists are now employed on the staffs of all the major universities both North and South, as well as in the National Institutes of Higher Education, the Institute of Public Administration in Dublin, and in various other centres. Courses on Irish politics now constitute core elements in the degree programmes of an increasing number of British universities, not least as a result of recent inter-governmental promotion of Irish Studies in the UK.

Yet Irish political science remains a fledgling discipline. Despite all of the recent interest, the formal and systematic study of Irish politics, and of politics in the Republic in particular, remains in its infancy. While there is now a substantial cumulated knowledge of party politics, for example, we are still groping our way towards an understanding of electoral behaviour and voter orientations. The newly-formed Centre for the Study of Irish Elections in University College Galway may go some way towards achieving the necessary improvement in understanding, but much more needs to be done. A full scale election study is urgently required, particularly in this period of political flux, and funds for proper scientific research are desperately needed.

We also need to look more closely at the political and policy experiences of our European neighbours and, in particular, at the experience of the other small democracies in Western Europe, which confront many of those same problems which now face the Republic. As both John Coakley and Brian Farrell emphasise in their chapters in this volume, Irish attitudes to political institutions and Irish modes of decision making are still far too constrained by the Westminster model and tend to neglect what are arguably more appropriate European examples. We also tend to neglect the lessons which can be learned from the industrial, fiscal and welfare strategies of the other small West European democracies which, as Peter Katzenstein has recently argued in his masterly *Small States in World Markets,* share dilemmas which are often similar to those of the contemporary Republic.

One of the goals of the PSAI is to heighten Irish awareness of these other political experiences and thus to broaden our domestic political horizons. Such an effort forms a natural companion to the more immediate task of promoting a better understanding of Irish politics itself, both at home and abroad, a task towards which the current volume is dedicated.

Michael Laver, Peter Mair and Richard Sinnott
Galway, Manchester and Dublin, July 1987

1. THE ROAD TO 1987

Tom Garvin

Irish party politics have traditionally been seen as eccentric and incomprehensible by outside observers, accustomed as they commonly are to the practices of the larger and better-known western democracies. Our peculiar brand of proportional representation, for example, which we share only with Malta, has encouraged a style of electoral competition which blends intense parish-pump intrigue with an equally thoroughgoing pragmatism at national level.

Newcomers to the system are particularly bemused by the intense and emotional rivalry that exists between Fianna Fáil and Fine Gael, parties whose names have unknown meanings for the majority of voters. (Indeed their meanings are doubtful even to those who are proficient in the official vernacular of the Republic, as distinct from those who can merely speak English).

A particularly confusing aspect of the Irish party system is the belief, borne out by most survey research, that voters see these two arch rivals as occupying approximately the same centre-right position on the ideological spectrum. In other western countries, the parties are normally arrayed along a generally understood left-to-right scale and, when one party is spoken of as being to the left or the right of another, this statement has a meaning for ordinary people. Irish voters cannot, however, say this of Fianna Fáil and Fine Gael; indeed survey evidence suggests not only that the parties are very close together on the spectrum but that they also have occasionally even exchanged places on it. Those who pine for the clarities of (say) Italian, French or Portuguese politics complain that the Irish party system looks rather like a psephological *Alice in Wonderland*, in which Tweedledum and Tweedledee incessantly fight over that nice new rattle.

Historically, the Irish parties have their origins in a small but intensely bitter civil war, a war which soured relations between leaders far more than it did among the general population. This was so partly because, unlike most civil wars, the casualties were made up disproportionately of leaders and activists rather than of their followers and of innocent civilians. From the point of view of the non-combatant population, the Irish conflict was a spectacle to be watched passively rather than a trauma to be experienced, lacking the now almost obligatory massacres of civilians, the bombings of towns, the rapes, or murders of children. By the low standards of twentieth century warfare, the Irish Civil War was a very well-behaved affair.

Subsequent parliamentary politics forced the combatant elites to act out their mutual hostility in a more-or-less peaceful and legal fashion, via electoral competition. As each party's leaders cared far more about defeating the other party than they did about the wishes of the voters, and as PR gave enormous power into the hands of a rather apolitical and bemused electorate, party politics became an extraordinarily contradictory mixture of nationalist fanaticism, Catholic fundamentalism, humorous common-sense and pork-barrel parochialism.

Irish parties competed against each other for decades in a game of ideological beggar-my-neighbour. Up to the mid-1950s, for example, Fianna Fáil and Fine Gael each tried to 'out-Catholic' the other by attempting to prove itself the more pious and the more orthodox. Each also tried to be more noisily patriotic than the other, Brit-bashing being a profitable political sport at the time. General Richard Mulcahy of Fine Gael offered a simple and probably honest explanation for his party's support for the declaration of the Republic and the leaving of the British Commonwealth in 1948: Fine Gael was fed up with being labelled less patriotic, less Anglophobic and less separatist than Fianna Fáil.

From the mid-1950s on, the rules of this game of political beggar-my-neighbour changed. Each party began to represent itself as more in favour than the other of welfarism, of lower tariffs, of 'planning' and of a thing called 'Europe'. The older issues of piety and patriotism were relegated, temporarily as it has turned out, to the back burner. Similarly, in the 1960s, each party busied itself with being more in favour than the other of a *rapprochement* with Stormont and with Northern Unionism, Fine Gael's quiet overtures to elements of the Unionist middle-class being trumped in 1965 by the Whitaker-Lemass visit to Stormont and Fianna Fáil's subsequent stage management of an all-too-brief era of good feelings between North and South. From 1969 on, however, Fianna Fáil went through the political equivalent of a nervous breakdown. This was because the party's traditional association with republican anti-partitionism conflicted with its more recently acquired benign view of Northern Ireland. The competition between Fianna Fáil and Fine Gael had switched to the issues of security and Anglo-Irish affairs.

With the coming of the economic depression of the 1980s, the parties competed first on welfarism and then on anti-welfarism, while increasing economic insecurity and rapid cultural change encouraged a reversion to the politics of piety.

The fiscal crisis of the state which grew gradually from the mid-1970s has generated an extraordinary new version of this beggar-my-neighbour process. The older 'I can spend more than you can' competition has gradually and confusingly been replaced by an 'I can fashion a more uncomfortable hairshirt than you can' competition. For a number of years each party tried to compete on both fronts at the same time, yielding fascinating examples of philosophical schizophrenia and even of attempts at idelogical bilocation by the party leaders. 'Wet' and 'dry' wings appeared at the tops of each party hierarchy.

Since the 1987 election, however, the transition from the politics of the handout to the politics of the hairshirt appears to have been more-or-less completed. Garret FitzGerald's 'soft' version of retrenchment has been replaced by a 'hard' version espoused by Fianna Fáil in office and tacitly supported after the departure of FitzGerald by the increasingly dry leadership of Fine Gael. Once again, the parties have leapfrogged each other on the left-right spectrum, this time with Fianna Fáil trying to outflank Fine Gael on the right. This is despite the fact that, right up to election day, Fianna Fáil was clearly signaling its position as being to the left of Fine Gael. Fine Gael has yet to try to 'out-right' Fianna Fáil, but this particular era, of course, has only just begun.

It could be argued that the 1987 election saw the end not only of the welfarist version of beggar-my-neighbour politics but also of the religious version. The truly fundamentalist dinosaurs of the twenty-fourth Dáil did not get reelected, Fine Gael in particular ridding itself of some of its most conspicuous ultra-traditionalists. In recent years, under FitzGerald's leadership, Fine Gael has attempted to corner secular liberalism or 'pluralism' as an ideological property. It had succeeded to a substantial extent, though its vocal and articulate diehard traditionalists had also succeeded in causing the leadership some considerable embarrassment.

The situation is, of course, more complicated than this. Since the late 1960s, the Irish party system has sprouted a noisy, disunited and occasionally brilliant left, a left which Fianna Fáil, wrestling interminably with Fine Gael, has not been able to swamp electorally as it had managed to do with the previous lefts that have emerged since the 1920s. This 'new left', consisting of a somewhat expanded and urbanised version of the traditional Labour Party, a small and determined hard-left Workers' Party and some independents, has had serious difficulties in achieving a common political purpose. Among other things, its members are divided on the national question, which one might imagine all good Marxists to have by now transcended.

More recently, Fianna Fáil's travails have supplied us with a 'new right', in the form of the Progressive Democrats under Desmond O'Malley, a group who, although led mainly by Fianna Fáil veterans, have offered their main electoral challenge to Fine Gael. For the first time ever, the Irish party system has a left group and a right group, while the two major parties compete against each other for a centre vote which, for the moment at least, is rather less dominant than it was in the good old days of Irish hyper-consensus.

A further complication has been introduced by the revival of political moralism over the past ten years. Neither the new left or the new right adhere to traditional Irish Catholic views on issues such as divorce, sexual morality or the relationship between the Catholic Church and the Irish state. A majority of Fine Gael and an indeterminate but significant proportion of Fianna Fáil supporters have also ceased to accept these traditional views unquestioningly. On such issues, Fianna Fáil clearly stays most loyal to the ideological and moral house that Dev built in the 1930s. So far, however, the party has been careful not to get itself into a philosophical straitjacket and has followed public opinion rather than, as Fine Gael has done, trying to lead it. An effect of the 1986 referendum on divorce, in which a proposal to introduce divorce was supported by Fine Gael, the new left and the new right but opposed by Fianna Fáil, has been to lock Fianna Fáil, at least temporarily, into the traditionalist corner.

However, the economy has dominated the minds of both politicians and voters in recent years and the emergence of small new left and new right blocs at the edges of the traditional Civil War party system are outward symptoms of a general economic unease. This unease is perhaps rooted in a dawning realisation that the old political games that politicians have continued to play throughout the crisis years of the 1980s have simply encouraged our leaders to ignore the national interest in pursuit of short-term partisan gains and personal survival.

This unease about the future of the Republic has become pervasive in recent years; the obsession of various small groups with the politics of morality and the similarly overwhelming preoccupation of many politicians with the minutiae of party competition have obscured the general worry and confusion with which many ordinary people have increasingly viewed the economy. Oddly, it is middle-aged people who seem to worry most about a country that appears to offer so many young people so little future; the young themselves appear to accept the situation with the confidence of youth.

The warnings of economists over the last ten years, warnings often sneered at by political leaders who ought to have known better, have become the forebodings of hundreds of thousands of people. A growing impatience with the politics of beggar-my-neighbour was clearly, if illiterately, expressed by the anonymous slogan pinned to telephone poles all over Dublin in May 1987. This urged voters to oppose ratification of the Single European Act by popular referendum. It read: 'WHY BELIEVE POLITICIAN'S (*sic*) PROMISES? VOTE NO'.

Many, particularly in the deprived and rotting cores of Irish cities and towns, took the advice; many others at least took the point. It also seems that the message has finally percolated through the party system, where even the Irish political leadership has eventually realised the truth of TANSTAAFL: there ain't no such thing as a free lunch.

The new Taoiseach, Charles Haughey, had previously come to terms with this in 1980 but had, for reasons of party competition, subsequently abandoned any real public commitment. In office once more in 1987 he has now embarked on a series of expenditure cuts that have horrified many of his most ardent supporters. The question that remains is whether Fianna Fáil, with its fabled internal solidarity, and with a renowned ability to follow its leader loyally around the most hairpin-like of U-turns, will succeed in doing the same this time. Past experience suggests that it will.

2. THE CAMPAIGN

Brian Girvin

THE COLLAPSE OF THE COALITION

The collapse of the Coalition Government in January 1987 was greeted by the *Irish Times* with an editorial to the effect that 'it was the best of Governments; it was the worst of Governments'. This seemed to refer to the relief which had been expressed by the *Irish Times*, among others, when the Coalition replaced the short lived and disaster-prone Fianna Fáil administration in November 1982 and instituted four years of relatively stable government. Yet the promise of this new Government was not realised and, even before its fourth anniversary, the signs were not auspicious. To all intents and purposes the election campaign opened long before the formal dissolution. By mid October 1986 serious divisions had appeared between the Fine Gael and Labour components of the Government. These disagreements centred on budgetary strategy and Fine Gael used its cabinet majority to override the objections of the Labour minority. This action set the scene for the manoeuvering that took place over the next three months as well as setting the political context for the dissolution of the Dáil and the general election itself. Conflict between the Coalition partners also placed the 1986 Fine Gael Ard Fheis in sharp relief.

Although the Taoiseach, Garret FitzGerald, believed that there would not be an election before June 1987, he recognised that this was the last party conference before that election. The substance of his Ard Fheis speech, however, indicated that he was already preparing for an election, perhaps at an earlier date. He took the opportunity to review the four years in office and to offer guidelines for the future. FitzGerald identified a number of successes for the Government; inflation had fallen to 3% from 21% when the Coalition had taken office; there had been some change in the taxation system; while the Family Income Support Scheme had helped the lower paid. The Anglo-Irish Agreement had, in addition, been a major success for Irish foreign policy. While continuing unemployment was indentified as the major source of instability in Irish society, FitzGerald argued that the most effective method of dealing with this difficulty was by reducing the government's debt. Unemployment was to be tackled in an indirect fashion through strict control of government borrowing and spending.

This concentration by FitzGerald on financial matters was supplemented by blaming the debt crisis on the behaviour of the previous Fianna Fáil Government. He suggested that Ireland's freedom of action had been seriously impaired by these policies and the Government was faced with a cruel dilemma. 'The simple truth is that Fianna Fáil's gross irresponsibility in those years has left us walking a tight-rope ever since. We have been facing the ever present risk of toppling over, on one side on to the rocks of tax increases and spending cuts so drastic as to destroy our hopes of economic recovery or, on the other side, into the abyss of national insolvency that would follow from failure to control spending and to keep borrowing on a downward path.'

This emphasis on fiscal and budgetary strategy was part of a wider strategy within the party which recognised that the existing Coalition Government would not continue after the next election. FitzGerald accepted that the Coalition could not continue in its existing form, because of fundamental philosophical differences between Fine Gael and Labour. Consequently, Fine Gael would seek a majority for its policies and, if this was not forthcoming, the party would seek other methods of realising its objectives. This implied that in any future Coalition Fine Gael would insist that its principles would be central to government formation and policy making.

Despite the obvious difficulties that his party had faced, FitzGerald remained optimistic that the broad trends in Irish society were working in Fine Gael's direction. One important section of his speech recalled his earlier commitment to a 'Constitutional Crusade', while simultaneously expressing a 'modernist' version of contemporary Ireland:

> 'The future Ireland, to which we dedicate ourselves, will not be inhabited by a fearful people, afraid to face reality. It will not be a backward-looking Ireland. It will not be an Ireland of narrow minded people, where personal, parochial or sectional interests hold sway over the common good. It will not be an Ireland of rigid or uncaring attitudes, nor an autocratic Ireland where political parties are personal dictatorships, with instructions handed down from the top. It will not be a male-dominated Ireland with women confined to a subservient or only a token role. It will not be a two-faced, dishonest, ambivalent Ireland - where the end is seen as justifying the means. The modern Ireland for which this party stands can be none of these things it if is to be worthy of the energetic and vital majority amongst the people who inhabit it. New times demand new approaches. Ireland can and will forge its own answers to its own problems, building on the best values and traditions of the past.'

By the time FitzGerald delivered this speech the modernist assumptions which it contained had received a number of setbacks and his government was in serious trouble. Fine Gael's identity had hardened under FitzGerald's leadership. On economic matters it had adopted a broadly neo-liberal stand, comparable to conservative and Christian Democratic parties in Western Europe. Fine Gael remained strongly committed to European integration, was decidedly secularist on the church/state issue and pursued a vigorous anti-Republican policy on Northern Ireland. Although Fine Gael's policies were coherent they did not, however, always attract wide public or political support.

The divisions within the Coalition in October 1986 exposed the main obstacles to the government's future and also the limits to Fine Gael's modernising appeal. The economic crisis which Ireland was experiencing appeared impervious either to the government's policies or to external stimuli. Unemployment stood at a quarter of a million, emigration was on the increase, while there was strong evidence that the country's industrial base, painfully built up during the previous decades, was contracting. Economic policy within the Coalition was framed by Fine Gael, but its impact had been mitigated by Labour and the continuing economic depression exacerbated the tension implicit in this situation. Fine Gael supporters often believed the policies were not going far enough, while Labour supporters feared that their influence was negligible. Thus, on both sides of the Coalition, pressure built up for a reappraisal. Within the Labour Party in particular, there was growing pressure on the leadership to withdraw from the Government because of its economic policies. This constrained the party leadership further and stiffened Labour resolve to resist any further move to the right.

This factor alone might have been overcome in the short run, but general political pressures exacerbated the pressure on the Government. In October 1986, following the Fine Gael conference, the Government narrowly escaped a vote of no confidence. The vote itself demonstrated the uncertain future for the Government, particularly as it was part of the Fianna Fáil strategy to decouple Labour from the Coalition by presenting itself as an advocate of working class interests. This uncertainty was compounded by the government's loss of its majority later in the year. Although the Government remained optimistic that it could survive, by January 1987 it could only command the support of 82 deputies out of 166. While there was no guarantee that an anti-government majority could be put together, the Government's drift into a minority position in the Dáil contributed to uncertainty in the run up to the publication of the budget estimates.

On top of all this the opinion polls did nothing to bolster the Government's confidence. Whereas the opinion polls had reflected considerable support for the Coalition when it entered office, this had soon evaporated. With the benefit of hindsight it seems that early Government successes in the polls were due more to hostility to Fianna Fáil rather than to a positive view of Coalition policies. In particular, the tight monetary policy adopted after November 1982 deflated the economy and alienated many sectors of the electorate. Moreover, with the exception of the middle classes, most other social categories did not accept Fine Gael's priorities on the debt, borrowing or state spending.[1] FitzGerald's popularity, always deemed an asset, dissipated once his Government introduced policies which increased unemployment and reduced living standards. His popularity ratings slumped quickly, satisfaction with his performance eroded while support for Charles Haughey, which had previously dropped to very low levels, received a considerable boost.

More ominously for the Government, a large section of its own supporters were disappointed with its performance. In November 1986 some two-thirds of Labour supporters expressed dissatisfaction with the Coalition's performance, while only a bare majority (53%) of Fine Gael supporters expressed satisfaction. Table 1 shows the levels of party support on four dates in 1986, and draws attention to the strength of Fianna Fáil and the continued weakness of Fine Gael.

Table 1: Percentage party support during 1986

	Feb	April	June	Nov
Fianna Fáil	42	48	52	46
Fine Gael	23	26	25	29
Prog. Democrats	25	17	15	15
Labour Party	4	5	4	5
Others	6	4	5	5

Source: MRBI. Undecided not included

A number of other factors weakened the Government in 1986, including the defeat of the Government sponsored referendum on divorce, during which it became clear that a large constituency in all parties supported traditional Roman Catholic moral teaching. This had two effects: it brought into the open the divisions within Fine Gael between the liberals and the traditionalists, demonstrating the weakness of the former; it also strained the Coalition, as the defeat convinced many Labour supporters that their social objectives could not be realised by this Government.

Another factor destabilising the Coalition was the emergence of the Progressive Democrats (PDs). Although originally a result of divisions within Fianna Fáil, it became clear that a sizeable chunk of the PD support was drawn from disaffected Fine Gael voters. In local opinion polls reported in November 1986, the PDs were shown to have very high levels of support in Galway West and in Cork City. In the latter the PDs had overtaken Fine Gael in their level of support, an outcome attributable to defections from Fine Gael.[2]

What was surprising during 1986 was the continued strength of Fianna Fáil, despite the establishment of the PDs and the subsequent defection of a number of its TDs and other members. Indeed, by the end of the year, Fianna Fáil support remained strong and its policy framework was becoming well established. Fianna Fáil has often been characterised as a 'catch all' party, but under the leadership of Haughey it developed a coherent conservative policy profile on a number of issues. If Fine Gael can be characterised as a modern liberal and/or Christian Democratic party, Fianna Fáil emphasised a traditionalism which reinforces the status quo. This is particularly reflected in its defence of the 1937 Constitution, its deep suspicion of liberalism (usually on moral issues), and its vigorous articulation of sovereignty and nationalism. Its economic policies remained unclear at this stage but, in contrast to Fine Gael, it retained an interventionist tradition which emphasised economic growth and activism by the state. The defeat of the coalition's divorce referendum demonstrated that Fianna Fáil's moral traditionalism had wide appeal. Haughey has also on a number of occasions returned to a theme which links his party ideologically with the preservation of the Constitution. 'Fianna Fáil today is more than ever left alone as the guardian of the republican tradition and the Constitution of this state, in which that tradition is enshrined. We are a constitutional party in the fullest sense, in that we support totally and unequivocally the Constitution of our country. Fianna Fáil see that Constitution as giving substance and meaning to Irish national life and to our freedom and independence.'[3]

This stance led not only to Fianna Fáil's opposition to the referendum on divorce, but also to consistent opposition to the Anglo-Irish Agreement, as well as to misgivings concerning the ratification of the Single European Act. The ideological firmness of Fianna Fáil is particularly evident on the Anglo-Irish Agreement, since a policy of general opposition was maintained despite the fact that the Agreement was perceived positively by most Irish voters. Fianna Fáil's popularity in the opinion polls, therefore, did not rest on its Northern Ireland policy. If anything, Haughey's commitment to renegotiate the Agreement could easily have become an electoral liability.

The party's popularity rested on general public disappointment with Government policies and a belief that Fianna Fáil would offer a viable alternative. Such was the headway that was made in public opinion that Haughey was able to claim, with little resulting criticism, that the state of public finances had been better under his own most recent administration than it was under the Coalition.

Even before the Coalition collapsed, therefore, the outline of the ensuing campaign was reasonably clear. What was not clear was Fianna Fáil's specific policy package. Just two days before the dissolution, Haughey addressed this question. Anticipating the election, he claimed that the Government would 'prolong the agony' with a long campaign. In a carefully measured speech Haughey sought to offset any advantage that a long campaign might have for Fine Gael by attempting to dictate the main issues.

First and foremost Fianna Fáil's objective was to obtain an overall majority in the Dáil. A vote for either the PDs or Sinn Féin would not only be wasted, Haughey claimed, but would also be politically disruptive, contributing to further governmental instability. This reflected Haughey's concern that these parties could erode enough of Fianna Fáil's republican and middle class support to deprive him of a majority. The criticism was not aimed at their policies but rather at the electoral consequences of voting for them. The reasoning behind this was that the '. . . issues can only be tackled by a single party Government united on the policies it intends to pursue'.

Dealing with the substance of these policies, Haughey claimed that economic problems could not be resolved by a 'no growth' mentality. Fianna Fáil would promote a comprehensive approach to economic development and no opportunity for growth and development would be ignored. Haughey's commitment to economic development implied that there would be considerable state intervention; he maintained that a 2-3% growth rate over a four or five year period could be achieved. This, however, would be achieved while observing 'prudent fiscal management'. Haughey proved reluctant to make more specific commitments at this stage but he did offer a general outline of Fianna Fáil policy in an effort to direct attention towards specific themes.

Despite voices being raised in some quarters about the possibility of a 'Grand Coalition' between Fianna Fáil, Fine Gael and the Progressive Democrats as a solution to the nation's economic crises, Haughey explicitly rejected this approach. 'My simple answer to that idea would be that all the instabilities and uncertainties that are inherent in a small coalition of two parties would be simply magnified in a bigger coalition. What we say is that the economic collapse is of such a magnitude that it will require a consistent programme of policies by a single party Government united on these policies over a four or five year period.'

He also refused to become involved in the Northern Ireland question, arguing that it should not be made an election issue. Perhaps sensing his vulnerability on it, he claimed that Fianna Fáil would not dispense with the Agreement but added: 'the process of government will be to continue Anglo-Irish relations. We do not accept the Constitutional implications of Article 1. What we do about it is something we will have to consider. But I do want to give the assurance that as far as any progress is made or has been made, and there's not much progress very evident, or is possible, we are not going to interfere with that.'[4]

The Campaign

Against a political background less and less propitious to the Coalition Government, internal events in both parties set in motion the process of dissolution. In November 1986 the Government narrowly escaped defeat when two Labour deputies, Frank Cluskey and Mervyn Taylor, reluctantly agreed not to vote against the Government. Within the Labour Party there was increased tension between those, such as Cluskey and Taylor, who were convinced that it was necessary to withdraw from the Government, and those, represented by Spring and Desmond, who advocated continued participation. At the end of November some advantage remained with those who wished to continue the Coalition; over the subsequent five weeks this advantage was progressively eroded. This process took a number of forms.

Haughey predicted at the beginning of December that an election was inevitable and that this would now take place in February 1987. This view was echoed, to a greater or lesser extent, by the three national dailies. This psychological pressure was accompanied by a Fianna Fáil strategy which involved an attempt to split the Coalition on major issues, while simultaneously harrassing the Government in the Dáil.

The release of the unemployment figures in early December increased these pressures. With the official unemployment rate standing at 18% Labour was placed in a cruel dilemma; if it remained in government it would be identified with the negative state of the economy, but if it withdrew it could not guarantee its ability to retain its electoral support. This dilemma was faced on the 8 December by Senator Flor O'Mahony who argued that Labour should be prepared to bring down the Government on the budget. He urged the party to withdraw in advance of cabinet agreement on the budget estimates, failure to do so would lead to a loss of credibility if the budget thus accepted were to be subsequently rejected, an outcome which Senator O'Mahony believed likely.

In fact, by this stage both Fine Gael and Labour were reported to be preparing their respective election manifestos. This was given added urgency when Alice Glenn resigned from Fine Gael after severe criticism for making a speech describing the non-Catholic churches, among others, as 'enemies of the people'. Following the resignation and her announcement that she would not support cuts in social welfare, the Government lost its overall majority. From the 10 December, the Coalition could not guarantee a majority on any issue; therefore it was only a matter of time before an issue would arise which would lead to dissolution.

At first, both FitzGerald and Spring appeared optimistic. FitzGerald reiterated his belief that the budget cuts were required, while Spring suggested that agreement was possible if certain guarantees on welfare and the public sector were made. By mid-December, however, these hopes had dissipated. FitzGerald had attempted to generate all party support for the budget, but his proposal was rejected by the PDs and Fianna Fáil. He then returned to the Fine Gael view that the budget would be introduced in January and if defeated the party would campaign on it. On 20 December the Coalition won the adjournment debate, but there was a widespread belief that, notwithstanding the Government's apparent unity, there would be no agreement on the budget.

This view was confirmed during the Christmas recess. Opinion hardened on both sides. Fine Gael believed that the October decision on the estimates should be the basis for any budget and that such a budget should be introduced even against the wishes of the Labour cabinet members. Opinion within Labour moved in the opposite direction. There was intense pressure on Spring from the party to withdraw prior to the introduction of the budget. This had been Senator O'Mahony's view, and by early January it had been accepted by most sections of the party. This view was supplemented by the fear among Labour supporters that it would not be able to maintain the support of its traditional constituency unless it publicly repudiated the proposed cuts prior to their acceptance by the Cabinet. As an election was inevitable due to the probable rejection of the budget, the Labour Party was committed to withdrawal on its return after the recess. Fine Gael would have preferred to introduce a budget, but without Labour support this would prove impossible. In early January Fine Gael decided not to compromise on their proposals and to submit them to the Cabinet. Consequently by 20 January the stage was set for the dissolution of the Dáil.

The collapse of the Coalition and the conclusion of four years of government could not have occurred in a manner more suited to Fianna Fáil. The incompatible ideological bases of the governing parties was demonstrated in their exchanges over the proposals for the 1987 budget. The context for Labour's withdrawal had been set in October when the Government had adopted what were essentially Fine Gael monetary targets. These formed the basis of a budget that was to remain the core of Fine Gael's election campaign. The budget proposals drew the comment from the *Irish Press* that Fine Gael '... is now signalling a strong desire to lose this much avoided General Election'.[5]

At the heart of the Fine Gael approach was the belief, not shared by the Labour Party or by other critics, that the debt incurred in the 1980s remained the main obstacle to economic recovery and that its reduction should take precedence over all other objectives. Substantial cuts in public spending were therefore envisaged; the overall reduction in spending would be 3.5%, though the reduction in social welfare would be lower at 2.2%. These cuts were supplemented by a number of other objectives linked to reducing public expenditure. These included five priorities: to strengthen the incentive to work; to maintain the level of state support for those in real need; to charge those who can afford it for state services; to restore better balance to the income of the Social Insurance Fund; and to raise productivity in the public sector. In fact, the overall emphasis at this stage rested firmly on a belief in the need to reduce government intervention in the economy and in particular to reduce government spending.

This was an approach which the Labour Party could not support. While not disagreeing with the need to contain spending limits, there was deep concern on how any adjustment would, in fact, take place. In particular Labour believed that any changes should be assessed in terms of their social consequences and that they should not endanger existing social programmes. The proposed changes, according to Dick Spring amounted to 'a fundamentally unacceptable imposition on insured workers and on the poorest sections of the community'.

When the Coalition Government had been formed Labour had recognised that, because of the actions of Fianna Fáil, difficult decisions would have to be taken. Spring acknowledged that it was 'for that reason I have participated in, and defended, a series of tough and unpopular decisions in the last four years. I was, and remain, convinced of the necessity of these decisions, even though I was also aware that there were many in my own party, and among those who supported the party, who resented many of the decisions taken'.

Circumstances had now changed, however. Fine Gael were monopolising the formation of policy. Under these conditions 'social justice' and 'equity' were being ignored and this left Labour with little option but to resign from the Government.[6]

THE CAMPAIGN PROPER

Fine Gael took the offensive during the early days of the campaign. It had certain advantages as the caretaker Government and sought to seize the initiative. Conversely Labour, by leaving the Government, gave up some of the advantages that might have helped it with its campaign. Fine Gael openly admitted that the proposed budget was a particularly tough one, but argued that the long-term benefits would be very positive. Stressing the importance of controlling spending, the manifesto and party publicity juxtaposed two scenarios. The first concentrated on what was termed the 'vicious circle' of high public spending, leading to high taxation and borrowing, which in turn led to high interest rates and job losses. This was contrasted to the Fine Gael approach, 'The Path to Growth', which concluded that the circle could be broken by lower spending, leading to lower borrowing, taxation and interest rates; this in turn would lead to increased investment and more employment. Fine Gael's objective was to create a low borrowing, low spending and low taxation economy.

The main thrust of this approach was neo-liberal, essentially embracing the economics of the New Right, a matter discussed in greater detail by Peter Mair in the following chapter. One method of achieving this was the privatisation of virtually every major state company including Aer Lingus, Bord Telecom and Irish Steel. In most cases outright privatisation was not envisaged, instead companies would dispose of 49% of their equity. Privatisation was aimed at reducing spending rather than being based on a belief in the superiority or efficiency of the market.

Although the manifesto advocated radical tax reform, its main proposal was one which would probably perpetuate the existing anomalies, a self assessment method for farmers. Indeed the party believed that, while there might be inequities in the system, the problem and the solution lay elsewhere. 'The real inequities are in the way we misuse the taxpayers' money. Reform must begin with reform of spending. If, because of excessive borrowing, there is not room for a real reduction in the level of taxation, tax reform can mean only that for every pound of inequity relieved in any one part of the system an additional burden is created somewhere else in the system. That is the major obstacle to tax reform at the present time. Real tax reform must involve reductions in the overall levels of tax. This can come only from reduced spending.'

Fine Gael envisaged a policy mix which has now become common among conservative parties in many liberal democracies. Large scale spending cuts would allow a reduction in taxation which would stimulate investment and economic endeavour. At the heart of the policy is the belief that economic activity is a mix of incentive (low taxation) and personal psychology (a strong work ethic). To this end, and here a consensus among the PDs, Fianna Fáil and Fine Gael appeared to emerge, the objective of tax policy would be to create a situation where at least two thirds of tax payers are on a standard 35% rate. This would be supplemented by creating personal pension schemes to enhance mobility, while there would be different salaries for new and experienced workers in the same employment. The argument here is that workers may not only price themselves out of employment, but that those in jobs exclude others by demanding that all entrants to the labour market be paid at existing levels. To secure better labour relations, Fine Gael proposed that the 1906 Trade Union Act would confer immunity only if certain procedures were followed.

While Fine Gael emphasised the fiscal/budgetary aspects of policy, it also addressed a number of other issues. There were proposals on agriculture, forestry, and tourism; and some suggestions were made on broadcasting and television. The policy document also promised to abandon the medical card scheme and planned to introduce a new system which would be closely related to income level and family responsibilities. Changes were also advocated in family law, particularly in relation to marriage and marital breakdown. The most radical noneconomic proposal concerned electoral reform. Fine Gael made a commitment to promote a referendum which would introduce single seat constituencies for two-thirds of Dáil representation. This would be achieved by transferable vote. The main objective of the reform appeared to be to exclude small parties, as there would be a 5% threshold which a party would have to achieve nationally before it could be represented in the Dáil.[7]

Despite Fine Gael's attempt to control the debate during the first week of the campaign, this was not successful. The impact of the budgetary proposals on Fine Gael's popularity was extremely limited. Most attention was paid to prospects of the PDs and to the possible proposals which Fianna Fáil would reveal in its manifesto.

The release of the first opinion poll on 28 January confirmed the worst fears of the Fine Gael strategists. Fianna Fáil - still in its pre-manifesto days - received 52%, while Fine Gael received 23% and the PDs 15%. The Labour Party received 5% but over a fifth of those polled remained undecided.

The first campaign poll also identified the main issues of concern to the electorate. Over 80% of those polled considered unemployment to be the main issue, concern over this issue was even stronger among the 18-34 age group. Taxation (45%), prices (26%), and government finance (20%) were the other issues considered significant.

These findings boosted the morale of the PDs. As a new and untested party it could appeal to disaffected Fine Gael and Fianna Fáil voters; particularly those with weak links to either party. In Desmond O'Malley the party had a popular, if not a charismatic, leader. Moreover, the PDs' insistence on the importance of the tax issue and the link between taxation, a reduction in public spending and employment introduced a very specific focus of policy into the campaign. Drawing explicitly on supply side arguments the PDs argued that low taxation would stimulate employment.

The difficulty for the PDs occurred when both Fianna Fáil and Fine Gael began to adopt policies similar to, but not as radical as, those they advocated. While O'Malley believed that this was an acknowledgement of the PDs ability to dictate the issues, he recognised that the party could become vulnerable to a Fine Gael counter attack. By the end of January he found it necessary to assert the PDs distinctiveness. During the launching of the party document on justice, O'Malley sought to present these proposals in radical terms. The document proposed to reduce the number of TDs to 120, to streamline the working of the Dáil and to restructure the law enforcement agencies and the legal profession. There was also a proposal to abolish the Senate

This document drew attention to the importance that the PDs place on institutions, particularly on the independence of state institutions. This gave the party a certain distinctiveness in the Irish context, since it advocates a minimal, but not a weak, state. The state should not be hindered by unnecessary involvement in the economy or social affairs but when it does become involved, its power should be used decisively.

The party also insisted on a more explicit distinctiveness associated with its disavowal of 'civil war politics' which it claimed characterised the two main parties. O'Malley insisted on a number of occasions that the PDs were a party of a new type in Irish politics, one that was clear on policy and not socialistic. Policy consistency was of particular importance, O'Malley claimed, if there was no majority for a single party after the election. There was a constituency for their policies and, while the PDs would enter negotiations to form a new Government, any agreement would have to accommodate the party's policies. O'Malley refused to compromise the party's position prior to the election itself, maintaining that the PD party would not '. . . barter its pivotal position in the election for an alliance with any group'.[8]

The PDs attempted to reinforce this distinctiveness when they launched their manifesto on 2 February. The party offered a radical approach to tax policy by advocating a progressive reduction in the basic rate to 25% by 1991. This process would be launched by a 2% reduction in the current year. The tax cuts would be paid for by the receipts from privatisation, from a reduction in public spending, and by deferring public sector pay increases. The costings by the PDs were detailed and suggested that the tax cuts and other costs would not lead to extra expenditure. In fact, the figures suggested that some £100 million would become available to the Government from the disposal of public assets; this would allow the Government to reduce borrowing, stabilise the budget deficit at its 1986 level and reduce exchequer borrowing to 11% of GNP.

Although the policy document addressed a number of other issues such as justice and social welfare its main concern was to establish the party as the main New Right organisation in Ireland. The aim of the proposals, as has been the case elsewhere with the Right, was to stimulate growth through major tax concessions. The proposals were aimed at securing overall living standards without wage increases, in order to attract workers out of the black economy, and to give larger wage increases to the lower paid. This legitimised the philosophy of the party. 'The essential step to achieve these two cuts (tax and interest rates) is to reduce government spending and borrowing. Once government borrowing is reduced, interest rates can begin to fall to the levels prevailing in other European countries, which are as much as 7% below Irish rates (or half our levels). If government borrowing is to be cut, then the only way in which to finance tax cuts is by reductions in government spending.   There is no other way to achieve these two essential steps on the road back to increased employment and improved living standards.'[9]

Although the PD manifesto bears some similarity to that of Fine Gael there is also a contrast.   Despite O'Malley's personal popularity the party did not attempt to function as a 'catch all party', instead it identified specific policies and linked them to an appeal to certain social strata.

The emergence of the PDs as an importance component in the Irish party system created a very high degree of uncertainty.   It remained extremely difficult throughout the campaign to predict both the impact of the new party and which of the other parties it would most affect. This uncertainty was enhanced when O'Malley hinted that he would not be prepared to support either FitzGerald or Haughey as Taoiseach after the election.   He believed that there would not be an overall majority in the new Dáil, but the PDs were not prepared to come to any preelection arrangements with the other parties.

The initial decline in Fine Gael support and the important of the PDs focussed attention on Fianna Fáil.   Entering the campaign as favourites to obtain an overall majority, Fianna Fáil were poised to be the main beneficiaries at the election.   The emphasis in the Fianna Fáil manifesto, published on 29 January, differed somewhat from that of Fine Gael or the PDs, but the importance of the tax issue pervaded all three.[10] The main commitments made by Fianna Fáil were to contain expenditure at 1986 levels and not to increase taxation or borrowing. In addition, they pledged to reduce the standard tax rate to 35% when - and if - this proved feasible. The party, however, refused to give any details on possible cuts, nor would it accept the Fine Gael budget estimates as a basis for future policy.   In contrast to the other two parties, Fianna Fáil proposed that growth would be at the centre of its economic policy; not only would this be of general benefit but it would provide extra revenue for the state.

When introducing the manifesto Haughey insisted that the recovery of the economy was linked to the success of Fianna Fáil at the election. Fianna Fáil's success would generate a consumer boom, a boom which had been predicted in 1986, but which had not occurred because of political uncertainty and the policies of the Government. 'As well as careful control of the public finances, there must be a development thrust to economic policy. . . economic growth is something that will only take place in response to the right policies and the right public mood and outlook.'

According to Haughey the pressure for a consumer boom existed and a Fianna Fáil election victory would 'generate the confidence needed to secure it.' In contrast to Fine Gael and the PDs, Fianna Fáil was basing its policies on growth in the short term. As they presented it, the problem with the Irish economy was not essentially fiscal but psychological; this in turn was due to the absence of positive policies. Haughey argued that the business community in Ireland was more interested in the type of government on offer rather than on the type of economic analysis available.

Haughey's apparent belief in growth drew on a Fianna Fáil tradition going back to the 1950s, and identified with Sean Lemass in particular. While Haughey recognised the budgetary and fiscal constraints, his main objective remained that of reviving production. 'In Ireland today there is absolutely no doubt of the main problem we face - unemployment and how to tackle it. We have set out in our programme a comprehensive, far reaching range of measures, policies, approaches. The emphasis will be on growth, of bringing all our resources, human and material, into the main stream of production.'

Fianna Fáil hoped to gain the initiative at this stage of the campaign by forcing the other parties to address the question of growth rather than that of taxation or borrowing. For Fianna Fáil taxation and borrowing were important but, without growth, employment could not be created whatever the success of other policies. A target of 2.5% growth in GNP per annum was set; this would be generated by a consumer boom rather than by direct government spending. Furthermore, the manifesto rejected the PDs approach, which concentrated solely on tax cuts. In an attempt to attract a section of the trade union and working class support base the manifesto also committed Fianna Fáil to renew the process of tripartite consultation and social partnership which had been a feature of government policy during previous Fianna Fáil administrations.[11]

If Fianna Fáil had hoped to control the policy debate subsequent to the publication of the various manifestos, it was quite successful in achieving this in the short term. Fine Gael characterised the Fianna Fáil manifesto as a 'non-document', the proposals in which would lead to more spending. In an attempt to regain the initiative Fine Gael attacked the Fianna Fáil reticence on the budget calling this approach 'cowardice masquerading as cuteness'. O'Malley welcomed what he believed was Fianna Fáil's conversion to the PDs tax policy, but criticised the manifesto for not detailing the cuts necessary to achieve these ends. FitzGerald dismissed the Fianna Fáil programme as 'waffle and fudge' and predicted that the electorate would reject it. He added that 'if I am proved wrong, then there will be consequences, not just for me, not just for my party, but for the whole of our society'.

Manifestos were also issued by the Labour Party and the Workers' Party. As each of these parties represent segments of the Left in Irish politics, the main objective in both documents was to counter the offensive from the Right. The Workers' Party issued its manifesto on

27 January and placed the defence of the public sector and tax reform at the centre of its programme. It promised to expand the economy in order to create additional employment, while at the same time rescheduling the national debt or freezing repayments. A 10% cut in PAYE would be introduced and the loss incurred to the exchequer would be offset by the collection of additional taxes from the self employed.

The Labour Party document, issued on 30 January, was not unlike that of the Workers' Party. Labour continued to believe that the state would play a strongly interventionist role; only thus could a 4% growth rate be achieved and employment enhanced. The taxation system could only be reformed, Labour believed, if large farmers and big business were confronted. Labour insisted that social welfare would have to be protected and rejected the dominant right wing view on borrowing. It argued that borrowing was fully justified once there is a return on the subsequent investment sufficient to cover the cost of servicing the debt.

The two main left wing parties were placed in invidious, although different, positions. Together they could not hope to form a Government; nor could they hope to influence its composition. The Workers' Party, however, could function as an alternative for disaffected Labour supporters, as was reflected by its strategy for the campaign. Labour had placed itself outside the process of government formation, but at the same time was in danger of suffering from its association with the policies of the outgoing Coalition. At the beginning of the campaign Labour was clearly in danger of losing a number of seats. Its strategy concentrated on maximising its influence in selected constituencies while attempting to challenge the dominance of the three parties to its right. The other major problem facing the Left was its continuing inability to appeal to the working class; most working class voters continued to support Fianna Fáil or, to a lesser extent, Fine Gael.[12] (The changing social patterns of party support in Ireland are discussed in detail by Laver, Mair and Sinnott, below).

When the parties entered the second half of the campaign at the beginning of February, their policy positions and tactical objectives were well established. Fianna Fáil was seeking an overall majority in the belief that only in this way could economic recovery be achieved. The PDs were attempting to draw support from both Fianna Fáil and Fine Gael and thereby hold the balance of power. The Labour Party hoped merely to survive as a parliamentary force, while Fine Gael's position remained the most difficult.

This was because the PDs remained attractive to traditional Fine Gael voters who would not consider voting for Fianna Fáil, while middle class electoral volatility appeared stronger throughout this campaign than during previous elections. This attractiveness was enhanced by the saliency of the tax issue for the middle classes. The anti tax sentiment appeared to be strongest among those strata where Fine Gael would normally expect to receive support. Fine Gael was probably also proving vulnerable to Fianna Fáil's appeal to sections of the lower middle class and skilled workers who had voted for Fine Gael in 1981 and 1982. By early Feburary, Fine Gael had concluded that its main objective should be to deprive Fianna Fáil of its hoped-for majority in the belief, presumably, that almost any alternative was preferable.

Fine Gael assumed that Fianna Fáil's weak spot was its commitment to growth and the control of public spending. In particular, Fine Gael attempted to portray Fianna Fáil as a party of high taxation and spending. In 'The Hidden Cost of the Fianna Fáil Manifesto' Fine Gael claimed that, in order to achieve its objectives, Fianna Fáil would have to increase taxation by £904 million over a five year period. The assessment was carried out by the economic consultants Davy Kelleher McCarthy, using a model based on the main objectives which Fianna Fáil had set itself:

1. To stabilise and reduce the level of public debt as a percentage of national income;

2. To achieve 2.5% growth in production;

3. To hold government spending constant as a share of national income.

The Minister for Finance, John Bruton, insisted that Fianna Fáil's policies were contradictory. Fianna Fáil rejected the claims and maintained that their aims were achievable. They in turn accused Fine Gael of misleading statements. The entire exercise proved controversial as Department of Finance officials had refused to do the costings during an election campaign. Department officials also refused to attend the press conference at which the Minister introduced the document.

Fine Gael followed this up with an advertising campaign which claimed that Fianna Fáil's policies would lead to a standard tax rate of 45%. The half page advertisements which appeared in the Irish Times, the Irish Independent and the Cork Examiner angered Fianna Fáil and led them to lodge a complaint with the Advertising Standards Authority. The sensitivity of the tax issue becomes apparent from the letter sent to the Authority. 'Fianna Fáil have never published anywhere, nor indeed stated, that they would increase the tax rate as stated by Fine Gael... The Fianna Fáil pledge is to have two-thirds of income tax payers pay tax at the standard rate....'[13] In response to this, and clearly believing that this was an issue which would stick, Fine

Gael retorted that their costings were valid and that, given Fianna Fáil's reluctance to cost their own policies, the construction in the advertisements was reasonable.

By the end of the first week of February Fine Gael had regained some of the initiative on the tax issue, but not always in the way intended. Fianna Fáil were on the defensive but this did not lead to a swing in support to Fine Gael. Fianna Fáil's response was to deny the claims made and to commit the party more solidly to a cautious fiscal strategy. In a sense Fine Gael forced Fianna Fáil to make clear its tax and spending policies, which proved to be not a great deal different from those of Fine Gael. In doing so Fine Gael may have enhanced Fianna Fáil's attractiveness to some sectors, for Fianna Fáil was in a position to assert its commitment both to growth and to a cautious fiscal policy. In contrast, despite its apparent success in this matter, the Fine Gael campaign came across as essentially negative, reflecting an obsession with numbers and a lack of any identifiable positive appeal to the electorate. In these circumstances Fianna Fáil was able to maintain its credibility.

Although economic issues remained central to the campaign, Fine Gael successfully introduced the Anglo-Irish Agreement as a major issue during the final ten days. Fianna Fáil had hoped to avoid becoming involved in controversy over the pact, recognising that it was an area where Fine Gael held the advantage. While the Agreement generally had a low priority among the electorate, this might always have been because of a widespread support for it, rather than the result of a general lack of concern.

In a speech to the Young Fine Gael Northern Ireland Group FitzGerald set out to maximise any benefits that might be derived from the Agreement. He believed that relations between Ireland and the United Kingdom had improved dramatically since the Coalition had come to office in November 1982. The Agreement had been a product of the new relationship, one which should be contrasted to the deterioration of relations under Haughey. FitzGerald also maintained that there were major differences between the Northern Ireland policies of the two parties. Fine Gael aimed to achieve a balance between the two communities in Northern Ireland; this reflects an earlier concern of FitzGerald's that his main interest in Northern Ireland was the elimination of the IRA.

In a radio interview Peter Barry and Desmond O'Malley pressed the Fianna Fáil spokesman Gerry Collins on the issue. Barry accused Fianna Fáil of ambiguity on the Agreement and urged the party, if indeed it had reservations on the matter, to test its constitutionality in the Supreme Court. O'Malley suggested that Fianna Fáil were giving the Agreement conditional support for electoral reasons and compared this with their decision to expel Mary Harney when she supported the

Agreement. Collins's response appeared confused; on the one hand he seemed to say that Fianna Fáil would respect the pact and 'honour its implications', while at the same time refusing to accept the constitutional implications. When interviewed later, Haughey continued to claim that it was not an election issue, but reiterated his view that the Agreement was unconstitutional.

Peter Barry returned to the attack in the belief that Fine Gael held the initiative. He criticised Haughey's statement on the pact suggesting that the electorate should carefully evaluate what Fianna Fáil would do if returned to office. The ambiguity on the issue, Barry added, was '...not only seriously immoral, but dangerous to constitutional democratic government in our country'. In response, Haughey again reiterated his opposition but added significantly: 'When we get into government we will have to accept the situation as it is. A government cannot just renege on international agreements signed by their predecessor.' This did not satisfy Barry who questioned how an administration which believed that an international agreement was unconstitutional could continue to operate it. Such an approach would seriously impair what had already been achieved. Following this up, FitzGerald suggested that any attempt by Fianna Fáil to alter the Agreement, particularly Article 1 which provided for the recognition of the status of Northern Ireland, would undermine the entire arrangement.

Haughey remained on the defensive throughout the campaign on the issue of Northern Ireland. When the two party leaders engaged in a set debate on television, FitzGerald used the issue with devastating effect against Haughey. Under severe pressure Haughey appeared to withdraw an earlier suggestion that he would use political and diplomatic pressure to alter Article 1.[14]

With the exception of the Anglo-Irish Agreement the television debate on 12 February added little to the campaign. Both leaders reiterated their policies and set about criticising the other. Haughey stressed the need for growth and employment, while FitzGerald stressed the spending implications of Fianna Fáil's policy and urged the need for fiscal caution. Although any evaluation of such a contest is subjective and impressionistic, FitzGerald clearly dominated on the Anglo-Irish Agreement. On the economic issues, however, it is probable that Haughey held the advantage. His presentation was clear and straightforward, while that of FitzGerald was often technical and negative in tone. It is probable that the debate did not significantly alter the image of the two main parties in the voters' eyes. Certainly, Haughey was unable to maximise his party's advantage, despite his promotion of economic themes during the debate.

The Fine Gael strategy to box in Fianna Fáil on the issues of taxation and borrowing had been quite successful, but in the last few days of the campaign a change of tactics occurred. Fine Gael's position remained precarious. All the opinion polls indicated that they were not attracting their expected share of the vote. The focus of the Fine Gael campaign now shifted to presenting a more positive image of its policies in the hope of improving its position. This was linked to the hope that opinion among the electorate would shift away from Fianna Fáil by election day. Fine Gael estimated that, if the Fianna Fáil vote fell to between 45% and 47%, then Haughey would not have a working majority. If Fine Gael could capture at least 30% of the vote this would improve their chances of influencing the formation of a new Government.[15] This was also reflected in a renewed appeal by FitzGerald for a consensus approach to economic policy. FitzGerald promoted the idea of an Economic Forum, along the lines of the New Ireland Forum, which would seek agreement on the economic difficulties facing Ireland. This case was either ignored or rejected by the other parties, each of whom continued to assert their autonomy in policy terms. Haughey, in particular, ruled out any form of National Government as a denial of democracy.

FitzGerald's appeal for an economic consensus was an attempt to preempt the election results by forcing the other parties to commit themselves to a particular course of action. When that proved unsuccessful, he concentrated on devising a strategy to prevent Haughey from becoming Taoiseach. On the Saturday prior to the election, he advised his supporters to give their second preferences to the PDs. In an RTE interview he justified this approach by claiming that the Fianna Fáil lead in the polls had slumped and that there was now a realistic alternative. 'The only alternative Government possible is a Fine Gael Government with support from the Progressive Democrats, who have shared broadly our analysis of the problem and who have faced the fact that for some years to come we have to control public spending.'[15]

The last opinion poll of the campaign was released on the Sunday prior to the election and tended to reinforce FitzGerald's claim. However, Fianna Fáil moved its emphasis back to the long standing claim that it was the only party which could form a stable Government. Fianna Fáil hoped that the issue of government formation would allow it to escape from the difficulties which it had encountered on the Anglo-Irish Agreement and the economy. For Fianna Fáil the question of a majority was central, because it was an area of weakness in the Fine Gael's claim to offer an alternative. In the event the Fine Gael strategy collapsed because O'Malley refused to advise his supporters on how to use second preferences beyond urging them to 'vote for candidates whose principles and policies are, in the voter's judgement, closest to our own'. This might have been construed as conditional support for Fine Gael, but it might also have been a careful calculation on the part of a new party whose support was not as 'firm' as that of its competitors. The last MRBI poll found that 34% of Fine Gael and Progressive Democrat voters would transfer to one another but that 21% of the PDs would transfer to Fianna Fáil.[16]

By election day there remained a considerable degree of uncertainty about the outcome, despite the public optimism of the parties. Table 2 traces the movement in public opinion during the campaign and suggests that, while Fianna Fáil support remained remarkably stable, the main changes occurred among Fine Gael and PD supporters. In particular, it is noticeable that any reduction in the size of the 'undecided' group, still a significant factor right up to election day, tended to work to the advantage of the PDs and Fine Gael rather than Fianna Fáil.

Table 2: Percentage party support January-February 1987

	Jan 28 MRBI	Feb 5 MRBI	Feb 14 MRBI	Feb 4 IMS	Feb 13 IMS	Feb 15 IMS
Fianna Fáil	40	40	40	43	41	38
Fine Gael	18	19	20	20	22	25
Progressive Democrats	12	11	13	15	14	11
Labour Party	4	4	5	5	6	4
Others*	5	5	5	6	6	6
Don't Know/ won't vote	22	21	17	11	11	15

Source: MRBI and IMS polls. *Includes Worker's Party and Sinn Féin

In retrospect, the campaign was a quiet but interesting one. There was a fear, reflected in newspaper editorials, that the electorate might prove apathetic, given the presidential style of campaigning. Yet, while the presence of party leaders is important, the local candidate and local party retain considerable influence over the outcome. This can be readily observed in the activities of both Fianna Fáil and the Labour Party. Fianna Fáil had targetted fourteen constituencies where they were likely to win seats and the party organised considerable resources in an effort to achieve the maximum gains. (These matters are discussed below by David M. Farrell). In a similar manner Labour attempted to meet the threat to sitting TDs by concentrating on retaining a local electoral base through hard work at the constituency level.

The Campaign

By election day a number of trends were observable. The opinion polls indicated a sizeable proportion still undecided, though it could be inferred that those among the undecided who voted would not vote for Fianna Fáil in significant numbers. Despite great optimism, Fianna Fáil had found itself unable to dictate the campaign agenda. Though emphasising growth and unemployment, the party was effectively deflected from these issues by Fine Gael and had to respond on terms dictated by its opponents. Unemployment never became a major campaign issue despite its significance in the opinion polls, nor could Fianna Fáil make it so; within a week of launching its manifesto serious discussion of this theme had been dropped.

It may be that the two of the issues that did become salient in the media, the Anglo-Irish Agreement and fiscal policy, placed Fianna Fáil at a disadvantage. As Laver, Mair and Sinnott show below, however, the Anglo-Irish Agreement does not seem to have been very salient with *voters*, whatever about its treatment by the media. Certainly the party was forced to adopt positions not of its own making on both of these policy areas. It would have suited the party to be more interventionist on the economy and more republican on the Agreement, but it also had to appeal to voters who did not share these views. The evidence suggests that Fianna Fáil failed to do so.

Fine Gael's success, however, was also very limited. Having pursued a negative campaign it was unable to make up for its loss of popularity when in government. The most novel feature of the campaign was the challenge posed by the PDs to the established parties. For the first time in 40 years a new party was playing a pivotal role in Irish politics. As an anti-tax party it successfully placed this issue at the centre of the debate and forced Fianna Fáil and Fine Gael to address it seriously.

Overall, the main issues in the campaign were defined by Fine Gael and the PDs rather than by Fianna Fáil. The politics of economic growth, once the main feature of Irish politics, has been replaced by the politics of fiscal constraint. On top of this the politics of Irish unity, as expressed in the Constitution, has been seriously modified by the Anglo-Irish Agreement. Although Fianna Fáil remains the largest single party, it must now share the centre-right of the political spectrum with two other parties. All three parties share some common ground, but on many issues there is considerable disagreement. This has so far resulted in increased electoral competition between the parties and such a development may prevent Fianna Fáil from obtaining an overall majority in the foreseeable future.

3. POLICY COMPETITION

Peter Mair

CONTEXT AND CHANGE

One of the great enduring myths about Irish political divisions is that they represent the democratic continuation of the civil war conflict. More than sixty years on, so the argument goes, modern Irish politics is still replaying the old issues of the early 1920s. The mutual hostility of Fianna Fáil and Fine Gael, for example, is seen to be comprehensible only by reference to the armed internecine struggle of their ancestors. The persistent failure of Labour seems understandable only by pointing to the party's irrelevance in the civil war conflict, and its subsequent inability to push social and economic issues onto an agenda dominated by arcane nationalist concerns. In effect, the myth of the maintenance of civil war politics represents the default option in any attempt to account for the puzzles of Irish politics and, in particular, appears to offer an easy understanding of the persistence of traditional political alignments as well as of their evident peculiarities.

More recently, a new myth has emerged which is intended to challenge this long-standing interpretation. According to this new myth, Irish politics ceased being about civil war politics in the mid-1980s. Proponents of this new view, point to the Anglo Irish Agreement which was signed in November 1985, and to the way in which this was successfully sold to the general public in terms which quite explicitly relegated Irish unity to a secondary position in the order of national priorities. The new myth is also reinforced by the evidence that Fianna Fáil met with little success on the ground when it sought to articulate a fairly unreconstructed irredentist nationalism during the immediate wake of the Hillsborough meeting. The break up of civil war politics seemed further confirmed by the departure of Des O'Malley and Mary Harney from the Fianna Fáil ranks, and by the subsequent success of their new party, the Progressive Democrats. These were the mould breakers par excellence, touting an apparent translation of Thatcherism while at the same time heralding a pluralist and essentially anti-irredentist version of the national interest; few if any parties have ever seemed less set in the civil war mould.

But despite their evident appeal - to journalists, to academics and even to the politicians themselves - neither of these myths is easily sustained by the evidence of the actual party policies. On the contrary, even a quick perusal of the parties' election programmes reveals that civil war politics died long before the mid-1980s and emphasises that, for all their continued enmity, both Fianna Fáil and Fine Gael have long eschewed traditional nationalist divisions in their attempts to mobilise electoral support.

Hence, while the Progressive Democrats may have cast themselves in a mould breaking role, their view of this mould as having been set in the 1920s was essentially misconceived - at least as far as the actual policies of the other Irish parties are concerned. As will be argued here, the most recent patterns of policy competition suggest not only that 1987 failed to inaugurate a wholly new repertory of concerns, but also that the emergence of the PDs as a significant electoral force precipitated an actual revival of earlier political themes, with the fragmentation of the anti-Fianna Fáil block encouraging a return to a language of political competition that had lain dormant for some time. The 1987 contest may well have signified a change in the recent pattern of policy competition in Irish politics; in and of itself, however, it represented little that was new.

THE POLICY CONTEXT

In order to understand the significance of the 1987 contest, it is necessary to underline that, when Irish parties have competed, they have done so on the basis of their social and economic programmes and at most they have simply paid lip service to traditional nationalist shibboleths.

At one level, these social and economic programmes were characterised by a substantial degree of consensus; at another level, however, substantial differences have existed in terms of the parties' respective priorities and in the manner in which these priorities have been justified. Fianna Fáil, Fine Gael and Labour all remained committed to the maintenance of the welfare state throughout the 1960s and 1970s, for example, yet they differed significantly in the priority that they gave to the need for a redistribution of resources. To be sure, these differences did not easily lend themselves to a simple left-right characterisation of party policy; nevertheless they were real, they were consistent, and they also made eminent sense of an alignment of the party system around the fundamental opposition of Fianna Fáil to both Fine Gael and Labour.

But before elaborating further on these differences, it is first necessary to understand the parameters of the policy consensus which did exist before 1987. An analysis of the election programmes issued between 1961 and 1982 reveals five crucial concerns which were common to all three main parties. Each of these concerns ranked among the ten most frequently mentioned themes in the election programmes of each of the parties. In order of importance these were: first, a commitment to the expansion of social services including education; second, a commitment to represent the major social interests; third, a commitment to economic growth and employment; fourth, a commitment to administrative efficiency; and fifth, a commitment to strong and effective government. The relative emphasis on these themes varied from party to party. Fianna Fáil, for example, laid significantly more emphasis on the need for strong government and economic growth than did either Fine Gael or Labour, while Labour laid more emphasis on the need to expand the social services than did either Fianna Fáil or Fine Gael. Notwithstanding such differences in emphasis, however, it is important to recognise that all five concerns were common to all three parties, while all five were also relatively straightforward and uncontentious, leaving Irish parties looking no different from their counterparts in most West European states.

This consensus is not the whole story, of course, for there were other issues which were emphasised by one or two of the parties but not by all three. Both Fianna Fáil and Fine Gael, for instance, have stressed support for private enterprise and both also stressed the need for social solidarity, yet neither of these themes was emphasised by Labour. Labour and Fine Gael on the other hand shared an emphasis on the need both for government control of the economy and for social justice, with neither theme being emphasised by Fianna Fáil. Each of the three parties was also characterised by its own individual priorities. Thus Labour proved singular in its emphasis on both democratic rights and quality of life issues, although neither concern came anywhere near to dominating the Labour policy agenda. Fine Gael, on the other hand, was singular in its emphasis on fiscal rectitude, while Fianna Fáil stood alone in emphasising law and order and the need for Irish unity. This last theme represented the only real incursion of the traditional nationalist appeal onto the policy agendas of the three main parties. Even then it barely registered, however, for it occupied only tenth position in the list of Fianna Fáil's ten most frequently cited appeals.

This initial survey of the pattern of consensus and conflict in the policy agendas of the parties in the 1961-1982 period, together with a more sophisticated statistical analysis of the overall programme contents (which is not reported here), offers a clearer understanding of the underlying basis of policy competition in this period.[1] It thus permits a more rigorous assessment of the extent to which the 1987 contest represents a real rupture with the past. In effect, it enables a definition of the principal policy dimension along which the parties have competed, thereby identifying how, if at all, the parties have been divided.

One end of this broad policy dimension is characterised by an emphasis on three specific policy themes: first, the emphasis on strong government; second, the emphasis on social solidarity and the national interest; and third, the emphasis on economic growth. Together these constitute what might be loosely defined as a generalised corporatist appeal, and they combine to encapsulate what is particularly distinctive about the Fianna Fáil position under Lemass and Lynch. The other end of the dimension is simpler, and reflects an emphasis on, first, social justice and, second, the need for government control of the economy. This particular combination constitutes a generalised social-democratic appeal and encapsulates the position of Labour. In between these two 'extremes' lies Fine Gael, approximating to the Labour position in its emphasis on social justice and the need for government intervention, and approximating to the Fianna Fáil position in its emphasis on social solidarity. The average positions taken by the parties on this policy dimension are shown in Figure 1.

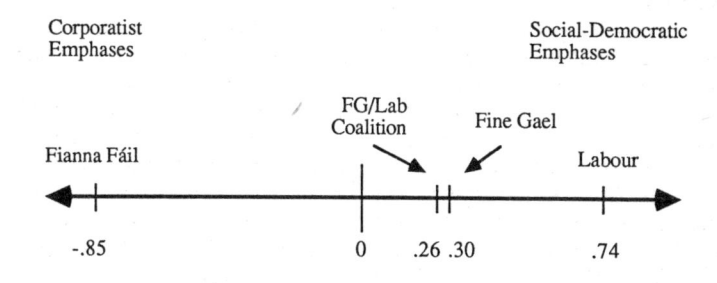

Figure 1: Average policy positions of Irish parties 1961-82

It is also interesting to note that if we study the movements of the three main parties along this dimension between 1961 and 1982 we see a significant trend in the position adopted by Fine Gael which, with the publication of its *Just Society* programme in 1965, shifts markedly towards the social-democratic end of the dimension.[2] Indeed by 1969, which was the last election predating the Fine Gael-Labour Coalition of 1973, the two opposition parties were clearly aligned on the basis of a common commitment to a social democratic appeal which, in turn, lay at quite a remove from the corporatist appeal of Fianna Fáil.

But what did these clear differences signify in more substantive terms? In what sense did the corporatism of Fianna Fáil differ from the soft social democratic appeal of Fine Gael and Labour ?

In brief, the difference lay in the relative emphasis on redistribution. In the 1960s and 1970s, and arguably also in earlier years, the Fianna Fáil commitment to welfarism was essentially contingent. While the party's first General Secretary was certainly justified when he recalled that 'the backbone of Fianna Fáil was the dispossessed class', nevertheless postwar party policy never really sought to represent the interests of the working class, the small farmers or the poor in any *exclusive* sense.[3] Party policy was certainly articulated as being of benefit to have-nots of Irish society, but the promised gains were to be measured in absolute rather than in relative terms. The have-nots would benefit in a context where all would benefit, and while their share of the national pie would remain unchanged, the commitment to growth would ensure that the pie itself would expand in real terms. In Lemass's famous phrase, 'the rising tide would lift all boats' and the party would not admit to privileging any specific social constituency.

As far as Labour, and later Fine Gael, were concerned, this proved an inadequate commitment. Like Fianna Fáil, both parties emphasised the need to build a welfare state but, while Fianna Fáil was more or less content to promise an expansion of the social services in the context of an expanding economy, the two opposition parties linked their commitment to welfarism to a further commitment to social justice, calling for a degree of redistribution of national resources. The rising tide might eventually lift all boats but, for Fine Gael and Labour, there were some boats which simply could not wait for the tide and which required more immediate attention. The shareout of the expanding national product needed readjustment. It was this common ground between the opposition parties which was to facilitate their later alliance in 1973.

The Labour commitment to social redistribution is unsurprising. The party has always articulated some version of reasonably left-wing policies. The shift in Fine Gael, on the other hand, does need to be underlined, for it represented a significant transformation of the party's traditional appeal. As recently as the late 1950s, for example, the then party leader John A. Costello had defined Fine Gael's appeal in terms of the need to claw back the state and to ensure the maximum of individual freedom. Twenty years later, by contrast, Fine Gael had appeared to align itself firmly in a social democratic mould and Garret FitzGerald could proudly proclaim to the Árd Fheis that 'the single great issue that makes us different from Fianna Fail as any two parties could be is our commitment to social justice'.[4]

This then was the essence of policy competition in the 1960s and 1970s: a consensus at one level but a significant divide at another, with Fianna Fáil pledging gains for all, and with Fine Gael and Labour combining to emphasise the need for a more effective redistribution of resources. By 1987, this pattern had been thrown into disarray.

THE CHALLENGE OF RECESSION

While the causes of the recent economic recession may be disputed, and while the prescriptions for a solution may be the subject of wideranging debate, the impact of recession on party policy was quite clear: by the mid-1980s, no party could plausibly pledge prosperity. Ireland was characterised by a politics of retrenchment, in which the promise of gains for all was replaced by the threat of cuts for many. The consequences for the policy strategies of the major parties were considerable.

One of the first and most telling consequences of the recession was a challenge to the plausibility of Fianna Fáil's postwar corporatist appeal. Fianna Fáil's appeal had been based on a commitment to welfarism in a context of strong government, of social solidarity and above all, of economic growth.[5] Given that overall growth meant an expanding national pie, then all sections of the community - farmers, workers and employers - would benefit from Fianna Fáil government. In the 1980s, however, and particularly in the wake of Fianna Fáil's expansionary swansong in 1977, the pie had clearly begun to get smaller and the promise of gains for all had quickly been transformed into a reality of hardship for many. At the same time, however, Fianna Fáil survival was still dependent on its capacity to bind together a broad cross-class constituency. And, if the corporatist appeal of Lemass and Lynch was no longer adequate to this electoral task, then an alternative mode of electoral mobilisation was required.

In the event, the party sought an alternative in its own past traditions and resurrected the original traditionalism of de Valera in an effort to forge a ready replacement for its faltering corporatist appeal. Thus, by the early 1980s and under the new leadership of Charles Haughey, the party found itself returning to past shibboleths. Evidence of this can be seen in Fianna Fáil's insistence on a unitary state solution in the New Ireland Forum discussions; its opposition to the Anglo-Irish Agreement in the Dáil; its strident advocacy of the constitutional ban on abortion and its effective opposition to the removal of the constitutional ban on divorce. As Dick Walsh concluded in his recent study of the party, Fianna Fáil was 'marrying religious and political fundamentalism - the partners of the past - with an eye to electoral opportunity'.[6]

The problem was that even these traditional appeals no longer proved so effective. To be sure, a majority of the voters in the constitutional referenda ended up on the same side as Fianna Fáil, and the campaigns undoubtedly undermined the new pluralist appeal of Fine Gael in particular. The strident position on irredentist nationalism proved significantly less popular, however, and the generally lukewarm response to the revival of traditional Fianna Fáilism suggested that it could not provide a sufficient basis for a winning electoral platform. The shift also had significant repercussions within Fianna Fáil itself. The resurrection of traditional virtues precipitated quite a significant wave of intra-party dissent, and eventually forced the departure of O'Malley and Harney and the later formation of the Progressive Democrats. Far from reconstituting Fianna Fáil hegemony, therefore, Haughey's revival of traditional appeals seemed set to leave the party even more vulnerable than before.

The recessionary context also had an impact on Fine Gael policy, forcing the party to adapt to middle-class discontent and to move away from its relatively new found commitment to social democracy. Increasing taxation, a growing public debt and the rapid growth of welfare had produced a quite unprecedented level of class/status polarisation in Irish society which had undermined such commitment to social justice as had existed among the more privileged. As the recession bit more deeply, Fine Gael found it increasingly difficult to balance the interests of its traditional middle-class constituency with those of the working-class voters whom the party had begun to attract in growing numbers during the 1970s.

Fine Gael's new-found commitment to social justice in the 1960s and 1970s had reaped significant rewards in working-class constituencies. As recently as 1979, FitzGerald had been quite unequivocal in stating that 'Fine Gael is now seeking to become the acknowledged party of the working man and woman',[7] and opinion polls on the eve of the November 1982 election revealed that 28% of working-class respondents preferred his party.[8] At the same time, however, the party had managed to retain a substantial proportion of its traditional middle-class constituency, as well as its traditional support among farmers.

This electoral balancing act had been largely achieved through persistent appeals to the altruism of the party's more privileged voters, and these appeals in turn had been largely made possible by overall economic growth. A slowdown of growth, on the other hand, was likely to threaten the electoral balancing act, given that any appeal to altruism might then fall on deaf ears. In other words, if and when resources began to contract, self-interest would be more likely to gain the upper hand and the prospects of a welfare backlash would become ever more likely. As FitzGerald himself pointed out in an interview with Magill, 'we have to face the reluctance of a majority of the people to accept a reduction in living standards in favour of the minority.[9] This reluctance is most evident in a no-growth period, as during the recent crisis, whereas when prosperity is increasing it is easier to win acceptance of redistributive measures'.

As the recession deepened, therefore, so also did the level of discontent within Fine Gael. Left-right tensions emerged quite explicitly, with fiscal rectitude quickly replacing social justice as the key rallying point within the party. In the process, relations with Fine

Gael's long-term coalition ally, Labour, became increasingly fractious, while disputes between the Labour leadership and the more conservative wing of Fine Gael became ever more public. This inter-party, intra-coalition conflict eventually culminated in the withdrawal of Labour from government in January 1987, thus precipitating the February election.

LEFT AND RIGHT IN THE 1987 ELECTION

The single most important element which intervened to distort the pattern of policy competition in the 1987 election was the birth of the Progressive Democrats, the first child of the recession. The formation of the new party had been prompted initially by internal Fianna Fáil discontent with the neo-traditionalist appeal espoused by Charles Haughey. As the party emerged with some force in early 1986, however, it was clear that its basis of appeal extended far beyond a simple commitment to a more pluralist version of nationalism. Had that been the sole justification for its existence, there would have been little reason for it to maintain a stance independent from Garret FitzGerald's Fine Gael.

In practice, the new party moved beyond its initial opposition to Fianna Fáil and began to espouse a distinct middle-class appeal, urging a substantial reduction in taxation, a new programme of privatisation and a policy of fiscal rectitude which could only be achieved through swinging cuts in public expenditure. In effect, the PDs offered unambiguous voice to precisely those same demands which formed the basis of conservative reaction within Fine Gael. Where it differed from Fine Gael, however, or at least from Fine Gael prior to January 1987, was in its refusal to countenance a reliance on the left. Coalitions are not disastrous per se, the PDs' 'Notes for Speakers' pointed out during the election campaign: 'what is wrong with the coalition concept up to now in Ireland is that it has always involved the Labour Party, which is in favour of high spending'.

The PD intervention therefore presented a significant source of competition to the right of Fine Gael. The latter could only respond to this challenge by moving more firmly to the right itself and by effectively abandoning the last vestige of its recently acquired social democratic commitment. Thus, when Fine Gael launched its policies in the 1987 election, it campaigned on a basis which was quite at odds with that on which it had campaigned in the 1960s and 1970s and which, if anything, simply recalled the policies last enunciated in the late 1950s. The circle had been completed, its closure precipitated by both the deepening recession and the party's new need to compete to the right.

The Fine Gael programme in 1987 was quite unequivocal in its emphasis on the market in the process of economic regeneration. The key policies for job creation, for example, included commitments to cut public spending, to reduce taxation, to encourage enterprise and to 'free rigidities in the labour market' - this last commitment including a proposal to reduce starting salaries for young people seeking their first jobs.[10] The party also committed itself to broaden share ownership and to initiate a process of the privatisation or semi-privatisation of state assets.

These echoes of the Thatcherite economic strategy were also complemented by a more cautious approach to the social services, emphasising the need to reduce public spending by targeting it at those most in need. Thus, 'even when social spending has to be cut, Fine Gael believes that those who most need assistance must be protected and social provisions for them should be improved. This can be done only in one way. We must reform social policy so that it becomes more selective.'[11] To be sure, the more progressive liberal legacy of the party was not wholly ignored. The programme included a substantial commitment to social reform, for example, particularly in the areas of family law, marriage and civil rights, while the party also committed itself to the enhancement of women's rights. Nevertheless, and particularly in contrast to the programmatic ethos of the 1960s and 1970s, Fine Gael's commitment to social justice in 1987 was notable by its absence.

The PD programme was virtually indistinguishable from that of Fine Gael. The new party shared its larger rival's commitment to cuts in public spending, but also hastened to add that these cuts would be selective and that 'the less-well-off will be protected by having state benefits and services focussed primarily on their needs'.[12] More generally, PD policy also shared the Fine Gael emphasis on the market as the source of stimulating economic regeneration - 'without incentive there can be no prosperity' - but proved significantly more strident in its ideological assault on the role of the state.[13] What the country needs, stated the PDs' *Message to the Irish People*, is 'a truly republican view of the state, where the individual is master, and not slave to the system; where the state protects the needy, but encourages the brave'.[14]

In the same vein, the party's commitment to substantial reductions in taxation and to a policy of privatisation were justified in quite strong anti-statist rhetoric. Thus, *The Message to the Irish People* [15] went on to emphasise that

> 'we believe that the state must play a less dominant role in the economic and social life of the country This programme will result in a fundamental shift from the state back into the hands of the people. Irish people are highly individualistic. We have record levels of home ownership and land ownership. Yet we have the curiosity of a level of state involvement in economic activity which exceeds that in many socialist countries. Under the Progressive Democrats' policies, people will keep more of what they earn, rather than suffering automatic expropriation by the state.'

Such an appeal was hardly new to Irish politics; consider the following statements by John A. Costello, listing the principles underlying the Fine Gael appeal in 1954:[16]

> 'that, where possible, any assistance [to those in need] be stimulated and supported by state activity but not supplanted or coerced. . . that the electorate be encouraged to a recognition that any promises or benefits are, in effect, promises by politicians to take more money from the people and spend it for them. . . that [the] policy of increased incomes can be done less well by direct Government activity than by the stimulation of private enterprise. . .that in all directions a positive approach of encouragement replaces a negative policy of control.'

If Fianna Fáil could be seen to have resurrected the ghost of de Valera just a few years earlier, then Fine Gael and the Progressive Democrats could now be seen to have resurrected the ghost of John A. Costello. It is in this sense that one can begin to see 1987 as a revival of the old rather than simply as the emergence of the new. Where 1987 did make a break with more recent precedent, however, was in the clarification of an emerging polarisation between right and left.

The shift to the right in Fine Gael, together with the avowedly middle class appeal of the Progressive Democrats, inevitably forced Labour into a much more openly left wing stance. While the smaller party was at pains to emphasise an acceptance of the gravity of the economic crisis facing Ireland, and while it admitted the need to effect a more equitable balance between government revenue and government spending, its proposed solution involved a growth of revenue rather than a reduction in expenditure, and it also proved quite unequivocal in its support for increased state direction of the economy. Forcing attention away from an exclusive concentration on the fiscal crisis, Dick Spring launched the Labour programme by emphasising the party's concern with [17]

> 'the evils of unemployment and social injustice as the two great national problems which must be solved, and solved quickly. The Party puts forward a range of proposals which are consistent with its long held socialist principles while being based on the realities of the present and the needs of the future. We present no easy solutions based on deception or promises. We present political facts as they really are and offer the electorate a radical alternative based on democracy and socialism.'

The programme went on to emphasise the importance of increased state investment and of 'a new dynamic and more directive relationship between the state and the private sector', and called for a 'redistribution of income, wealth and power'.[18] Its policies included an extension of the role of the National Development Corporation; opposition to the privatisation of state assets and complete state ownership and control of the natural gas industry. The party also called for a redistribution of the tax burden in order to gain an increased yield from business, from the self-employed and from farmers. The subsequent increase in revenue would then contribute to reduce the budget deficit and borrowing, and hence reduce the pressure to cut spending.

At the same time, however, Labour's own commitment to the spending programme was not wholly unqualified. With echoes of the Fine Gael and PD programmes, the party did allow for what it called 'carefully targeted cuts in public spending', adding that these would be acceptable only if they were 'just'. 'The poor and ordinary employees should not be asked to take the burden, while other groups make no contribution. The crisis must be shared. The last target must be the poor.'[19] As such, while accepting the need for some cuts, Labour also advocated a 4% increase in welfare benefits and, in the area of health, condemned the Fine Gael proposals on prescription charges and outpatient fees. More generally, the whole tenor of the Labour was predicated on a belief in the achievement of real economic growth, which, in the longer term, would help to restore a balance in government finances.

The second voice on the left, the Workers' Party, also predicated its programme on growth, but it also proved more emphatic in its commitment to redistribution and in its opposition to cuts. Accepting that the scale of the national debt had to be seen as a major economic problem, the party castigated the idea that a solution could be found in curtailed spending:[20]

> 'The word 'cuts' in the mouth of Fianna Fáil, Fine Gael, the Progressive Democrats or Labour means cuts in social welfare payments and cuts in spending on health and education. It is a policy of making the needy - the victims of the crisis - carry the burden of the crisis. A policy of cuts in government spending on social services will only aggravate the problem by increasing the scale of poverty. The Workers' Party puts forward a policy of expansion rather than cuts. We must grow or slow down. The debt crisis must be met by massive growth in our Gross Domestic Product.'

The Workers' Party policies included proposals for an expansion of the public sector; the removal of all restrictions on state companies; a massive programme of job creation; opposition to all privatisation; spreading the tax-burden to incorporate business, the self-employed and farmers; and the establishment of a minimum income for all, regardless of age, gender or employment status.

The combination of the unequivocal left appeal of the Workers' Party - described by its leader Tomas Mac Giolla as 'the only serious socialist party in the state with the determination to take up the challenge of the new right' - and the more self-consciously left wing rhetoric of the postcoalition Labour Party underlined the importance of left-right divisions in 1987.[21] From an electorally weaker base, both parties acted to mirror the more rightwing emphases in the promarket austerity programmes of Fine Gael and the Progressive Democrats.

FIANNA FÁIL AND THE CENTRE

But this is only part of the story, for it neglects the crucial position of Fianna Fáil. As noted above, Fianna Fáil in the mid-1980s had sought to resurrect the ghost of de Valera and to revive its traditional shibboleths in an effort to compensate for the declining appeal of Lemass style corporatism. Diminishing resources and the evidence of an emerging class/status polarisation in Irish society had appeared to undermine an electoralism based on the appeal for strong government, social solidarity and the national interest. At the same time, as noted above, it was increasingly unlikely that traditional Fianna Fáilism would generate the support necessary to return the party to government. Haughey himself was aware of the difficulty: concluding his Dáil speech in opposition to the Anglo-Irish Agreement in 1985, for example, he stated - perhaps recklessly given the later U-turn in the first months of office - that 'regardless of whether it costs us votes or popularity, we are not prepared to surrender by deserting the constitutional nationalist position'.[22] But even then he was already qualifying his position for, despite his opposition to the Agreement, he told the Irish Times that Fianna Fáil would not make it a major campaign issue: the party would be 'going to the country on economic issues'.[23] So what were the Fianna Fáil issues? To begin with, they were decidedly domestic; Northern Ireland was accorded just one page in the party's glossy 71 page programme. While the policy did emphasise opposition to the Agreement and a commitment to a unitary state solution, Fianna Fáil's position was nonetheless qualified by endorsement of the all-party Forum Report and by wholehearted support for 'any worthwhile reforms or improvement in the position of the Nationalist community that could be brought about by the [Anglo-Irish] Conference'.[24] Fianna Fáil was intent on retaining its nationalist credentials but it was also not going out on a limb to do so.

The bulk of the remainder of the programme concentrated on social and economic issues and the party's approach to these issues was clear. First, as Haughey emphasised when launching the manifesto, Fianna Fáil stood for strong, single-party government and looked with horror 'at the prospect of another coalition government and the instability, bargaining and so on'. The launching speech constantly returned to this theme. 'We have in Fianna Fáil the confidence and the experience . . . we will generate the confidence necessary for growth. . . [business needs] clear leadership, restoration of confidence and good management of their affairs [and a government] which knows what has to be done and is prepared to do it.'[25]

Second, the party was insistent that unemployment was a more pressing problem than that posed by the fiscal crisis and that the only real long term solution lay in increased economic growth. Third, the party argued that this growth could only be achieved by everybody working together, by renewed national solidarity and, in particular, by achieving 'an industrial consensus' through the involvement of the social partners in the creation of a plan for national recovery.[26] Indeed, this latter proposal was accorded pride of place in the party programme, being linked with proposals for financial management and taxation to provide the necessary framework for recovery. Fourth, while accepting the need for spending cuts, Fianna Fáil was insistent that the burden should not fall on those most in need and reasserted its commitment to the maintenance of as complete a welfare programme as was made possible by existing resources. As far as immediate problems were concerned, Haughey committed a Fianna Fáil government to bring forward proposed welfare increases and to explore the possibility of removing prescription charges.

This catalogue of concerns had a familiar ring and signified that, despite all the recent emphasis on irredentist nationalism and the defence of traditional values, traditional Fianna Fáilism had now suddenly been abandoned. Indeed, the only ghosts to stalk the launch of the programme were those of Lemass and Lynch - de Valera had been forgotten, at least temporarily. The echoes of Lemass were quite resounding with the emphasis on strong, single-party government, particularly in the wake of a coalition break up; [27] the commitment to welfarism; the stress on economic growth; and, in particular, the attempt to incorporate the trade unions in national planning (a strategy which may well account for Fianna Fáil's stated opposition to a policy of privatisation).[28]

How can this quite abrupt change be explained? Consider the situation as it emerged in 1987. A combination of the recession and the challenge from the PDs had forced Fine Gael to the right of the political spectrum. As against this Labour had moved to the left, aligning itself with the Workers' Party in distinct opposition to Fine Gael and the PDs. In short, the anti-Fianna Fáil opposition had fragmented, dissolving the formerly quite cohesive alternative platform which had characterised opposition to Fianna Fáil in the 1960s and 1970s.

And where did this leave Fianna Fáil? Where else, but with an opportunity to regain the centre ground which it had lost when forced to confront the reasonably coherent, social-democratic and essentially redistributive platform which had characterised the appeal of both Labour and Fine Gael in the 1960s and 1970s. By 1987, Fianna Fáil found itself in the position which it favours more than all others - confronting a multi-party opposition which had left the centre ground unoccupied.

In other words, and against all the odds, Fianna Fáil under Charles

Haughey in 1987 now found itself more or less in the same position as Fianna Fáil under Sean Lemass in 1957. First, it was the only party which looked like having any chance of forming a government - it was most unlikely that left and right could combine to form an alternative coalition and it was also extremely unlikely that the right on its own, in the shape of Fine Gael and the PDs, would win sufficient seats to form a new administration. Second, Fianna Fáil's credibility as the only potential government had been enhanced by the break up of the Fine Gael-Labour Coalition, just as it had been following the collapse of the inter-party government in 1957. And third, Fianna Fáil was attempting to mobilise support in the wake of a series of weak, alternating governments and in the context of severe economic recession.

If the circumstances of 1987 can be seen to have echoed those of 1957, then so also did the policy positions of the parties: Fine Gael competed from the right; Labour had begun to rediscover a socialist heritage; and Fianna Fáil sought the centre ground through the revitalisation of its corporatist appeal. On the one hand, it could appeal to the left through its commitment to welfarism, job creation, growth, and the incorporation of the unions; on the other hand, it could appeal to the right through its encouragement of enterprise and in its role as the party of business. With left fighting right in 1987, Fianna Fáil was happy to stretch its hands out to both and, in the process, to lay undisputed claim to the vacant centre ground.

There were, of course, additional constraints in 1987. The Workers' Party, for example, represented an added ingredient in a new and articulate leftwing politics; the PDs were also an added ingredient, in that they challenged Fine Gael's monopoly of conventional conservatism. But it can be argued that these elements simply enhanced the prospects for Fianna Fáil, for they accentuated the fragmentation of the opposition and so underlined the larger party's claim to be the only plausible governing alternative.

In the event, however, the strategy proved only partially successful. While Haughey may have sought to emulate the appeal of Lemass in 1957, his party ended up with just over 44% of the poll, as against more than 48% in 1957. In 1987, Fianna Fáil managed to win just 49% of Dáil seats, and was obliged to form yet another potentially vulnerable minority government; in 1957, by contrast, the party had commanded more than 53% of the seats and ended up enjoying a comfortable four year majority.

One of the principal lessons to be learned from 1987, therefore, is that, regardless of the changed electoral circumstances, the once resonant corporatist appeal of Fianna Fáil has still failed to ensure widespread popular success. Strong government remains an important rallying cry, but there is now greater concern with the policy output of government rather than its simple administrative effectiveness. The promise of growth may be commendable, but voters have now learned to treat such promises with scepticism. The appeal for social solidarity and the pursuit of the national interest may still be regarded as crucial electoral cues, but such an appeal now carries less meaning in a society which is increasingly characterised by extremes of wealth, status and power.

TRADITIONALISM VERSUS PLURALISM

The situation has been further complicated as a result of the growing importance of the conflict between traditionalism and pluralism in Irish politics. This contrasts a more liberal or pluralist commitment vis-a-vis Northern Ireland, family law and religion, with the more traditional Catholic and nationalist emphases. It is a contrast which has already been highlighted during the debates over such issues as abortion, contraception, divorce and the Anglo-Irish Agreement. As opinion polls evidence and the referenda imply, this cleavage has been reinforced by both interregional and interclass divisions. What is more significant, however, is that it represents a set of issues which has the potential to unite - however contingently - the otherwise sharply divided anti-Fianna Fáil opposition.

The clearest example of this potential common ground can be seen in the parties' respective commitments vis-a-vis Northern Ireland and the Anglo-Irish Agreement, even though, as has been the case throughout the postwar years, the parties' policies on Northern Ireland constitute just a tiny proportion of their overall programmes. The Fianna Fáil position has already been noted and can be summarised briefly as one of unequivocal support for unity, coupled with a more cautious opposition to the Anglo-Irish Agreement. While Fianna Fáil did underline its support for 'any worthwhile reforms or improvement in the position of the Nationalist community' that could be achieved through the Hillsborough initiative, the party made little secret of its dissatisfaction with the degree of recognition afforded by the accord to the constitutional position of Northern Ireland.

Fianna Fáil stood alone in this opposition. Fine Gael, unsurprisingly, endorsed the Agreement completely and offered a lengthy catalogue of various practical reforms which had been achieved since Hillsborough. The party also emphasised that the degree of recognition afforded to Northern Ireland had 'removed all possible grounds for Unionist fears of unification being imposed on them' and insisted that the Agreement had 'effectively removed the British question from Irish politics, leaving decisions on Ireland's future to Irish people in Ireland'.[29] The Progressive Democrats also endorsed the Agreement, specifying a commitment to work for 'peace and reconciliation among the divided communities in Northern Ireland', while neglecting even to mention the prospect of territorial unity.[30] In a separate document outlining its policy on justice and law reform, the PDs also called for a rewriting of Articles 2 and 3 of the Constitution 'in order to make clear that we favour unity by consent'.[31]

The two left parties adopted a similar position, with Labour even going so far as to incorporate its Northern Ireland policy under the heading of 'Ireland and Our Neighbours'. The policy itself was brief. 'Labour is dedicated to the promotion of peace and stability in Northern Ireland, through reconciliation of the two traditions, and through a guaranteed voice for the minority community in Northern Ireland.' The remainder of the section expressed support for the policy of neutrality and for nuclear disarmament and pledged solidarity with the Third World.[32] The Workers' Party also neglected to mention territorial unity but was critical of the Anglo-Irish Agreement insofar as it had alienated the Unionist community. It urged an end to direct rule, the introduction of devolved government and the enactment of a Bill of Rights. The party also emphasised the need for class politics within Northern Ireland, claiming to stand alone 'in opposing the sectarian politics and parties of both the Unionist and Nationalist blocks'.[33]

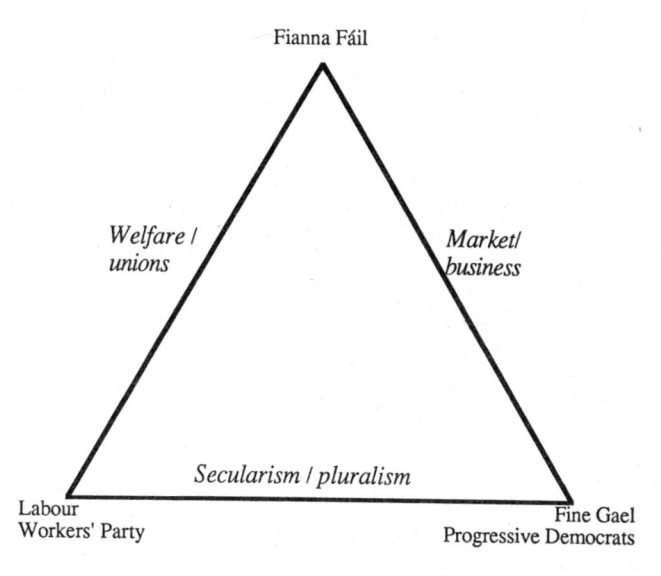

Figure 2: The ideological dimensions of modern Irish politics

While the absence of a strident irredentist politics offers perhaps the best example of the common ground forged by the left and right in opposition to Fianna Fáil, their shared concerns also spill over into more domestic issues. In particular they reflect a relatively united voice in support of a more pluralist and secular culture in the Republic itself.

The general effect, therefore, is that the combination of left-right divisions in social and economic policy with divisions on the dimension of traditionalism versus pluralism led to the creation of a crudely triangular alignment of the parties in contemporary Irish politics (see Figure 2).[34] This ideological configuration offers three potential bases for an inter-party alliances. On one side of the triangle, Fianna Fáil can attempt to find common ground with the left in resisting pressure for drastic cuts in public spending, while at the same time emphasising the need for a trade-union voice in the planning process. On another side, Fianna Fáil can attempt to find common ground with the right through an encouragement of the market and through an emphasis on private enterprise. Finally, left and right can find mutual common ground against Fianna Fáil in terms of their more pluralist and secular commitments.

In the end, however, it is this very complexity which may yet prove to be the salvation of Fianna Fáil. There seems little in terms of economic or social policy, for example, which could bring Labour and the Workers' Party into the same anti-Fianna Fáil lobby as Fine Gael and the Progressive Democrats. At the same time, as the party's recent statements on the Anglo-Irish Agreement indicate, it is likely that Fianna Fáil will attempt to circumvent those issues in the pluralist arena which might bring together its otherwise divided opponents. In this sense, the party may prove reasonably secure in office.

As against this, however, it must be emphasised that this analysis is based on the programmes of the parties as announced in the intensely competitive vote-seeking environment of an election campaign. Parties behave differently once the polls have closed and already there is clear evidence that Fianna Fáil have begun to embrace the sort of austerity programme which it took such care to denounce on the hustings. Yet, if anything, such a shift is likely to provoke only the opposition of the left, and that is something which the party can live with quite easily.

CONCLUSION

Regardless of the original imperatives underlying the formation of the Irish party system, there is no real sense in which the politics of postwar Ireland can be characterised as civil war politics. The society which the parties seek to govern has changed considerably over the decades and generations since independence and, in adapting to this change, the pattern of party competition has been modified almost beyond recognition. By the early 1960s, the essentially nationalist opposition which divided Fianna Fáil and Cumann na nGaedheal/Fine Gael in the early years of the state had been transformed and a new opposition had emerged which pitted the loose corporatist appeal of Fianna Fáil against the soft social-democratic emphases of Labour and Fine Gael.

By the early 1980s, however, there were signs that even this more recent pattern was undergoing a process of transformation. Severe recession and the emergence of a politics of retrenchment had undermined the electoral plausibility of Fianna Fáil. In response, and in an effort to restore its electoral fortunes, the party then appeared intent on resurrecting more traditional shibboleths even if, as was the case, such a move encouraged the secession of those elements within the party who had been nurtured within the corporatist ethos of Lemass and Lynch. The deepening crisis in the 1980s also strained Fine Gael-Labour relations, pushing the former to the right and encouraging the latter to revive a more explicitly socialist appeal.

Yet, by the time of the 1987 contest, and perhaps ironically, it was this clear fragmentation in the anti-Fianna Fáil camp which afforded Haughey the opportunity to rehabilitate the very appeal which he had once seemed so ready to discard. The centre ground had been vacated, a new confidence was required and the party found itself in a position to play the left off against the right while offering itself as the repository of the best virtues of each.

The pattern of policy competition in 1987 therefore represented a significant change from more recent elections, but it offered little that was new Fine Gael, now joined by the Progressive Democrats, sought to revive the principles last enunciated by John A. Costello in the 1950s. Labour, gingered on by the challenge from the Workers Party, sought to rediscover its socialist credentials. And Fianna Fáil, despite its recent greening, found itself echoing the appeals of Lemass in the late 1950s and early 1960s. The circle had indeed closed, even though the parties now confront an electorate which is more critical, more polarised and arguably more demanding than at any stage in postwar history.

4. CAMPAIGN STRATEGIES

David M. Farrell *

When writing about elections in Ireland there is an understandable tendency to focus on the local campaigns, on individual personalities and on particular trends in the forty-one separate constituencies of a political system where 'localism' is endemic. For some time, however, Irish parties have been placing increasing emphasis on their national electoral strategies and on the marketing techniques necessary to get them across to the electorate.

In 1977 Fianna Fáil took the initiative with a carefully prepared marketing strategy. In 1981 it was the turn of Fine Gael to set the trend in a campaign which, in terms of professionalism, was well up to the standards of national campaigning in other countries.[1] Six years later, it is interesting to see what has changed on the national campaign front; how the two big parties measure up to the upheavel in the party system; how the Progressive Democrats launched their bid for Dáil seats; and how the smaller parties are faring.

THE PREPARATIONS OF THE PARTIES

Fianna Fáil

With the formation of the majority Coalition Government in November 1982, Fianna Fáil found themselves in the position, for the first time since Haughey's election as party leader, of having an extended period of time to prepare the party machinery for an effective campaign at the following election. The party was at rock bottom in terms of campaign readiness and candidate talent.

Work to correct these deficiencies progressed on several fronts and in much the same fashion as it did in Fine Gael after FitzGerald's election as leader in 1977.[2] The European Parliament election campaign was approached primarily as a morale booster but also as a first attempt at a nationwide strategy of vote-management.[3] The 1985 local elections also served the function of boosting morale, though their main role was to promote new candidates. In July 1985 the party set up a 'constituencies committee' chaired by Charles Haughey. This was to head-hunt talented candidates and supervise the nominating conventions.

The party also paid close attention to general organisational reform. In late 1983 'Operation Dublin' was initiated. At the time Dublin was Fianna Fáil's weakest region but it was also the area which held out the greatest scope for future electoral gains. Individual constituencies were targeted; 'paper' branches were closed down; close attention was paid to local organisational reform. Later similar attention was given to improving local organisational structures throughout the country. The final phase of organisational reform came after defections to the Progressive Democrats had the effect of removing factionalism within the party.

The party went on an election footing at the end of 1985. A special committee was set up, chaired by the party's press officer, P.J. Mara. This untitled and highly secretive committee carried out the functions of a communications committee. It was given a specific brief to produce initial plans for Fianna Fáil's message and tactics in the election. Members included people from public relations, advertising and the media. One of its first acts was to commission some qualitative research in the Spring of 1986. This research indicated that tax was not the big issue that the media and others suggested. The main issue was unemployment, followed by emigration and then tax reform.

Fianna Fáil speeches at the time reflected these findings. The research found that voters were weary of everyone blaming everyone else for the country's problems. Voters were looking for somebody to take charge, to provide leadership. At the same time favourable attitudes were expressed about Haughey, particularly about his leadership qualities. These findings suggested that the party's approach to the election should be positive and presidential. One other important finding was a significant fear among working class voters of the possibilities of a Fine Gael-Progressive Democrat coalition. The party commissioned a second national qualitative survey before the election. Its findings largely confirmed those of the earlier research. (During the election Fianna Fáil did not commission any further private research; instead, they received 'advice' from the agency they had been using before the campaign).

In early 1986 an election committee was set up, bringing together Mara's committee with selected organisational strategists. This was a nuts-and-bolts committee chaired by the party's director of elections, Paddy Lawlor. Its terms of reference were to finalise strategic preparations, including such things as preparing artwork and stencils for material produced by the constituencies and attempting for the first time to achieve a standardisation of publicity materials. The committee also organised the design and production of such things as leader's posters, issue leaflets and lapel stickers. Innovations included the renting of time on the 'Scannervision' sign on O'Connell Bridge in Dublin; planes with banners; and large helium balloons. Much work also went into preparing advertisements and party political broadcasts. O'Kennedy-Brindley (a subsidiary of the giant Saatchi and Saatchi advertising agency which has been used since 1979 by the British

Conservatives) were given the contract to design the party's advertisements and preliminary drafts were ready before the election was called.[4] Fianna Fáil refuse to provide any information about the numbers of posters and the amount of election literature printed. Nor will the party say how much was spent in the campaign. One estimate is that national headquarters spent one million pounds, while another million was spent by the constituencies.[5]

Fine Gael

Fine Gael preparations were modelled closely on their earlier campaigns. Most party strategists had worked on the 1981-1982 election series and knew exactly what was expected of them. However, there were several important differences. First, Fine Gael had spent four years in office as the senior partner in a very unpopular Government; the product would need a hard sell. Second, a lot of the 'heavyweight' strategists were no longer available, disqualified by public appointment, sickness, or simply pressure of work. This was to affect decision-making efficiency. Third, the remaining strategists worked in an uneasy atmosphere caused by close media scrutiny of their role as the 'national handlers'.[6] In some cases this appears to have limited their effectiveness.

Fine Gael preparations began in September 1986. As in earlier elections, a number of committees were set up to organise matters such as finance, the manifesto, candidates and media coverage. These were grouped into two strands, a strategy committee and a communications committee. These merged just before the election into a single election committee. The strategy committee which worked, among other things, on co-ordinating the campaigns in the constituencies. The party's general secretary, Finbar Fitzpatrick, organised a series of meetings with the constituency officers. In November, a 'constituency briefing manual' was circulated, detailing what to do before and during the campaign and what to expect from national headquarters in terms of posters, election literature, as well as stencils and artwork. Also in November 16,000 leader's posters (without a slogan) were circulated, to cover against the possibility of a sudden election.

The communications committee was much more compact than in earlier elections, reflecting the absence of some key strategists and the greater confidence of those involved. It met every Saturday from September onwards. To see where they stood, the committee commissioned a national qualitative survey in mid-1986. This found that by far the most important issue for voters was unemployment, much as Fianna Fáil's research had noted a few months before. Just as happened within Fianna Fáil, the findings of the qualitative research encouraged FitzGerald to make speeches stressing that unemployment was a more urgent problem than taxation.[7]

Campaign Strategies

In terms of the party's image some of the findings of the qualitative research were not too surprising. There were a number of criticisms of the party's, and of FitzGerald's, performance in government. What was interesting, however, was that respondents, when engaged in conversation by the interviewer, began to look at the party in a more favourable light. This suggested that a long election campaign could prove beneficial to Fine Gael. The researchers found a distinction among voters between a desire to return to the simple, sheltered, old ways of life and an understanding of the need to look forward to new, more modern ways of living. Fine Gael respondents tended towards the latter emphasis. This indicated that the party's best strategy was to push for change, for something of the order of FitzGerald's 'constitutional crusade'.

It was around this time that the party's press secretary, Peter White, commissioned an advertising specialist to devise a new party logo. The party, for the first time, dropped the traditional green colour and adopted the 'more marketable' blue.

The research also examined attitudes towards Fianna Fáil. Many respondents felt that there was no substance to the party, that the party was reducible to the leader, Charles Haughey. Fine Gael strategists later argued that in running a very low key campaign Fianna Fáil simply played into their hands, confirming to voters that Fianna Fáil had no substance, no new ideas. The research indicated that any personal attacks on Haughey would be a bad idea.

Fine Gael's private market research provided a useful backdrop to the committee's marketing preparations, which were designed with two features in mind. First, the Fine Gael campaign was going to be much more subtle than before. This was partially a reflection of the greater experience of the strategists who realised that a lot of expenditure in earlier elections on such things as press advertisements had been unnecessary and wasteful. It also reflected a more limited budget and a realisation that the 'sign of the times' warranted a campaign less reliant on gimmicks and razamataz. Second, the campaign was going to be a long one. The research recommended this and the strategists clearly expected it. In an interview in early September 1986, Fitzpatrick was quite explicit. 'In the past we went for a 21-day campaign instead of a 28-day one and that may change.' [8] This meant the campaign would have to be planned in such a way as to maintain momentum over an extended period.

Marketing preparations were much as in earlier elections, involving the design and production of posters, election literature and merchandising items. One of the new developments was the provision of extra material for canvassers who were to be in the frontline of antagonistic feedback and would need as much help as possible. Three canvassers' guides' were printed setting down the achievements of the

Government, stressing the importance of job creation and pushing for a majority Fine Gael Government. The committee also produced plastic coated 'issue cards' on taxation, state borrowing, agriculture, jobs, mortgages and social welfare. The idea for these had come from the German Christian Democrats who had been visited in the summer of 1986 by some members of the communications committee in a trip financed by the Konrad Adenauer Foundation. These cards provided a quick summary of the party's standpoint on the issues which could be handed out at the doorstep whenever any of the items arose in conversation.

The party produced more than 60,000 leader's posters and a few thousand larger posters and banners. Apart from the election addresses and canvassers' cards there were also more than 1.7 million canvassers' guides and issue leaflets; and about 450,000 'issue cards'. One important development was the use of a professional distribution agency (Swift Couriers) to transport material throughout the country within a day. In total, party headquarters spent about £800,000 on the campaign, with the constituencies spending anything from another £5,000 to £15,000 each.

There was no preelection billboard campaign. The strategists had doubts as to its value and they wanted to avoid provoking any unnecessary election mongering. Instead, the preelection campaign activities of Fine Gael consisted of a leader's tour which served the purpose of boosting morale, reducing FitzGerald's touring load during the election proper, and helping the strategists prepare for the election tour itself.

Progressive Democrats

Inevitably, the party which had to put the most effort into its campaign preparations was the Progressive Democrats, which had only been founded at the end of December 1985. The party lacked the grassroots network of experienced activists enjoyed by the established parties. One strategist estimated that two-thirds or more of the party's members had never before been active in politics. The party, in every sense of the word, was 'new'. The business of preparing it for the election was in the hands of the general secretary, Pat Cox, and the party's director of policy and press relations, Stephen O'Byrnes. The first phase in their preparations was a party conference which served the dual purpose of unveiling party policy and of consolidating the national organisation, introducing the members to each other for the first time.

The second phase of preparations took the remainder of the summer of 1986. Only a few months earlier, O'Byrnes had researched a book on Fine Gael, *Hiding Behind a Face*. Much of what he learned when doing this was useful in informing the preparations of the Progressive Democrats. The party set up two committees, a strategy committee under Cox and a communications committee which was initially chaired by O'Byrnes. The committees merged in November into an election committee.

The strategy committee was charged primarily with setting up an efficient organisational infrastructure, using an approach which was essentially three-pronged. First, each constituency in which the party was operating was examined, with close attention to such things as members, branches, finances, local issues and candidate potential.[9] Second, a detailed election planning manual was drawn up setting out a structure for local party organisations and an A-Z guide of how to conduct an election. Third, the committee organised canvassing seminars aimed at demonstrating to first-timers the exhilaration of campaigning and encouraging activists to engage in some preelection canvassing. The first of these seminars was held in July and the proceedings were videotaped, edited by Cox with commentary and circulated to all branches.

The communications committee was concerned with drawing up marketing plans. Irish Marketing Surveys (IMS) were commissioned to poll 18 selected constituencies in late August and early September to identify the characteristics of existing Progressive Democrat supporters and potential supporters ('convertibles'); to evaluate the party's image; and to identify 'the aspirations and expectations' of the party's supporters and of the electorate in general.

Progressive Democrat supporters were found to be predominantly middle class and located in urban centres and in the Munster region. They tended to be drawn more from Fine Gael than Fianna Fáil (a ratio of almost two to one). The poll indicated once more that the overriding issue was unemployment, particularly youth unemployment. Issues next in line included the need to reduce government spending and to cut taxes. Issues of secondary importance among Progressive Democrat supporters included the need to crack down on crime and to confine welfare payments to those most in need.

The IMS poll came up with three other important findings worth mentioning. First, the report noted 'evidence of a more 'go-ahead' attitude among Progressive Democrat supporters, revealed with (sic) a high degree of agreement with the statement that 'we are quick to begrudge the success of others''. (Sixty-seven percent of Progressive Democrat supporters agreed with the statement as opposed to 48% of all respondents). Second, the report found that possible Progressive Democrat 'convertibles' tended to opt for some form or another of coalition agreement involving the party. Twice as many of this particular subgroup would prefer a coalition arrangement with Fine Gael (20%), as opposed to one with Fianna Fáil (9%). Third, the party's leader, Desmond O'Malley was found to be associated with the party 'to a far greater extent than any other individual'.[10]

Kenny's advertising agency was commissioned in late Autumn 1986 to design an advertising campaign to launch the party in the marketplace. As far as the Progressive Democrats were concerned, one of their distinguishing features as a 'mould breaker' was to be a shift away from the cult of personality. However, the IMS poll clearly indicated that the party's greatest electoral asset was its leader. A very reluctant O'Malley was persuaded that he had to feature at least in the party's initial advertisements. The communications committee booked billboard sites in October-November 1986 to guard against a possible election and, if there was no election, to show a Progressive Democrat presence. The IMS poll's findings on the importance of O'Malley and of the 'go-ahead' attitude among Progressive Democrat supporters were linked together in the slogan 'Dessie Can Do It'. The 'can do it' approach was promoted by the party's strategists as the best means of gaining credibility, showing that nothing should be considered impossible, not least 'breaking the mould'. There was an initial uncertainty as to whether the surname or forename should be used (reflected in some Autumn press advertisements where the slogan was 'O'Malley Can Do It'). In the end the strategists got their way and the forename was used, stressing the human touch of the leader. Ultimately the slogan was retained for the election.

About 100,000 posters, 5.2 million canvassers' cards and 2.2 million election addresses were printed centrally, with some local input by the constituencies using artwork provided by headquarters. The party also produced 40,000 paper hats, 800,000 lapel stickers, 50,000 car stickers and 5,000 rosettes. Campaign expenditure by headquarters amounted to £450,000, with another £330,000 by the constituencies.

Labour

Labour's preparations started in the Autumn of 1986. A strategy group was set up under the party's Administrative Council with the function of providing guidance for the overall planning of the campaign. This was designed to take into account the possible circumstances in which the election might occur, circumstances which were difficult to predict. The group made the assumption that the most likely scenario would be a failure to agree on a budget and that this would occur in January-February. On that basis they booked a number of billboard sites and designed their advertising plans appropriately. Financially this was a big risk, but it paid off.

A Public Relations Unit was set up with about five members working in the areas of art and design. Their brief was to produce artwork and layouts, particularly for posters, and to provide a backup service for constituencies. Unlike the larger parties, all posters were printed centrally, guaranteeing standardisation.

Three sets of posters were printed: candidate posters in the first week, followed by leader's posters and issue posters. These latter, 'stop the lights' posters, signified the first use of issue posters by Labour. In all 140,000 posters were printed, at a cost of about £50,000. The party also printed election addresses, 250,000 issue leaflets, a manifesto and an 'alternative budget'. In total about £150,000 was spent on the campaign by national headquarters, with another £100,000 or so by the constituencies.

The Workers' Party

Despite its very limited financial resources, the Workers' Party also paid substantial attention to preparing a national strategy. As with Labour, all posters, canvass cards and election addresses were printed centrally and distributed directly from the printers to the constituencies. Party activists worked on design and artwork themselves. The only outside agency used was for the production of the party's party political broadcast. The Workers' Party leader, Tomas Mac Giolla, travelled around the country from Christmas onwards as a morale booster.

The Workers' Party spent £80,000 on the entire campaign. Among the items produced were 75,000 candidates' posters, several thousand issue posters, about 120,000 issue leaflets and more than two million canvass leaflets and 'postal manifestos'.

THE CAMPAIGN TRAIL

By the time the election was called each of the parties had its machinery ready for action. Posters and election literature were printed and distributed; policy documents, manifestos and the itineraries for the leaders' tours were finalised; national headquarters were set on an election footing with the recruitment of extra staff and the installation of any extra equipment needed for the campaign such as FAX machines and the like. Each of the parties was ready to start an election campaign. The question now - particularly in the context of a four week campaign - was whether they could see the campaign through, whether momentum could be maintained.

Leaders' tours were prepared with the same meticulous attention as in earlier elections. The difference this time, was that each of the party leaders made only brief excursions, returning each evening to Dublin. These were not the national whistlestop tours of 1977 or 1981. This fact, together with the decision to play down the razamataz and the fact that the tours tended to have less novelty, meant that they did not receive as much national media coverage as in earlier elections.

The three remaining communication vehicles on which the parties built their national campaigns were television coverage, press advertisements and the party manifesto, together with subsidiary policy documents.

The television campaign

The general consensus among party strategists was that, in 1987, the emphasis would be on television. Fianna Fáil took out an exclusive contract with Carr Communications. All leading Fianna Fáil politicians were given crash courses in television presentation, with particular attention being given to the six individuals selected as the principal party spokespeople for television and radio.

In the past Fine Gael have also made use of Carr Communications. Because this service was not available to them in 1987, however, the Fine Gael press officer set up a video camera at national headquarters and personally organised the training sessions with party spokespeople. Much the same approach was followed by the other three parties.

In every election there is always at least some tension between broadcasters and politicians over quantity and balance of media coverage. In this election such problems were compounded by the presence of five Oireachtas parties, which complicated the already difficult rules of balance, particularly on panel discussions. The amount of coverage is traditionally calculated on the basis of first preference votes in the previous election. Special allowance had to be made for the Progressive Democrats, however, given that the party's formation postdated the November 1982 election.

RTE decided that Fianna Fáil and Fine Gael should receive the bulk of the coverage; that their leaders should be offered the possibility of meeting in debate; and that all other parties should receive coverage proportionate to Dáil strength and candidate numbers.[11] Needless to say, frequent complaints were made by the parties over whether a fair balance had been achieved. Fine Gael was particularly unhappy with the balance of RTE news coverage throughout the campaign. Under Section 31 of the Broadcasting Act, RTE was not able to interview, or to broadcast recordings of speeches by, members of Sinn Féin, who were contesting the election for the first time on a non-abstentionist platform. This situation provoked protests from several quarters as well as, predictably, from Sinn Féin.

There were also disagreements over the party political broadcasts (PPBs) which many broadcasters feel have long outlived their usefulness. RTE sought to reduce the number and length of PPBs. The parties were not happy with this, each putting forward arguments as to why they deserved more time. Eventually a compromise was reached.[12]

Much of the preparation for Fianna Fáil's PPBs were done long in advance of the election. Following the advice of their qualitative research the emphasis was on a positive presentation, elaborating on the party's policies and stressing leader image. Their PPBs were produced at Windmill Lane Studios with much attention to snappy style and professionalism.[13]

Because of Fine Gael's decision to play down the razamataz and the fact that the party had a complicated message to put across the party's PPBs lacked the stylishness of earlier elections. They were produced by Anner Films Ireland Ltd. the day before presentation.

The Labour party concentrated their limited resources on their second PPB. The first PPB consisted of a straight piece-to-camera with the party leader. The second one was put together by their advertising agency using the theme of a pack of cards to elaborate on the differences between the parties.

The Progressive Democrats' PPB was produced by James Dillon Promotions. This concentrated on introducing the party's candidates to voters. The PPB was not, in the event, seen as being very effective. This may well have been because, since the tape of the original had been stolen, it was necessary to edit together a new broadcast very quickly.

It was generally accepted that the most impressive PPB in the campaign was that of the Workers' Party which, involving minimum expenditure, developed the theme of the popular quiz programme 'Mastermind'. This PPB was also produced by Anner Films with the assistance of an experienced RTE producer.

Advertising and policy

Fine Gael started the election with the release on consecutive days of their budgetary proposals and manifesto. The party's advertisements were produced by Arks. In the first week or so of the campaign these elaborated on Fine Gael's central campaign theme, 'breaking out of the vicious circle'. Originally Fine Gael had planned a campaign to run in two phases. First, an all out attack on Fianna Fáil and then, in the second half, a presentation of Fine Gael's proposals (a positive campaign), together with some attacks on the Progressive Democrats. Fianna Fáil's decision to stay out of the limelight in the first week disrupted Fine Gael's plans, and their attacks on Fianna Fáil did not really begin until the third week of the campaign. As recommended by the party's research, these attacks were not personalised; they concentrated rather on the costings of the Fianna Fáil programme.

The second part of Fine Gael's original strategy also had its difficulties. First of all, there was the problem of the Progressive Democrats. Opinion in Fine Gael was divided over whether the party should launch a tough attack on the Progressive Democrats in order to try to win back some of their own supporters, or whether they should try to come to some form of accommodation with the PDs, so as to maximise inter-party vote transfers. The latter group prevailed and, working through intermediaries, the party entered into discussion with the Progressive Democrats.

Accounts differ as to what happened. According to Fine Gael strategists, the two parties were agreed that FitzGerald would make a speech towards the end of the campaign recommending transfers and that O'Malley's response would, at worst, be a neutral one. The Fine Gael strategists put O'Malley's subsequent unequivocal 'no' down to last minute panic and indecision. For their part, the Progressive Democrat strategists argue that Fine Gael overtures were initially rebuffed, that ultimately some discussion did take place, but that there was no agreement between them. All that can be concluded is that somewhere down the line there was a misunderstanding.

At any rate, because of these discussions Fine Gael strategists were distracted and unable to attack the Progressive Democrats. The point has been made that perhaps the Progressive Democrats agreed to talk to them for this very reason. There were some critical speeches made by Fine Gael spokespersons and a few advertisements in evening newspapers declaring 'Dessie Can't Do It' but these represented little more than a 'shot across the bows'.

A second problem with the last part of the Fine Gael strategy was in trying to get across their positive message, explaining what Fine Gael proposed to do. Their advertisements in the final week of the campaign concentrated on selling this message with much stress on the party leader. Billboards went up throughout the country with pictures of FitzGerald sitting at his desk late at night and the slogan 'At the end of the day, you know who cares'.

Also in the final week of the campaign, media attention turned to the Anglo-Irish Agreement, examining Haughey's stance on it. Fine Gael argued Haughey was being inconsistent. This issue tended to distract attention from Fine Gael's attempts to put forward a positive emphasis and the Fine Gael arguments tended to give the impression that they were raising the 'Haughey factor', personalising their attacks on the Fianna Fáil leader.

Fine Gael strategists intended to use the television debate at the end of the campaign as a key opportunity for FitzGerald to elaborate on party policy. Great effort went into preparing for the debate. FitzGerald was ordered to spend the day away from the campaign trail and the previous night and during a lot of the next day several key advisors (including a former RTE journalist) went through practice sessions with FitzGerald, working with the index cards which it was intended he would use on the night. An agenda, proposed by the current affairs programme, *Today Tonight*, was agreed with the parties, although Fine Gael sought some changes. The major items their sequence and the order of speakers for each heading were known so that the cue cards could be put in order.

Due to a misunderstanding, however, the first question put to FitzGerald at the opening of the debate was not what he had expected and, as a result, he found himself unable to follow the order of the index cards. This seriously damaged the well-laid plans of Fine Gael to push its positive image, but to some extent it was probably an important factor in FitzGerald's winning of the debate. To compensate for his inability to use the index cards, FitzGerald adopted a more aggressive approach than had been intended, and than had been expected by Haughey. This culminated in FitzGerald scoring a very important point over an inconsistency of Haughey's in relation to the Anglo-Irish Agreement.

Haughey, for his part, was probably over-prepared. While he was well on top of his brief, the impression was that too much effort had gone into appearance and suitable poses which, on the night, did not work well. He had been advised by his consultants at Carr Communications to appear relaxed and dignified. In the face of FitzGerald's repeated onslaughts, however, this tended to give a more furtive impression.

Fianna Fáil's advertising approach took a longterm perspective. The party ran a billboard campaign in October-November 1986 (around the same time as the Progressive Democrats) and speeches were made attacking the Government on unemployment, emigration and the health cuts. The Fianna Fáil approach was to concentrate their attacks on the period before the election. Their qualitative research recommended a positive strategy during the campaign: 'taking the high ground and being positive'. Voters were fed up with politicians bickering with each other. The strategists wanted to exploit this and to tie in the impression that Fianna Fáil was the natural party of government.

On the face of it Fianna Fáil's overall campaign was nothing if not positive. A conscious decision was taken that, whatever the Government may have planned, Fianna Fáil were going to campaign only for three weeks, the argument being that a four week campaign was both difficult to maintain and wasteful in terms of trying to influence voters. On the Thursday of the second week Fianna Fáil released its manifesto, *The Programme for National Recovery*.

The launch was carefully designed to be 'presidential', and 'dignified'; the emphasis being less on content than on image. To maintain momentum and to develop the positive theme the strategists arranged for the launching of supplementary policy documents, at the rate of about two a week for the remainder of the campaign, on such topics as forestry, crime, financial services and youth. For each of these the party called a press conference, thus attempting to set an issue for the day and to compensate for the lack of media attention to formal prereleased scripts.

Whatever about Fianna Fáil's intention for the campaign, the emphasis was not in fact entirely positive; nor, indeed, was it only concentrated into the final three weeks. If anything, the party's advertisements mirrored those of Fine Gael. As we have seen, Fine Gael started by explaining their proposals; they then turned to attacking Fianna Fáil; and finally they ended with further explanations of their proposals. In contrast, Fianna Fáil opened their campaign in the first week with advertisements pointing out the weaknesses of coalition government, following the recommendations of their qualitative research. This was also a means of showing a campaign presence prior to the delayed release of their manifesto and helped to counter Fine Gael's and Labour's attempts to distance themselves from their record in government. The second stage of the Fianna Fáil advertising strategy coincided with the release of the manifesto and lasted up to polling day. The theme was 'there is a better way', with a selection of advertisements picking out particular aspects of Fianna Fáil policy. The third stage, running side-by-side with the second, emerged during the last few days of the campaign. This appears to have been somewhat in response to poll trends which indicated there was the possibility of a Fine Gael-Progressive Democrat coalition. Fianna Fáil published advertisements elaborating on 'the choice' facing voters between 'stable' Fianna Fáil government and an 'unstable' coalition.

The Progressive Democrats had one major aim, to establish credibility. Great emphasis was put on producing policy to show that the party meant business. The party released detailed policy documents before the election on such areas as tax reform and the environment. During the campaign, apart from the manifesto which was released in the third week, the party brought out policy documents on social justice and on language and culture. The party wanted to show with these that they could not be dismissed as an 'irresponsible opposition'. The policies also served the function of agenda setting.

To demonstrate organisational readiness, O'Malley was whisked around the constituencies by helicopter in the first seven days, attracting considerable newspaper coverage. One strategist makes the point that the party's campaign in the first week filled a news vacuum left by a non-participating Fianna Fáil and a low key Fine Gael campaign. RTE, however, stuck to its rules of balance and much of the Progressive Democrats' campaign went unreported. Press advertisements (and another billboard campaign) were designed primarily to show how new a product the party was.

The Labour Party's campaign concentrated on health. The health cuts proposed in the 1987 budget were the main reason for Labour's withdrawal from government and the party was determined that Fine

Gael should not divert attention away from the issue. The party had a very small advertising budget (£40,000) and virtually all of this was spent on emphasising health. The advertisements (produced by the agency Quinn McDonnell and Pattison) were concentrated primarily in newspapers with high working-class readerships, i.e. *The Sunday World* and the Dublin evening papers. The party also hosted three major press conferences and its leader, Dick Spring, toured around some of the key constituencies.

The Workers' Party had no money for an advertising campaign. A few advertisements were designed by party workers, at minimal expense and placed in some interest group publications and in the magazine, *In Dublin*. The party's campaign concentrated on traditional working class issues such as unemployment, social welfare and tax reform. Strategy was largely designed to maximise media exposure, particularly in the target constituencies.

CONCLUSION

When attempting to compare the campaign strategies of the Irish parties with those in countries such as Britain, West Germany or the United States, it is important to take into account some of the constraints which restrict Irish parties. First, while Irish parties, like those elsewhere, increasingly tend to campaign on television, their success at maximising coverage is very much dependent on the structure of the medium itself. The television broadcasting monopoly enjoyed by RTE in Ireland undoubtedly reduces the quantity of election coverage. It may also, as some parties argue, affect its quality. Another limitation is the small size of the Irish political system which reduces the scope for economies of scale for parties wanting to introduce expensive new campaign tools such as fully integrated computer systems.

The 1977 and 1981 elections had witnessed major changes in the campaign strategies of Fianna Fáil and Fine Gael. For the first time the parties were marketing themselves as products and had adopted a wholly new approach to electioneering. Six years later this process seems to have reached a new equilibrium. The campaign strategies of the three larger parties in 1987 were all very similar. The fact that Labour and the Workers' Party ran less flashy campaigns seems more the result of financial constraints rather than of any particular ideological hang-ups.

While there may have been few startling developments in campaign strategy in 1987 this does not imply that the strategists are not considering them. Plans are afoot to extend the use of computers and telecommunication links, as a means of improving internal party communications, and to develop direct mailing of target groups in the electorate. The parties are increasingly making use of qualitative market research which provides a richer source of data than the more traditional opinion polls. Further feedback developments will probably include panel studies and some form of 'fast feedback' system with selected samples of voters. The next election, indeed, should witness a substantial growth in the professionalized marketing of the parties.

5. THE OUTCOME

Michael Gallagher

At the five previous general elections, from 1973 to November 1982, there was really only one question which needed an answer from the country's returning officers: would the next Government be controlled by Fianna Fáil or by a Fine Gael-Labour coalition? Only those with a particular interest in the minutiae of Irish politics cared greatly about the myriad of other statistics to emerge from each election. In February 1987, things were very different. The big question seemed to have been answered already: hardly anyone doubted that the next Government would be a Fianna Fáil one led by Charles J. Haughey. But there were many questions whose answers were eagerly awaited. Would Fianna Fáil achieve the 84 seats needed for an overall majority? Would Fine Gael lose all the ground it had gained under Garret FitzGerald since 1977? Would the Progressive Democrats' bubble burst when the first real test arrived, or would their opinion poll support translate into seats and, if so, at whose expense? On the left, could the Workers' Party overtake the ailing Labour Party, demoralized after four years of participation in a Government regularly castigated as austere and heartless?

At first sight, the results spelt disappointment for all the parties except the Progressive Democrats (PDs), who made the most dramatic electoral debut of any party for nearly 40 years. One striking set of statistics illustrates the setback received by the three established parties. Fianna Fáil won its lowest share of the national vote since 1961; Fine Gael won its lowest share since 1957; Labour won its lowest share since 1933. At a stroke, it seemed, the PDs had shaken the hitherto stable edifice of the Irish party system.

However, the message of the ballot boxes was unambiguously gloomy only for Fine Gael, which found itself transported back to its feeble position of the late 1950s. The other parties could all draw at least some comfort from the results. Fianna Fáil did not win its overall majority but it did gain seats, enough to return to office. Labour staved off the threat from the Workers' Party, while the Workers' Party itself, though failing to alter decisively the balance of power on the left, doubled its Dáil strength.

The outcome

VOLATILITY

For years it has been the conventional wisdom that the Irish electorate is becoming increasingly volatile, though before 1987 there was little hard evidence to support it. Perhaps it was only a matter of time before the evidence appeared. As Peter Mair has observed, the decline of unquestioning loyalty to parties has been a feature of recent West European politics and the ground has been ready for some time for an upsurge in electoral volatility in Ireland.[1] In 1985, before the formation of the PDs, Michael Marsh wrote that 'many of the factors that might produce considerable levels of volatility are present', and suggested that 'there are ample grounds for expecting electoral changes in Ireland to be more dramatic than they have been'. The evidence of opinion polls, he argued, constituted 'grounds for expecting something to happen, or for not being surprised when it does'.[2] In February 1987, it did.

The concept of 'volatility', and the problem of how to measure it, have both produced a good deal of debate. One of the most straightforward measures is calculated by summing the percentage gains of the parties which gained relative to the previous election, and the percentage losses of the parties which lost, adding these together and dividing the result by two.[3] Ignoring changes in the electoral register and those people who switch to or from abstention, this index measures the minimum number of voters who must have changed their vote. Its value can range from 0 to 100. A figure of 100 would denote that every voter changed his or her voting behaviour; a figure of zero would mean that every party received exactly the same share of the votes as at the previous election. Of course, the actual number of voters changing parties is likely to be higher than this index, since some vote-switchers cancel each other out and therefore do not show up in the overall gains and losses.

Table 1 gives the volatility figure both for 1987 and for the two elections of 1982. It shows the exceptional nature of the 1987 contest: at least one in every six voters altered their voting behaviour and the net volatility produced was about five times higher than in either of the 1982 elections. In fact, it is necessary to go back to 1943 (when the net volatility figure was 20.3%) to find the last election to show so much change.

Table 1: Net volatility at elections, 1982-1987

Percentage change in support for:	Feb 1982	Nov 1982	Feb 1987
Fianna Fáil	+2.0	-2.1	- 1.1
Fine Gael	+0.8	+1.9	-12.1
Progressive Democrats	n.a.	n.a.	+11.8
Labour	-0.8	+0.3	- 3.0
Workers' Party	+0.6	+1.0	+0.5
Sinn Féin	-1.5	-1.0	+1.9
Others	-1.2	0	+1.8
Total change	6.9	6.3	32.2
Volatility	3.4	3.2	16.1

Note: The 1981 H-Block vote is taken as a Sinn Féin vote

At the level of individual constituencies, the figure for volatility was even higher than at the nationally aggregated level, mainly because most parties, and especially Fianna Fáil, made gains in some constituencies while losing in others. Table 2 shows that the most volatile constituencies were, as might be expected, in Dublin, the most urbanized part of the country, and the least volatile were in Connacht-Ulster, the least urbanized. Of the 11 most volatile constituencies, seven were in Dublin, the others being Limerick East, Galway West, Cork South-Central and Tipperary South, in each of which an incumbent TD changed parties between elections. The four constituencies where volatility was lowest (the two Mayos and the two Donegals) are all in Connacht-Ulster.

One obvious sign of this increased volatility was the large number of seats to change hands. Whereas, in both February and November 1982, seats changed in only 14 constituencies, in 1987 there was a change in 26 constituencies. This involved a total of 30 seats, since two seats were affected in Dublin Central and Galway West and three in Limerick East (see Table 3). Another manifestation of volatility was the much more widely dispersed nature of power in the Dáil. From 1973 to 1982, two large blocs - Fianna Fáil and the Fine Gael-Labour alliance - commanded nearly all of the seats in the Dáil. After the 1987 election there were four substantial political groups, each pursuing an independent strategy. In the aftermath of the election Ireland clearly had a multi-party system, and the Dáil was more fragmented than after any election since 1961.

Table 2: Constituency volatility, by province, 1987

	Average volatility (%)
Dublin	21.8
Rest of Leinster	16.2
Munster	19.8
Connacht-Ulster	13.0
Ireland	**18.2**

Table 3: Seats changing hands November 1982-February 1987

Fianna Fáil
Gains (9): Dublin Central, Dublin N, Dublin SC, Kerry S, Longford-Westmeath, Meath, Sligo-Leitrim, Tipperary N, Wicklow.
Losses (3): Galway W, Kerry N, Limerick E.

Fine Gael
Gains (1): Kerry N.
Losses (20): Carlow-Kilkenny, Cork E, Cork SC, Dublin Central (2), Dublin N, Dublin NE, Dublin S, Dublin SE, Dublin SW, Dublin W, Dun Laoghaire, Galway W, Limerick E, Limerick W, Longford-Westmeath, Sligo-Leitrim, Waterford, Wexford, Wicklow.

Progressive Democrats
Gains (14): Carlow-Kilkenny, Cork NC, Cork SC, Dublin Central, Dublin S, Dublin SE, Dublin SW, Dublin W, Dun Laoghaire, Galway W, Limerick E (2), Limerick W, Waterford.

Labour
Gains (2): Galway W, Wexford.
Losses (6): Cork NC, Kerry S, Limerick E, Meath, Tipperary N, Tipperary S.

Workers' Party
Gains (2): Cork E, Dublin NE.

Others
Gains (2): Limerick E, Tipperary S.
Losses (1): Dublin SC.

THE FORTUNES OF THE PARTIES

The most important figures to emerge from the election are set out in Tables 4 and 5, which give the breakdown of votes and seats by party and by province and also show the changes in the parties' strengths compared with the November 1982 election. The main story of the election is undoubtedly the emergence of the PDs and the slump in Fine Gael support, but the fortunes of the other parties also require detailed analysis.

Table 4: Party shares (in %) of the vote 1987; *change since November 1982*

	Dublin	Rest of Leinster	Munster	Connacht-Ulster	Ireland
FF	40.5 *+2.2*	45.7 *-0.5*	42.7 *-3.4*	49.7 *-2.1*	44.1 *-1.1*
FG	23.7 *-17.4*	27.3 *-11.5*	26.9 *-9.3*	31.8 *-9.9*	27.1 *-12.1*
PD	13.6 *+13.6*	11.0 *+11.0*	15.0 *+15.0*	5.6 *+5.6*	11.8 *+11.8*
Labour	7.1 *-3.4*	9.5 *-2.3*	6.8 *-4.5*	1.2 *-1.1*	6.4 *-3.0*
WP	7.5 *+1.0*	2.2 *+0.3*	3.2 *+0.3*	1.4 *+0.3*	3.8 *+0.5*
SF	2.2 *+2.2*	1.6 *+1.6*	0.9 *+0.9*	3.2 *+3.2*	1.9 *+1.9*
Others	5.5 *+1.9*	2.7 *+1.3*	4.5 *+1.0*	7.0 *+3.9*	4.8 *+1.8*
Total	100	100	100	100	100

Table 5: Party seats 1987; *changes since November 1982*

	Dublin	Rest of Leinster	Munster	Connacht-Ulster	Ireland
FF	21 *+3*	19 *+3*	22 *0*	19 *0*	81 *+6*
FG	13 *-9*	12 *-4*	16 *-4*	10 *-2*	51 *-19*
PD	6 *+6*	1 *+1*	6 *+6*	1 *+1*	14 *+14*
Labour	4 *0*	5 *0*	2 *-5*	1 *+1*	12 *-4*
WP	3 *+1*	0 *0*	1 *+1*	0 *0*	4 *+2*
Others	1 *-1*	0 *0*	2 *+2*	1 *0*	4 *+1*
Total	48	37	49	32	166

Fianna Fáil

Until the formation of the PDs in December 1985, there seemed every possibility that at the next election Fianna Fáil could emulate its 1977 achievement, when it won more than half of the popular vote and acquired a record 20 seat overall majority. In mid 1986, it still seemed that not even the PDs could prevent a Fianna Fáil landslide. Even though four of the new party's deputies (Des O'Malley, Mary Harney, Pearse Wyse and Bobby Molloy) had originally been elected for Fianna Fáil, it was obvious that the PDs were drawing support mainly from dissatisfied Fine Gael voters. The MRBI's June 1986 survey found that Fianna Fáil was the choice of more respondents (45%) than supported all the other parties combined (43%). During the election campaign itself, at least until the last few days, a Fianna Fáil overall majority was the conventional prediction. Where, then, did things go wrong?

The most disappointing aspect of the results for Fianna Fáil was that it actually lost votes. This was especially remarkable given the November 1982 base from which it started. This, at 45% of the votes, already represented its weakest performance for over twenty years. Given that only Fianna Fáil could credibly offer the prospect of stable government after the election the loss of votes was, even after making allowances for the impact of the PDs, a surprise.

Altogether Fianna Fáil lost ground in 18 of the 41 constituencies and made gains in the other 23. Three of its four biggest losses were, predictably, in those constituencies where one of its deputies had defected to the PDs: Limerick East, Galway West and Cork South-Central (see Table 6). It gained votes, however, in Dublin South-West despite the loss of Mary Harney. But there were three other constituencies where its share of the votes dropped by over 5%: Limerick West, no doubt partly due to the Des O'Malley factor washing over the boundary from Limerick East; Cork North-Central, and Kildare, where its vote was down 5%.

Turning to the constituencies where Fianna Fáil made its largest gains, once more we see no clear pattern. It might be thought that the party would do best where the PDs offered no candidate, but this is not the case. Of the five constituencies where its vote rose most (see Table 6), all bar Dublin North-West were contested by the PDs. Of the eight constituencies not contested by the PDs, Fianna Fáil won votes in five and lost in three (Donegal North-East, Kerry North and Roscommon).

Table 6: Parties' best and worst performances in February 1987, compared with November 1982

BEST Constituency	Change (%)	WORST Constituency	Change (%)
Fianna Fáil			
Dublin NE	+ 8.6	Limerick E	-21.1
Kerry S	+ 8.2	Galway W	-15.4
Dublin NW	+ 8.1	Limerick W	-10.9
Longford-Westmeath	+ 4.6	Cork SC	- 6.9
Dublin W	+ 3.9	Cork NC	- 5.3
Fine Gael			
Kerry N	+ 9.1	Dun Laoghaire	-21.9
Mayo W	+ 0.4	Dublin S	-21.6
Mayo E	- 3.2	Dublin W	-21.0
Clare	- 4.7	Dublin SW	-20.8
Tipperary N	- 5.1	Dublin Central	-19.2
Progressive Democrats			
Limerick E	+37.1	Sligo-Leitrim	+ 5.5
Cork SC	+25.0	Tipperary N	+ 7.3
Galway W	+21.5	Dublin NC	+ 8.3
Dublin S	+20.9	Meath	+ 8.8
Dun Laoghaire	+19.8	Wexford	+ 8.9
Labour			
Waterford	+ 3.4	Tipperary S	-10.8
Wexford	- 0.2	Meath	- 9.7
Dun Laoghaire	- 0.5	Kerry N	- 9.5
Donegal NE	- 0.6	Kerry S	- 9.4
Dublin NC	- 0.7	Dublin SW	- 8.6
Workers' Party			
Dublin SW	+ 6.0	Waterford	- 3.0
Dun Laoghaire	+ 4.6	Dublin Central	- 1.8
Donegal SW	+ 1.8	Dublin W	- 1.8
Dublin NW	+ 1.8	Carlow-Kilkenny	- 1.0
Cork E	+ 1.8	Dublin NE	- 0.8

Note: The PDs offered no candidate in eight constituencies, Labour in nine and the Workers' Party in fifteen

There is, it is true, a relationship between the change in Fianna Fail's support and whether or not the PDs contested the constituency. As Brendan Walsh points out, Fianna Fáil's vote dropped by 1.0% on average in the constituencies with PD candidates, but rose by 1.2%

where there was no PD candidate.[4] Moreover, there was a strong relationship across the country between the size of the PD vote and the change in Fianna Fáil support. For the 33 constituencies where the PDs stood there was a negative correlation (of 0.71), between these two factors, indicating a pronounced tendency for Fianna Fail to do best where the PDs did worst, and vice versa.[5] This relationship is hardly surprising, but it does not tell us under what circumstances, or in what type of constituency, the swing from Fianna Fáil to the PDs was likely to be highest.

A striking feature of Fianna Fáil's performance was the very uneven nature of the swing to or from it across the country. This led to mixed performances in its marginals (see Table 7). It picked up seats which required a large swing (Dublin Central, Longford-Westmeath and Cavan-Monaghan) while failing to take five of its eight best prospects (Clare, Carlow-Kilkenny, Dun Laoghaire, Kildare and Wexford), as well as losing one in Kerry North even though there was no PD candidate there.

Table 4 shows the regional variations in voting patterns (see also the maps in the Appendix). Only in Dublin did Fianna Fáil improve on its November 1982 performance, with gains in every constituency bar two (Dublin South and Dun Laoghaire). The net gain in Dublin, though, was small and the party's level of support still leaves it below its position between 1977 and February 1982.[6] Fianna Fáil gained only two seats in Dublin as a result of winning votes from other parties (in Dublin Central and Dublin North); its third Dublin gain, in South-Central, owed more to the acquisition of former independent TD John O'Connell. The party failed to pick up either Dun Laoghaire or Dublin South-East, two constituencies on which it had lavished a lot of attention but where its team of candidates, the incumbent deputies apart, still lacked voter appeal. In the end, it was in Dublin North-East that Fianna Fáil came closest to recording its fourth Dublin gain, Sean Haughey being just 235 votes behind Pat McCartan on the final count. In general, the party did best in Dublin in the more working class constituencies, (North-East, North-West, South-West - despite the defection of Mary Harney - and West), and less well in the most prosperous ones.

Table 7: Fianna Fáil marginals at the start of the campaign

Constituency	Swing required (%)	Outcome
Possible Fianna Fáil gains		
Tipperary N	0.1	FF gain
Clare	0.2	No FF gain
Meath	0.7	FF gain
Carlow-Kilkenny	0.9	No FF gain
Kerry S	1.2	FF gain
Dun Laoghaire	1.6	No FF gain
Kildare	1.8	No FF gain
Wexford	2.3	No FF gain
Sligo-Leitrim	2.4	FF gain
Dublin N	2.7	FF gain
Wicklow	2.9	FF gain
Cork NW	3.0	No FF gain
Cork SW	4.2	No FF gain
Cavan-Monaghan	4.7	FF gain
Cork NC	4.9	No FF gain
Longford-Westmeath	5.4	FF gain
Dublin SE	6.7	No FF gain
Cork SC	8.5	No FF gain
Dublin Central	8.5	FF gain
Possible Fianna Fáil losses:		
Kerry N	0.2	FF loss
Laois-Offaly	1.1	No FF loss
Dublin SW	1.3	No FF loss
Cork E	1.8	No FF loss
Galway W	2.1	FF loss
Waterford	2.2	No FF loss

Notes: (i) The concept of 'swing' in multi-party systems is a complex one. The figure used here and in Table 15 under 'swing required' for Fianna Fáil to gain a seat refers to the number of votes it needed to take from the party which won the last seat if it was to win an extra seat. As the results showed, this did not necessarily mean that the Fianna Fáil vote had to rise by that amount, or indeed at all.

(ii) In Cavan-Monaghan, FF needed the swing specified merely to retain their three seats, given that only four seats were at stake since Tom Fitzpatrick was returned automatically as outgoing Ceann Comhairle.

In the rest of Leinster, the party's losses were small and it picked up three seats. One came in Meath, where the outgoing Government at each of the last four elections has lost a seat and where Fianna Fáil came, remarkably, within striking distance of taking four of the five seats. Yet in the adjacent constituency of Kildare, very similar in both socio- economic and political terms, its share of the votes fell by over 5%. Fianna Fáil's other successes here were in Longford-Westmeath and Wicklow (where it lost votes), but it missed out in the more enticing constituencies of Carlow-Kilkenny and Wexford, partly due to a failure to pick the strongest possible team of candidates.

The party's real disaster area proved to be Munster. It lost votes quite substantially there, and its current level of support, 43%, is its lowest since 1948. It was able to pick up only two seats, the long-targeted Kerry South and Tipperary North, but these were neutralised by losses in Kerry North and Limerick East, where its vote dropped by nearly half. Moreover, it was unable to capture a third seat in Clare, contrary to most predictions, or to improve its position in Cork. Although some attribute the party's poor state in Cork to a lingering 'Lynch factor', historically Cork has never been a Fianna Fáil stronghold; the party's share of the votes there has been below its national average at every election since it was founded, apart from the three at which it was led by Jack Lynch. Consequently, it was no real surprise that it failed to gain a second seat in the paper marginal of Cork North-West, let alone pick up an extra seat in long-shots like North-Central or South-West.

Connacht-Ulster, as usual, was far removed from the real battleground of the election, with only three constituencies in any doubt. Fianna Fail's strength held up fairly well and the area remains the party's heartland. It regained the seat in Sligo-Leitrim which it had lost in November 1982, but was unable to win back the Galway West seat which Bobby Molloy took with him to the PDs in 1986. In Cavan-Monaghan - reduced from a five- seater to a four-seater because Tom Fitzpatrick was the outgoing Ceann Comhairle - it did well to hold on to its three seats.

Fine Gael

Ever since the emergence of the PDs, the opinion polls had recorded Fine Gael's support at around the 25-30% level. Party optimists insisted that this was too bad to be true, but their belief that PD support would melt away proved unfounded. Fine Gael lost votes in 39 of the 41 constituencies, the exceptions being Mayo West, where its vote went up very marginally, and Kerry North, its one real bright spot, where

Jimmy Deenihan added over 4,000 to his 1982 first preference total to give the party its first deputy there since Ger Lynch lost his seat in 1977. In the rest of the country Fine Gael could aspire only to damage limitation and success meant holding on to seats despite losing votes. In all, Fine Gael lost seats in 19 different constituencies. In one of them, Dublin Central, where both of its 1982 deputies had left the fold by 1987, it lost two seats, a fate which had just once previously befallen any party in any constituency. It emerged as the strongest party in only one constituency (Dun Laoghaire), compared with 12 in November 1982.

Fine Gael's losses were generally heaviest in urban areas. There were 11 constituencies where the party's vote dropped by more than 15%, of which seven were in Dublin, three were in other relatively urban constituencies (Cork South-Central, Limerick East and Galway West), and only one could be described as rural (Longford-Westmeath). Dublin, hitherto the area where Garret FitzGerald's leadership had borne the richest fruit, was where it suffered most. In November 1982 Fine Gael won 41% of the votes there, its best performance in the capital since its forerunner Cumann na nGaedheal won 48% in September 1927. At a stroke, this advance was wiped out, and the party plunged back to 24%, a lower point than Fine Gael or Cumann na nGaedheal had ever touched before, and little more than half of its 1982 level. It lost seats in all but three Dublin constituencies (North-Central, North-West and South-Central). In four Dublin seats, its vote actually dropped by over 20% (see Table 6).

Even if the party's losses outside Dublin were less devastating than in the capital, they were still sufficiently substantial to bring it back to levels it had not known since the 1950s. It lost four seats in the rest of Leinster and two in Connacht-Ulster, besides failing to make its anticipated gain in Cavan-Monaghan (see Table 3).

Fine Gael was undoubtedly hit hard by the PDs. Walsh observes that its losses were much heavier where the PDs stood (12.9% on average) than where there was no PD candidate (5.4%), and most of the seats it lost went to the PDs.[7] But it is clear that Fine Gael would still have lost a lot of votes, mainly to Fianna Fáil, even if the PDs had not existed. In Cavan-Monaghan and Dublin North-West the Fine Gael vote fell by more than 11%, and in Roscommon and Donegal South-West it dropped by over 9%, despite the absence of PD candidates in any of these constituencies.

The Progressive Democrats

The PDs went into the election with their support in the polls running steadily at around 15%, but with lingering doubts about the commitment of their professed supporters. The fact remained that not a single vote had been cast for a candidate standing on the PD ticket, and it still seemed conceivable that the PDs would prove to be the media creation alleged by some of their opponents. Consequently, the 12% of the votes and 14 seats won by the new party meant that it had most reason to feel satisfied with the election results.

The party fared best in urban areas; only two of its seats came from predominantly rural constituencies and its vote in constituencies with a significant urban population was over 6% higher than in the rural constituencies it contested.[8] Regionally, it did best in Munster and Dublin and worst in Connacht-Ulster (see Table 4 and the maps in the Appendix). Within Munster, it fared particularly well in Limerick, home base of its leader Des O'Malley, and Cork, the bailiwick of Jack Lynch, the man seen by many, accurately or otherwise, as its spiritual godfather. In Limerick East the PDs won two seats and outpolled each of the other parties, the only place where they achieved either feat. John McCoy's victory in Limerick West, upsetting a pattern of two Fianna Fáil seats and one for Fine Gael which had held consistently since 1948, was perhaps the most surprising of the election. In Cork South-Central Pearse Wyse won more votes than he had for Fianna Fáil in 1982 and the PDs took 25% of the votes, their second best performance in the country. In Cork North-Central, former Fianna Fáil candidate and councillor Mairin Quill comfortably took a seat. In Waterford, Martin Cullen, who had attracted just 350 first preferences when standing unsuccessfully as an independent for the Corporation in 1985, pulled off a surprise victory.

Cullen's success, though, was something of an exception for the PDs in Munster, for elsewhere they made little impact outside Cork City and Limerick. Their candidates in the three Cork county constituencies, Kerry South, and the two Tipperary constituencies never figured seriously as challengers for a seat. Only in Clare, where David O'Keeffe missed a seat by fewer than three hundred votes (the margin by which he trailed Madeleine Taylor-Quinn on the seventh count), does there seem to be the basis of a seat in the near future.

The PDs took a further six seats in Dublin. Three of these were in the most prosperous constituencies (South, South-East and Dun Laoghaire), and two others represented successful defences of their seats by defectors Mary Harney and Michael Keating. The sixth seat, in Dublin West, was won by Pat O'Malley, a relative of the party leader.

The PDs also came within a thousand votes of seats in North-East and South-Central.

In the rest of Leinster the PDs fared rather disappointingly, polling more than 10% of the votes in five constituencies but more than 12 % in only one. This was Carlow-Kilkenny, where Martin Gibbons, son of former Fianna Fáil TD and anti-Haugheyite Jim Gibbons, won the party's only rural Leinster seat. The PDs wrote off most of Connacht-Ulster in advance as unpromising territory. They contested only three constituencies and won in just one, Bobby Molloy retaining the Galway West seat he had occupied for Fianna Fáil for over twenty years. Molloy's running mate lost his deposit, as did the PD candidate in Sligo-Leitrim, but in Galway East Joe Burke won 17% of the votes to make this the PDs' ninth strongest constituency, and finished less than 900 votes behind Fianna Fáil's Noel Treacy.

Not since 1948, when Clann na Poblachta won 13% of the votes, has a party performed so strongly on its general election debut. Where did the PDs' votes come from? It is not difficult to say where their 14 seats came from. Eleven were taken from Fine Gael, with one coming from Fianna Fáil (in Limerick East) and one from Labour (Cork North-Central). The fourteenth seat was won in Galway West, where both the PDs and Labour gained a seat while Fianna Fáil and Fine Gael each lost one. However, the fact that most of the PDs' seats were gains from Fine Gael does not, of itself, prove that former Fine Gael votes made up the bulk of PD support. In a multi-party system, the fact that party A gains a seat in a constituency while party B loses one does not necessarily mean that former supporters of B have switched to A; it may be that supporters of B have switched to C, and some of C's supporters have switched to A, or the chain may be even longer and more complex. Even so, given that the PDs' 12% of the votes practically matches the drop in Fine Gael's support, it is tempting to assume that nearly all PD voters had switched from Fine Gael. However, a look at the regional breakdowns in Table 4 shows that the two movements do not correspond perfectly at this level. The lack of perfect symmetry is even more pronounced at the level of individual constituencies, where there were occasionally large differences between the size of the PD vote and the swing away from Fine Gael.

Of the 33 constituencies where the PDs stood, their vote was greater than the swing from Fine Gael in 17, and it was smaller in 16. A closer look at these differences, constituency by constituency, shows a clear pattern. In some areas, especially Dublin, the PD vote does not fully account for Fine Gael's losses; in others, especially Cork and Limerick, Fine Gael's losses do not fully account for the PD vote. The constituencies where Fine Gael's losses exceeded the PDs' vote are grouped particularly in Dublin and in parts of the rest of Leinster, notably Laois-Offaly and Longford-Westmeath. Of the ten Dublin constituencies contested by the PDs, the party's vote was smaller than Fine Gael's losses in all bar Dublin South-East, where the two are practically identical. The biggest differences in the country occur in Dublin West (a Fine Gael loss of 21% and a PD vote of only 12%) and in Dublin Central (Fine Gael down 19%, a PD vote of 13%).

At the other end of the scale, there were eight constituencies where the PD vote was significantly more than the drop in Fine Gael support. The largest difference was in Limerick East (PDs 37%, Fine Gael down 16%), followed by Limerick West (PDs 19%, Fine Gael down 10%), and the other constituencies in this category were Clare, Cork North-Central, Cork South-Central, Cork North-West, Galway West and Cork South-West.

Given that Fianna Fáil fared best in Dublin and worst in Munster (especially Cork and Limerick) and Galway West, it is clear that the flow of votes from party to party was different in different areas. It is plausible to suggest that the pattern of vote switching may have been as follows.

In Dublin, the great majority of PD voters were former Fine Gael supporters; some other 1982 Fine Gael voters switched to Fianna Fáil. In most of Munster (especially Cork, Limerick and Clare), and in Galway West, the PDs attracted both former Fine Gael voters and a number of (sometimes many) former Fianna Fáil voters; there was relatively little direct movement from Fine Gael to Fianna Fáil. Some of those Fianna Fail voters who switched to the PDs no doubt did so out of loyalty to deputies like Des O'Malley, Pearse Wyse and Bobby Molloy but the usually ignominious fate suffered by TDs who leave their party, shared at this election by Alice Glenn and Liam Skelly (former Fine Gael deputies who stood and lost as independents), shows that voters do not follow a deputy unless they believe in the course he or she has taken. Clearly, those former Fianna Fáil voters who moved to the PDs differed in some way from other Fianna Fáil supporters. Their motivation may have been dissatisfaction with Charles Haughey's leadership, discontent with the party's failure to adopt a liberal line on divorce and contraception, or a preference for the PDs' economic policies. To answer the question conclusively would require survey data of a depth not available, (although see the discussion by Laver, Marsh and Sinnott in the next chapter), but analysis of the voting figures may throw some light on the question.

Table 8 shows that the PDs did best in constituencies where support for divorce was highest in the 1986 referendum. But the relationship is not strong. The PD vote is little higher in areas high in support for divorce than in areas of medium support. Correlating the PD vote with the 1986 pro-divorce vote confirms this impression: for all 41 constituencies it produces a correlation coefficient of 0.36 and, for the 33 constituencies contested by the PDs, one of only 0.23. Another interesting feature of the PD vote is that it correlates more strongly with the decline in Fianna Fáil's vote (0.71) than with the decline in Fine Gael's vote (0.49). (Both figures relate to the 33 constituencies where the PDs stood; over all 41 constituencies, the respective coefficients are 0.58 and 0.60.) While there can be little doubt that a substantial proportion of the PD voters in 1987 had backed Fine Gael in November 1982, the flow of votes between Fine Gael, Fianna Fáil and the PDs was complex and would repay fuller analysis.

Table 8 : PD vote 1987, by pro-divorce vote in 1986 referendum

	Pro-divorce vote 1986			
	Low (less than 28%)	Medium (28-37%)	High (more than 37%)	Ireland
Average PD % vote per constituency	6.8	13.1	13.7	11.1
N of constituencies	14	13	14	41

Labour and the Workers' Party

The two parties of the left had mixed fortunes, both collectively and individually. The combined vote for Labour and the Workers' Party was only 10% of the total and, even if the votes of the Democratic Socialist Party candidates and left-wing independent Tony Gregory are added to this, the total left-wing vote is still lower than at any time since 1957 when Labour, then the left's sole flagbearer, won 9% of the votes. At the February 1987 election, the vote of Labour and the Workers' Party combined rose in only eight of the 41 constituencies, generally only very marginally. It should be remembered, of course, that the left in Ireland is weak at every election; the result in February

1987 differed only in degree from previous results.

Most interest focussed on the balance of power within the left, and whether the Workers' Party could deliver a death blow to Labour. In the event this did not happen, which provided considerable consolation for Labour given its otherwise poor showing. In terms of votes, certainly, the results could hardly have been worse for Labour. It is now only the fourth strongest party in the country, having been the third party ever since 1951. Its share of the votes, at just over 6%, represents its second worst total ever (the nadir came in 1933, when it won just under 6%). Its Dublin strength, at 7% is its lowest since 1938; its Munster strength of 7% is its lowest since 1933; in the rest of Leinster, its share of below 10% is a record low.

Compared with the previous election, the picture was one of setbacks almost everywhere. Of the 31 constituencies which Labour contested in both November 1982 and 1987, its vote rose in just one, Waterford, where Brian O'Shea overtook former Workers' Party TD Paddy Gallagher to give the party a prospect of regaining the seat held by Tom Kyne for nearly thirty years. There were another six constituencies where it held its losses to less than 1% (see Table 6 - the additional cases are Carlow-Kilkenny and Cork East). But there were eight constituencies where the Labour vote fell by more than 5%, and five were in Munster; the three others, besides those listed in Table 6, were Tipperary North, Limerick East and Dublin South-East.

When seats rather than votes are the object of analysis, though, the outcome is much less gloomy for Labour. Only in Munster did the dire predictions that the party might be virtually eradicated come close to realization. It lost five of the seven seats it had won there in November 1982: those in Cork North-Central (left by Toddy O'Sullivan, who crossed the River Lee to defend Eileen Desmond's South-Central seat), Kerry South, Limerick East, Tipperary North and Tipperary South (where Sean Treacy parted company acrimoniously with the party in February 1985 and stood successfully as an independent). There was a touch of luck even about the two Munster seats it retained: Toddy O'Sullivan would not have been elected in Cork South-Central had either Fine Gael or the PDs 'managed' their votes better (see below), and former Tanaiste Dick Spring's winning margin of four votes in Kerry North was the closest in the country.

In the rest of the country, the party actually made a net gain of a seat. Its only other loss came in Meath, where Frank McLoughlin's vote dropped to a mere 40% of its 1982 level, and this was balanced by Brendan Howlin's recapture of the seat in Wexford occupied for Labour by Richard and Brendan Corish from the foundation of the state until February 1982. In addition, Emmet Stagg's retention of the Labour seat in Kildare was a surprise to many, given that the previous Labour incumbent, Joe Bermingham, had left the party in 1986 in a dispute as to who should be picked to succeed him as Labour candidate, and many members of the local party organization were said to have left with him.

All four Dublin TDs were re-elected, even though three of them - Frank Cluskey, Ruairi Quinn and Mervyn Taylor - lost votes heavily and needed transfers to survive. The fourth, Barry Desmond, widely identified as the most vulnerable of Labour's deputies, saw his vote in Dun Laoghaire hold up well despite a substantial rise in the Workers' Party vote. Finally, in Galway West Michael D. Higgins regained the seat he had held from 1981 to November 1982. This too was a victory against the odds: Higgins's vote fell for the third election in a row, to a figure representing only about 40% of the quota, and Labour is now weaker in Galway West than it has been at any election since 1965. As a result of these unexpected successes, and in the face of speculation that the incoming group of Labour TDs might arrive at Leinster House in the back of a taxi, the party returned with 12 seats, only four down on the November 1982 figure, and only two down on its position at the dissolution, following the departure of Bermingham and Treacy.

The Workers' Party too had mixed reactions to the results. On the positive side, its vote went up in every region of the country (see Table 4) to a new peak of 4%. It doubled its Dáil strength from two to four, with Joe Sherlock recapturing the Cork East seat he had held from 1981 to November 1982 and Pat McCartan winning narrowly in Dublin North-East even though his vote fell from its 1982 level. In Dublin, the party repeated its feat at the 1985 local elections by overtaking Labour in votes; less significantly, it did the same in Connacht-Ulster. At national level, it closed the gap with Labour to about 3% and its share of the combined Labour and Workers' Party vote continued to rise (see Table 9). Nevertheless, the feeling remains that the Workers' Party may have missed an historic opportunity. Labour was more vulnerable in February 1987 than it is likely to be at any other election for some time to come. The best defence it could offer of its record in government was the uninspiring, even if accurate, claim that bad as things had been for those on low incomes they would have been worse if it had not been there. It is hardly likely that the party's four weeks in opposition after leaving the Government on 20 January had done much to alter its perceived degree of responsibility for the Coalition's record. Circumstances could hardly have been more favourable for the Workers' Party to establish itself as the main party of the left.

Table 9: Labour and Workers' Party shares of their combined votes, and of the total votes, 1981-1987

Election	Labour share of combined WP + Lab vote %	WP share of combined WP + Lab vote %	Lab + WP share of total vote %
1981	85.2	14.8	11.6
1982(1)	79.9	20.1	11.4
1982(2)	74.2	25.8	12.6
1987	63.0	37.0	10.2

The striking feature of the Workers' Party performance is how little its vote changed. Table 6 shows that in only three constituencies did its vote move more than two percentage points away from its November 1982 level, and one of these (Waterford) was a downward movement signalling the seemingly permanent loss of the seat it held for nine months in 1982. It made significant gains only in Dun Laoghaire, where it is still a long way from a seat, and in Dublin South-West, where Pat Rabbitte, an exceptionally strong candidate, overtook Labour's Mervyn Taylor on first preferences and seems likely to win a seat before long. Elsewhere it made little headway, and the strenuous efforts of hard-working candidates like Eric Byrne in Dublin South-Central, Andy Smith in Dublin South-East, Jimmy Brick in Galway West and John McManus in Wicklow seem to serve only to fasten Labour TDs in their seats by increasing the number of Workers' Party votes to be transferred. Each of these candidates appears to have reached a ceiling of support beyond which progress is difficult or impossible. The Workers' Party is not likely now to transform the balance of power on the left. By surviving the February 1987 battle, Labour may have sealed victory in this particular war.

Others

Sinn Féin, fighting the election for the first time as a registered party and on a platform of taking any seats it won, stood in 24 constituencies. It won 2% of the votes, nearly twice as many as in February 1982, the last election it had contested, but below the 2.5% won by the H-Block campaign in 1981. There was little in its performance to suggest that dropping the abstentionist policy will bring about any change in its fortunes. Of its 27 candidates, 24 lost their deposits. Its best results were in border constituencies: it won 8% of the votes in Donegal North-East, 7% in Cavan-Monaghan, 6% in Sligo-Leitrim and 6% in Louth. The border republican vote has existed since the 1920s, though, and, while durable, is not large enough to elect a deputy except at times of heightened nationalist feeling such as during the IRA campaign in 1957 or the hunger strikes in 1981. Sinn Fein's fifth best constituency was Dublin Central, where it won 5% of the first preferences and this probably represents its best prospect of winning a seat at some stage in the not very imminent future.

The Democratic Socialist Party contested four constituencies. Three of its candidates attracted negligible support but its only nationally known figure, Jim Kemmy, won back from Labour the Limerick East seat he had held from 1981 to November 1982. The Green Alliance/Comhaontas Glas ran candidates in nine constituencies. All lost their deposits, but there were a few signs that the party is taken rather more seriously than hitherto by the electorate: three candidates received more than 1,000 first preferences, and in Dublin South it outpolled the Workers' Party. The Greens won 0.4% of the total votes cast. The Communist Party of Ireland contested only three constituencies, running five candidates in all; it won a total of 725 first preferences.

Three independents were elected: Neil Blaney in Donegal North-East, Tony Gregory in Dublin Central and Sean Treacy in Tipperary South all retained their seats. Treacy was achieving a feat achieved only twice (by Blaney and John O'Connell) in the previous twenty years, of successfully defending as an independent a seat he had won on a party ticket. Although he won nearly 3,000 fewer votes than when he had last stood for Labour in November 1982, he still attracted almost 1,300 more votes than the Labour candidate. Two other incumbents lost their seats fighting as independents: Alice Glenn and Liam Skelly had both been elected in November 1982 for Fine Gael, but both had failed to win reselection as party candidates and both lost their deposits. Besides the three constituencies where independents won seats, there were just two others where the vote for independents exceeded 10%; Roscommon, where a candidate fighting on a platform opposing the closing of the county hospital won 13% of the votes, and Galway West, where a plethora of independents, headed by former Fianna Fáil member Michael 'The Stroke' Fahy, won 12%.

THE TRANSFER PATTERN

At each of the five elections in the period 1973-1982, there was a clear pattern of party competition and consequently a predictable pattern of transfers. Fine Gael and Labour were in alliance against Fianna Fáil and operated a formal or informal transfer pact. Under this, a majority of each party's terminal transfers (the votes distributed when the party has no other candidate available to receive them) passed to the other party and played a vital part in producing the election of coalition governments in 1973, 1981 and November 1982. The arrival of the PDs and the break-up of the Fine Gael-Labour coalition in January 1987 made the flow of transfers much harder to predict. The main points to emerge from analysis of the transfers are as follows.[9]

Fianna Fáil remained in a position of isolation; few transfers came its way, and most of the votes of its eliminated candidates became non-transferable rather than pass to candidates of another party.

The closest relationship was that between Fine Gael and the PDs. When the last Fine Gael candidate was eliminated, most of his or her votes tended to pass to the PDs, if a PD candidate was available to receive transfers. For example, in the five constituencies where both Fianna Fáil and the PDs were available to receive Fine Gael terminal transfers, Fianna Fáil received only 7% while the PDs received 72%. Similarly, when the PDs and Labour were in contention for Fine Gael transfers, the PDs received nearly four times as many as Labour (63% compared with 18%). Looking at all the cases where a Labour candidate was available to receive Fine Gael terminal transfers, Labour received only 39%, compared with between 69% and 86% at the previous five elections. The previous link between Fine Gael and Labour, though considerably weaker than during the 1973-1982 period, had not dissolved completely, however. Fine Gael votes transferred quite strongly to Labour (at a rate of 60%) when there was no PD candidate available to receive transfers. PD transfers favoured Fine Gael, though not quite as decisively. When both Fine Gael and Fianna Fáil had at least one candidate available to receive terminal PD transfers, Fine Gael received a total of 54% of them and Fianna Fáil only 19%.

On the left, just over a third (38%) of Labour terminal transfers passed to the Workers' Party where the latter had a candidate available to receive them. The figure for transfers in the other direction was very similar, at 37%, for the twelve constituencies where Labour, Fianna Fáil and Fine Gael all had candidates available to receive terminal Workers' Party transfers. When the choice lay between the two major parties, Labour voters showed a clear preference for Fine Gael over Fianna Fáil.

Transfers played a decisive part in determining the outcome of the election. Fianna Fáil was deprived of no fewer than 12 seats (one, in Dublin South-Central, twice over) which it would have won had not the other parties' transfers favoured each other more than they favoured Fianna Fáil (for the full list, see the article cited in footnote 9). The most common cause of this was the pattern of transfers between Fine Gael and the PDs, which cost Fianna Fáil a seat in nine constituencies. Fine Gael itself was the victim of transfers in three constituencies, two of them (Cork South-Central and Dublin South-East) because Workers' Party transfers gave a seat to Labour. The Workers' Party was deprived of a seat in Dublin South-West because Fine Gael transfers broke heavily in favour of Labour's Mervyn Taylor.

The main beneficiaries of transfers were Fine Gael and Labour, each of whom owed seven seats to the transfers received. Fine Gael in each case was dependent on transfers from the PDs, but Labour attracted transfers from nearly all quarters, especially when Fianna Fáil was the alternative. Two Labour TDs, Michael D. Higgins and Ruairi Quinn, actually received more transfers from other parties than they won first preferences.

Finally, it may be noted that it was through transfers that the Green Alliance made its first impact on Irish politics, by deciding the destination of the last seat in Dun Laoghaire, albeit only between two candidates of the same party. Monica Barnes was 53 votes ahead of Fine Gael running mate Liam T. Cosgrave on the first count, and the two remained neck and neck over the next eight counts. Seven of the transfers favoured Cosgrave, which would have won him the seat, but the remaining transfer, from the Green Alliance's Alan McGoldrick, went 112-37 in Barnes's favour, enabling her to edge out Cosgrave by just 21 votes.

STV, TACTICAL VOTING AND VOTE MANAGEMENT

Tactical voting can be very important under the single transferable vote (STV) electoral system in multi-member constituencies, contrary to the belief of some of STV's more enthusiastic proponents. The number of seats won by a party which attracts a certain number of votes in a particular constituency can depend to a considerable extent on how those votes are distributed among its candidates. The art of trying to ensure that the votes are distributed in such a way as to maximize the seats won has recently come to be known as 'vote management', although the technique itself has been practised in Ireland since the 1930s at least.

A good illustration from this election of the need for vote management comes from the Dublin West constituency. After the fifteenth count Fine Gael's Jim Mitchell had 7,964 votes, his running mate Brian Fleming had 5,508, and the PDs' Pat O'Malley had 5,973. Fleming was eliminated and both Mitchell and O'Malley were elected. Yet Fine Gael's two candidates, with 13,472 votes between them at this stage, had well over twice as many votes as O'Malley and the party could have won two seats if its votes had been divided more evenly. If any number from 466 to 1,990 of those who gave their first preference to Mitchell had switched to Fleming, both Fleming and Mitchell would have stayed above O'Malley and therefore been elected, the outcome undoubtedly desired by the overwhelming majority of Fine Gael voters. By voting sincerely rather than tactically, Fine Gael supporters gave their party one seat rather than two.

This case demonstrates one of the key rules in vote management. This is that, if a party is aiming to win two seats in a particular constituency, its best course is to try to ensure that its top two candidates have as nearly as possible identical numbers of votes at the final stage of the count. If one is too far ahead of the other, another candidate may, like O'Malley, fill the gap between them, even though he has less than half the combined votes of the party's two candidates. The same general principle operates if the party is looking for three or even four seats in a constituency. Trying to ensure that both candidates finish level does not necessarily mean allotting them identical numbers of first preferences. If one candidate is likely to attract more lower preferences than the other, perhaps because he comes from a more populous part of the constituency, it is best if that candidate starts with fewer first preferences than his running mate and gradually catches her up.

There are two additional points to make about vote management. The first is that it usually plays a part in only a minority of constituencies, since in most cases the number of seats a party will get is strictly determined by the number of votes won by it and the other parties. If a party has enough votes, no distribution can deprive it of one of its seats; if it has too few, no distribution can gain an additional seat. There is, though, a grey area in which the way a party's votes are spread among its candidates can play a vital part and it is in these circumstances that vote management becomes important.

The second point is that vote management is easier to describe than to effect. There are two difficulties in 'managing' votes. The first is that the party needs to know what will happen if it leaves its votes unmanaged; only then can it tell which candidate needs to be boosted and by how much. The private polls conducted by the main parties in marginal constituencies are usually the most reliable guide to the way the votes are breaking but perfect information is available only with hindsight.

The second difficulty is that, once a party organization has worked out how it wants to manage the votes, it is liable to encounter resistance from candidates and/or voters when trying to implement its scheme. In essence, vote management consists of siphoning votes from one candidate towards another who seems to need them more, normally by leafletting a particular area of the constituency between the various candidates' bailiwicks and asking party supporters there to give their first preference to the candidate who needs boosting. Obviously, the candidate from whom votes are to be taken may be reluctant to co-operate unless he or she is more confident of election than most candidates ever are. In addition, not all voters like to feel manipulated, and they may be especially loth to switch their support from a high profile candidate for whom they want to vote, or from a candidate generally thought likely to need every vote he or she can get.

Vote management proved to be a factor in eighteen constituencies at the February 1987 election, with the management of the Fine Gael vote being important in eleven. There were five constituencies where a good division of the votes between its candidates ensured it an extra seat and six where a bad division cost it a seat. Its five successes were in Clare, where the division, though far from perfect, was just good enough to keep out the PDs; Cork North-Central, where a bad division of the votes could have let in Labour; Cork North-West, where the distribution between its two outgoing deputies was perfect, and prevented a possible loss to Fianna Fáil; Dublin North-Central, another case of a near-perfect distribution between its two outgoing deputies, the consequence in this case of unrestrained competition between them rather than a vote management scheme; and Kildare, where a fairly even distribution between the high-profile Alan Dukes and backbencher Bernard Durkan ensured that Durkan did not lose his seat to the PDs.

On the debit side, Fine Gael forfeited six seats: to Labour in Cork South-Central (given that the PDs mismanaged their votes there - see below), by letting Peter Barry run too far ahead of Hugh Coveney; Dublin South-East, where Joe Doyle would have retained his seat at Ruairi Quinn's expense had 800 or more of Garret FitzGerald's supporters switched to him instead; Dublin West, already described; Limerick West, where Fine Gael made a different mistake, and by spreading their weak vote evenly among three candidates sustained a loss to the PDs which could have been averted; Waterford, where both Austin Deasy and Eddie Collins would probably have been reelected, at the expense of the PDs, had their combined votes been evenly divided between them; and Wicklow, where after the seventh count Gemma Hussey was 1,775 votes ahead of Godfrey Timmins, who lost his seat to Fianna Fáil by only 430 votes. It is significant that in five of these six cases, the exception being Limerick West, the candidate with too many votes was an outgoing minister, so the local party organization might have had difficulty in persuading the party faithful to desert him or her even if it had tried. This is especially true in Wicklow, where Gemma Hussey was thought by many to be in danger of losing her seat.

The distribution of the Fianna Fáil vote proved important in seven constituencies; in three it was good enough to earn an extra seat, but in four it cost the party a seat. In Dublin Central the distribution was heavily unbalanced, but was just good enough to earn Fianna Fáil a third seat; in Sligo-Leitrim it was excellent, so the party's second and third candidates finished within 14 votes of each other, and both were elected; and in Wicklow, though it was by no means perfect, it was better than Fine Gael's distribution and was responsible for the election of Dick Roche. On the other hand, Fianna Fáil lost a seat in Clare, where its two strongest candidates were allowed to run too far ahead of Frank Barrett (admittedly, not even a perfect distribution of the votes could have absolutely guaranteed a third seat); Dublin North-East, where Sean Haughey was left too far behind outgoing TDs Liam Fitzgerald and Michael Woods, who each had votes to spare; Kerry North, where Tom McEllistrim finished four votes behind Labour leader Dick Spring while the other outgoing Fianna Fáil TD Denis Foley was a further 311 votes ahead; and Wexford, where Lorcan Allen finished 350 votes behind Labour's Brendan Howlin while his running mates John Browne and Hugh Byrne each had nearly 600 votes to spare over Howlin.

For the other parties, winning enough votes to capture even one seat took precedence over managing their votes. Vote management was a factor for them in only two cases. One was in Cork South-Central, where an even division of the PD vote between Pearse Wyse and Eoin Curtin would have given the party the seat taken by Labour's Toddy O'Sullivan, even if Fine Gael had managed their own vote better. The other was in Galway West, where a more even division of the PD votes between Bobby Molloy and his running mate might have given the party the seat taken by Michael D. Higgins.

Vote management has implications both for the electoral system and for party organisations. It shows that STV, while free of many of the defects of other electoral systems, is not without its problems. I t cannot be denied that there is an element of chance in the outcomes it produces in cases like those discussed above, and that a party whose supporters vote 'sincerely' may be at a disadvantage compared with one which persuades its supporters to vote in a guided fashion. The only way of overcoming the problem would be to recalculate the quota (based on the total number of valid votes minus the non-transferables) every time votes become non- transferable, and start the count again from the beginning. This is discussed by Newland, but he does not recommend it, as it would complicate and greatly lengthen the count.[10]

With perhaps 12 cases of inadequate vote management, some might cast aspersions on the competence of party head offices. This would almost certainly be unjust. As already pointed out, it is only with the benefit of hindsight that one can tell how many votes needed to be 'managed', where and in which direction. Moreover, it is far easier to identify cases where a different distribution of votes would have earned an extra seat than it is for party officials, armed at best with nothing more than the findings of a privately commissioned opinion poll, to persuade harassed candidates to hand over hard won first preferences to a running mate whose entitlement to them seems, in the heat of the campaign, dubious in the extreme.

In addition to these cases where the management (or non-management) of a party's vote was important, there was one case where the crucial distribution lay between candidates of different parties, and where supporters of one candidate could best have helped their cause if some of them had voted against him. This strange situation arose in Dublin North-East, where after the ninth count Sean Haughey (FF) had 5,356 votes, Pat McCartan (WP) had 4,995 and Neil Holman (PD) had 4,971. Holman, as the bottom candidate, was eliminated, and his transfers ultimately took McCartan ahead of Haughey and into the last seat.

The crucial margin here was the 24 vote difference between McCartan and Holman. If McCartan had trailed Holman, he (McCartan) would have been eliminated, and those watching the votes being counted were agreed that in that event Haughey would undoubtedly have taken the last seat. Consequently, it would have been in Haughey's interests if 25 (or any number up to perhaps five or six hundred, depending on the precise breakdown of McCartan's second preferences) of his supporters had switched to Holman, thereby ensuring that it was McCartan rather than Holman who was eliminated. Indeed, if Haughey managed during his campaign to persuade 25 voters to switch from Holman to him, then we can now see that this actually *cost* him the seat. Haughey would thus have benefited had some of his supporters voted tactically (or simply deserted him) for Holman. The result is an illustration, rare in practice though much discussed in studies of voting theory, of STV's inability to guarantee the property known as monotonicity (which means that a candidate cannot possibly be harmed by additional support). In this case, a modest loss of support to Holman would have made Sean Haughey a TD, and given his father a crucial 82nd Dáil seat.

THE ELECTORAL SYSTEM

The suitability of the STV electoral system for Ireland has provoked considerable discussion recently, with two questions receiving most attention. Are the absence of single-party majority government and the large volume of constituency work performed by TDs bad things? If so, should the electoral system take the blame for them? Since these have both received an extended airing recently, the same ground will not be covered here.[11] Instead, we shall look at the aspect of 'positive responsiveness', which refers to whether a change in a party's share of the votes in one direction (either up or down) is accompanied by a change in its share of the seats in the same direction.[12] At this election, Fianna Fáil lost first preferences but gained seats, which also happened to it in 1969, while in 1973 it gained first preferences but lost seats. The explanations for the earlier cases are well-known: in 1969 Fianna Fáil benefited from a gerrymander of the constituencies, while in 1973 it suffered because Fine Gael and Labour voters passed on unused transfers to each other. Why did this apparently paradoxical outcome occur in 1987?

Table 10 shows that the election results deviated considerably from pure proportionality. The three long-established parties, especially Fianna Fáil and Fine Gael, were over-represented; the others, especially the PDs, were under-represented. A standard yardstick to measure the overall amount of disproportionality produced by an election is calculated simply by adding together the amounts by which the over-represented parties are over-represented.[13] The index for the February 1987 election is thus 9.1% (the sum of the vote-seat differences of Fianna Fáil, Fine Gael and Labour). This is a uniquely high figure for an Irish election. It is also considerably higher than average, though by no means a record, for an election conducted under PR.

This unusually disproportional result occurred for two main reasons. The first is the use of small constituencies; the second is that transfers between parties affect the relationship between seats and first preferences.

Table 10: Party shares of first preferences and seats, 1987

	% of first preferences	% of seats	Difference	Seats actually won	Seats on strictly proportional basis
Fianna Fáil	44.1	49.1	+ 5.0	81	73
Fine Gael	27.1	30.3	+ 3.2	51	46
Prog. Dem.	11.8	8.5	- 3.3	14	19
Labour	6.4	7.3	+ 0.9	12	11
Workers' Pty	3.8	2.4	- 1.4	4	6
Sinn Féin	1.9	0.0	- 1.9	0	3
Others	4.8	2.4	- 2.4	4	8
Total	100	100	0	166	166

Note: All calculations exclude the seat of the outgoing Ceann Comhairle, Tom Fitzpatrick (FG), who was returned automatically

Looking at the first, the average number of TDs returned per constituency is only four, fewer than in any other country using a PR electoral system. It is well known that, under any type of PR, the smaller the constituencies used, the less proportional the results become.

In Ireland, three-seaters usually deliver the least proportional results. Their impact was particularly strong at this election: with the quota in a three-seater standing at 25% of the votes, both the PDs and Labour usually fell short of what was required and consequently nearly all of their votes in the three-seaters were wasted. There are 13 three-seaters, returning 39 deputies, and Fianna Fáil and Fine Gael between them won 36 of these seats. The PDs took only one seat in a three-seater (in Limerick West), as did Labour (in Kerry North) and others (Donegal North-East).

The same pattern was evident in the fourteen four-seaters

(including Cavan-Monaghan), though not to the same degree: the PDs won just three seats, and Labour four. Both parties relied on the fourteen five-seaters to compensate for their shortfall in the smaller constituencies: the PDs won 10 of their 14 seats in five-seaters, and Labour 7 of their 12.

When disproportionality is permitted by an electoral system, through using small constituencies, strange outcomes can ensue, including parties gaining seats while losing votes. An additional reason why Fianna Fáil specifically benefited in this way is that the 'opposition' vote was much more fragmented than at any election for nearly forty years. Vote transfers between the PDs and Fine Gael, though respectable, were not as strong as internal Fine Gael transfers had been at past elections. Moreover, transfers between Fine Gael and Labour were, as we have seen, well down on the previous five elections. The lower degree of transfer solidarity among its opponents helped Fianna Fáil to a certain extent, though only two of its seats (in Dublin Central and Wicklow) can really be attributed to this factor, which was less important than the bonus the party derived from being the largest party and from small constituency size.

The reasons for the other cases of over-representation are not hard to identify: Fine Gael received a 'bonus' of seats because it benefited more often from PD transfers than the PDs benefited from Fine Gael transfers, and similarly, on the left, Labour benefited more than the Workers' Party from the flow of transfers between them.

Finally, in defence of the electoral system, it must be pointed out that Fianna Fáil's feat of gaining seats while losing votes was the outcome of different electoral currents in different constituencies. Of the eight constituencies where Fianna Fáil gained a seat, it gained votes in six; its overall loss in votes was brought about by its losing votes in 18 constituencies, in only three of which did this cost it a seat. So the only real 'paradoxes' arose in the two constituencies, Sligo-Leitrim and Wicklow, where the party lost votes but gained a seat. In Sligo-Leitrim, Fianna Fáil seems to have lost votes to Sinn Féin, but many of them returned through transfers. Wicklow, as already noted, was one of the two constituencies where Fianna Fáil benefited from a lack of transfer solidarity among its opponents; it did better from Workers' Party transfers, and Fine Gael did worse, than at the previous election. In addition, the PD to Fine Gael transfer fell just short of what was required for Fine Gael to save its second seat.

THE NEW DÁIL

The party breakdown of the new Dáil may differ significantly from past Dála, but is this also true of the backgrounds of Dáil deputies? Is the occupational profile of the Dáil changing; are deputies becoming better educated; are TDs, like policemen, getting younger? In this section, we shall examine some of the characteristics of the 166 deputies elected in February 1987.

Occupation

Table 11 shows the occupational backgrounds of deputies; full-time politicians are categorized according to their previous occupation and deputies with more than one job are classified according to their main one.[14]

Table 11: Occupations of deputies, February 1987

		FF	FG	PD	Lab	Other	Total
Manual	N	2	0	0	1	3	6
employee	%	2	0	0	8	38	4
Non-manual	N	9	4	2	6	0	21
employee	%	11	8	14	50	0	13
Commercial	N	22	14	3	0	2	41
	%	27	27	21	0	25	25
Farmer	N	11	9	2	0	0	22
	%	14	18	14	0	0	13
Lower	N	15	11	4	1	1	32
professional	%	19	22	29	8	13	19
Higher	N	22	13	3	4	2	44
professional	%	27	25	21	33	25	27
Total	N	81	51	14	12	8	166

The table shows the preponderance of professionals, who make up 46% of all deputies, and the small number of manual or non-manual workers (16%). The proportion of TDs with a 'commercial' background, mainly small business people, is still exceptionally high for a western parliament, but is continuing its seemingly inexorable decline. Since 1965, the proportion of commercial TDs has dropped from 34% to its present 25%, while the proportion of professionals has risen from 25% to 46%.[15] Since commercial TDs are the oldest occupational group (average age 48 at the time of the election) and professionals are the youngest (average age 43), this trend seems likely to continue.

Differences among the largest three parties are surprisingly minor. They all have roughly the same proportion of professionals among their deputies (45-50% in each case), and differences in other categories are also small. The marked dissimilarity in the social bases of these parties' electoral support (see the discussion by Laver, Marsh and Sinnott, below) is not reflected at the elite level. Only Labour is significantly different, with no farmers or commercial TDs and a high proportion of non-manual employees, all but one of them trade union officials.

Education

As after previous elections, the Dáil is unusual among western legislatures in the low proportion of deputies who have graduated from a university. Altogether, 68 (41%) have a degree (see Table 12), which represents a small rise since the last election, when the figure was 63 (38%). There has been a slow but steady upward drift in the educational attainments of TDs since the foundation of the state; earlier studies found that only 21% of pre-1948 deputies had anything more than secondary education, and by 1965 this figure had risen to 30%.[16]

Table 12: Educational backgrounds of deputies

		FF	FG	PD	Lab	Oth	All
Deputies with university degree	No.	31	21	8	5	3	68
	%	38	41	57	42	38	41

The table shows that four of the parliamentary groups contain very similar proportions of graduates, the exception being the PDs, who are by some way the most educated. The gap between the two main parties has narrowed considerably since 1982, when 44% of Fine Gael TDs had degrees compared with only 33% of Fianna Fáil TDs.

Having a degree is of course linked to having a professional occupation (76% of professionals have a degree, compared with just 11% of other deputies), and so graduates, like professionals, are to be found particularly among younger and newer TDs. The average age of graduate deputies at the time of the election was 43, while non-graduates averaged 48 years. Of the TDs who have entered the Dáil since January 1982, 48% are graduates, whereas only 32% of pre-1977 entrants are. It is overwhelmingly probable that the proportion of graduates in the Dáil will continue to rise, a trend which Dinan interprets as marking an increase in the number of 'ministerial' rather than 'ordinary' TDs.[17]

Gender

The number of women in the Dáil remains at 14, the peak it reached in November 1982. The number of Fine Gael women TDs has dropped from nine to five, and Labour's only female deputy retired, but there was an increase of one in the number of Fianna Fáil women TDs, and four PD deputies are women (see Table 13). Of the 14 women deputies, five were elected for the first time in February 1987, bringing to 42 the total number of different women TDs since 1922.

Table 13: Women deputies

		FF	FG	PD	Lab	Oth	All
Women	No.	5	5	4	0	0	14
deputies	%	6	10	29	0	0	8

As in the previous Dáil, women TDs have received more education than their male counterparts (71% of them have degrees compared with 39% of men), are considerably younger (37 years at the time of the election compared with 47), and are newer (first elected, on average, in February 1983, compared with October 1977 for men). Women TDs are less likely to have been local authority members before entering the Dáil; this applies to 57%, compared with 72% of men. Half of the women are related to previous deputies, compared to 24% of the men.

Routes to the Dáil

In Ireland, as in most countries (Britain is one of the few exceptions), it is common for deputies to belong to a local government body before they enter the national parliament. Studies of earlier Dala have shown that, ever since the 1930s, a consistent 70% or so of deputies have local authority membership in their backgrounds. Also, there are some signs that the number has been rising very gradually over the years.

Table 14: Local government background of deputies

		Became local authority member before entering Dáil	Became local authority member after entering Dáil	Never local authority member	Total
FF	N	60	15	6	81
	%	74	19	7	100
FG	N	34	4	13	51
	%	67	8	26	100
PD	N	7	2	5	14
	%	50	14	36	100
Labour	N	9	3	0	12
	%	75	25	0	100
Others	N	7	1	0	8
	%	88	13	0	100
All TDs	N	117	25	24	166
	%	71	15	15	100

This upward trend seems to be continuing, as 142 (86%) of the deputies elected in February 1987, compared with 78% of the previous Dáil, have at some time been members of a major local authority. Of these, 110 (66%) belonged to one at the time of the election.[18] Table 14 shows a certain amount of inter-party variation. The great majority (93%) of Fianna Fáil deputies have local authority membership in their backgrounds, but over a quarter of Fine Gael deputies do not. The PDs are most likely to have skipped this traditional route to the Dáil: over a third have never been local councillors, and only half of them filled this role before becoming deputies. There is a difference between the eight PD deputies elected for the first time in 1987 and the six who had already been TDs; five of the former, but none of the latter, have never belonged to a local authority. The new PD deputies really are new.

The other well-trodden route to the Dáil, being related to another deputy, has the same salience as it did in the November 1982 Dáil. On that occasion, 41 TDs (25%) were related to one or more previous or present deputies who had preceded them into the Dáil. The figure in February 1987 has risen to 44 (27%), with this factor being, on a subjective judgement, significant in the initial election of perhaps 27 of them.

Age and experience

The average birth date of the deputies elected in February 1987 was May 1941, giving them an average age, at the time of the election, of 45.8 years, about eight months older than the November 1982 figure. Of the main party groups, Labour TDs were the oldest (average age 47), followed by those of Fine Gael and Fianna Fáil (both at 46), with the PDs youngest, at 42 years old on average. Exactly half of the PD deputies were under forty, compared with only 31% of all deputies, while 58% of Labour TDs were fifty or more, compared with only 38% of all deputies. Just four TDs were aged under thirty, while thirteen were aged sixty or more. Even into the 1960s participation in the war of independence was still a feature of the background of a significant number of TDs, but there is now only one deputy, Tom Fitzpatrick of Cavan-Monaghan, who was even born before the state was founded.[19]

The average deputy first stood for the Dáil in February 1976 and was first elected in April 1978, nine years before the February 1987 election. The PD group is the newest (average date of entering the Dáil March 1981), and the Workers' Party and others group the most experienced (December 1975), with the average dates for the other three parties all falling in 1977 or 1978. Deputies can be divided into three roughly equal cohorts: 50 entered before 1977, 57 from 1977 to 1981 inclusive, and 59 since January 1982. Only two (Neil Blaney and Charles Haughey) sat in the Dáil with Eamon de Valera, and another 13 entered while Sean Lemass was Taoiseach. At the other end of the scale, 32 entered the Dáil for the first time in February 1987, and 10 former TDs returned to the Dáil after some time in the wilderness, the highest number since 1944. When first elected, the average deputy was aged 37, a little younger than the average November 1982 deputy; there is little difference among the main groups in this regard.

Deputies between them have stood for the Dáil on a total of 832 occasions (five times on average), and have been successful 683 times (about four times on average), a success rate of 82%. The most successful are PD deputies, who have lost only 7 of their 50 campaigns, a success rate of 86%. They are followed by Fianna Fáil (85%), Fine Gael (84%), Labour (74%) and others (64%). Most deputies (96 out of 166) were elected the first time they stood, but this factor varies greatly between the parties. Whereas over two-thirds of both PD and Fianna Fáil deputies were elected on their first candidacy, this is true of fewer than a fifth of Labour, minor party and independent TDs. The great majority (93%) of TDs had succeeded in getting elected by their third campaign; nine had to wait until their fourth campaign, two (Michael D. Higgins and Joe Sherlock) until their fifth, and Tomas Mac Giolla until his seventh. Most TDs (86 out of 166) have never lost an election, and 144, including the 32 first elected in February 1987, have been unbeaten since first being elected.

THE NEW MARGINALS AND THE FUTURE

Assessing the marginality of seats under STV is far from straightforward. While it is possible to say how many more votes the runner-up would have needed to have finished ahead of the last elected candidate, this may not be the real test of how marginal the constituency is, as the last candidate elected is not necessarily the most vulnerable. A party's first preferences do not always tell the full story of its real strength in the constituency, as some parties are much more likely to attract transfers than others. The concept of the last effective count is used in the analyses by *Magill* magazine to overcome this problem but, while it is often an improvement, it is not the complete answer.

For example, Fianna Fáil's last effective count strength in Waterford comes to 55.5% which, with the quota standing at 20%, suggests that the party is certain of two seats and close to a third. In fact, it reached this high last effective count figure only because of the specific pattern of earlier eliminations, and with a first preference strength of only 43% is still in danger of dropping to one seat, its fate in February 1982 when it won 49.5% of the first preferences. A swing of approximately 6% from Fianna Fáil to Labour in Waterford would give Labour one of Fianna Fáil's two seats. Another complication is that vote management can play a large part in deciding the destination of seats. Consequently, while it is possible to quantify the swing Fianna Fáil needs to gain a seat in marginals like Kerry North and Dublin North-East, it is also true that the party could win both without gaining a vote, if it managed its existing votes more effectively.

Table 15: Fianna Fáil marginals at the next election

Constituency	Swing required (%)	Gain from
Possible FF gains:		
Kerry N	0.01	Lab
Dublin NE	0.3	WP
Wexford	0.3	Lab
Cork NW	0.8	FG
Clare	0.9	FG
Dublin NC	1.1	FG
Meath	1.7	FG
Cork SW	2.2	FG
Dublin SC	2.6	FG/Lab
Kildare	2.8	FG/Lab
Galway W	2.9	Lab
Possible FF losses:		*Loss to*
Dublin Central	0.1	FG
Wicklow	0.5	FG
Sligo-Leitrim	0.7	FG
Longford-Westmeath	0.8	PD/FG
Galway E	1.3	PD
Limerick W	1.7	FG
Cork E	2.1	FG
Cork SC	2.1	PD/FG
Louth	2.8	PD

Table 15 lists the Fianna Fáil marginals based on the February 1987 results.[20] When a Fianna Fáil candidate and another party's candidate are involved in a fight for the last seat, the difference between their final count vote totals is taken as the gap to be bridged. In most other cases, the last effective count figures used in *Magill: Election February 87* are used as the basis of the calculation. The table shows that there are eleven constituencies where Fianna Fáil could make a gain with a swing of less than 3%, including five where the required swing is below 1 %. But there are also nine where the party would lose with a swing against it of 3%, including four it would lose on a 1% swing. It is apparent that the marginals are scattered across the country; no one region can be singled out as the key battleground.

Clearly, the result of the next election is very open, with seats liable to change between Government and Opposition in 20 of the 41 constituencies given a swing of 3%. With such a swing in its favour, or even with better vote management, Fianna Fáil could win a secure overall majority; with such a swing against it, it could be reduced to around 72 of the 166 TDs, with little prospect of forming a Government. A larger swing would affect even more seats: a swing of 6% towards it could mean another five seats for Fianna Fáil, and such a swing against it could cost it eight seats, in addition to those listed in Table 15. Given the pattern of the last ten years, with governments losing popularity because of cutbacks and increasing unemployment, the more pessimistic scenario for Fianna Fáil is the more probable.

Other factors too will work against Fianna Fáil at the next election. For one thing, the opposition is likely to be less fragmented. Fine Gael, freed from the burdens of office, can be expected to win back some of the ground lost to the PDs. History is against the PDs, for most 'new' parties in Ireland over the past fifty years have declined, steadily or rapidly, from the level of strength they reached at their first election. Clann na Poblachta, for example, who won 13% of the votes at the 1948 election, were reduced to 4% by the next election. The PDs have a professional headquarters organization and a leader with wide appeal, but will find it increasingly hard to define what it is that distinguishes them from Fine Gael. They will not disappear overnight, but there is a question mark as to whether they can sustain themselves in the long term as a significant political force.

On the left, Labour can be expected, now that it is back in opposition and committed to remaining there, to eat into Fianna Fáil's working class support although, given the number of breaks that the party got in February 1987, this will not necessarily mean more Labour seats. Indeed, if the next election comes too soon, Labour might even lose seats. The Workers' Party will be pressed to defend the gains it has made since 1981. The transfer rate between Labour and the Workers' Party on the one hand, and Fine Gael and the PDs on the other, is likely to rise as the Fianna Fáil administration alienates ever more sections of society and creates a fragile identity of interests among its opponents. Fianna Fáil's strongest card, though, remains the absence of any alternative government. With Labour and the Workers' Party determined not to enter a coalition government with anyone, the only possible alternative government to Fianna Fáil is a Fine Gael-PD coalition. But with only 39% of the votes, and 65 seats, between them at the February 1987 election, those two parties' chances of being able to form a Government seem remote. Irish politics are in an abnormally fluid state and it may require allegiances hitherto untried if majority government is to be provided in the years to come.

6. PATTERNS OF PARTY SUPPORT

Michael Laver, Michael Marsh and Richard Sinnott

Voter volalatility was much heralded in Ireland in the early 1980s; it arrived in 1987. As Michael Gallagher has just shown, the February 1987 election was an exceptional contest - at least one in every six voters changed their voting behaviour. This means that the electorate was about five times more volatile than in either of the 1982 elections and more volatile in fact than in any election since 1943. Dramatic changes in party policy, however, were much less in evidence, even taking into account the arrival of a new 'mould breaking' party the Progressive Democrats (PDs). Thus Mair, on the basis of a comprehensive analysis of the party manifestos, concludes above that 'the pattern of policy competition in 1987. . . represented a significant change from more recent elections but it offered little that was new'.

So what were the voters doing and thinking? Who changed and why? How did voters react to the packages offered by the parties? Equally importantly, how were voting decisions affected (indeed were they affected at all) by either the record of the Government or by the unfolding pattern of political events? The country, after all, had experienced a deepening economic crisis, a fundamental initiative in Anglo-Irish relations and two referenda that raised the issue of Church-State relations in a way that had not been seen since the Mother and Child controversy of the early 1950s. Finally, how important was political leadership? The 'Haughey Factor' had been much touted in earlier campaigns, Fine Gael had a high-profile leader in Garret FitzGerald, while the new PDs, for reasons discussed by David M. Farrell above, had decided to play on Des O'Malley's wide popularity with their 'Dessie Can Do It' campaign.

Some tentative pointers can be gleaned from close analysis of the actual results themselves. For example, Gallagher shows that, in Dublin, Fianna Fáil did best in the more working class constituencies and less well in the more prosperous ones while, over the country as a whole, the PDs tended to do somewhat better in constituencies where support for divorce was highest in the 1986 referendum.

Aggregate voting figures can only take us so far, however. They can tell us the net winners and losers, but not who changed their votes. They can tell us that the PDs did well where support for divorce was high, but not whether it was in fact the PD voters who favoured the introduction of divorce. For a more comprehensive and detailed treatment of these issues, therefore, we must turn to a body of opinion poll research which, well in advance of the election, had set about looking at the impact of factors such as class, attitudes and leadership images in a more systematic way than had previously been attempted.

In the three sections that follow, we look at three of the most important aspects of the patterning of party choice in Ireland. In the first, we look at the class basis of voting behaviour in Ireland, against the background of an argument that posits that this is a system of 'politics without social bases'. In the second, we look at the link between issues, attitudes and party choice. This discussion is set against the background of conflicting views on the matter of whether voters take their attitudes on issues from the party of their choice, or whether voters choose parties on the basis of their policies on important issues. In the final section, we look at the relationship between leadership and voting choice, against the background of a decade in Irish politics which had increasingly developed into a head-to-head confrontation between two dominating party leaders, Charles Haughey and Garret FitzGerald.

The survey data on which this discussion is based comes largely from the Market Research Bureau of Ireland (MRBI), who conducted three polls for the *Irish Times* in the run-up to the campaign. We were very fortunate in two respects. The first is the wholehearted co-operation of MRBI and the *Irish Times*, which allowed Laver and Sinnott a major input in designing the series of questionnaires. This enabled the surveys to go some way towards filling the role of a proper election study, which Ireland has always lacked. The second fortunate event was the fact that there was hardly any movement in public opinion during the period over which the three MRBI/*Irish Times* polls were taken. This exasperated Fine Gael strategists, who were waiting for a bandwagon to roll in and rescue them, and infuriated media commentators, who were waiting for things to liven up one way or the other. But it was very helpful as far as an analysis of the survey data goes, since it allows the three surveys to be combined into one. This enables a more complex and detailed analysis than would otherwise have been possible.

Michael Marsh was involved in analysing the data for the series of polls conducted by Irish Marketing Surveys (IMS) for the *Irish Independent/Sunday Independent* group, and this information is used in the discussion of leadership factors.

There is no substitute for a full-scale election study but, given that no funds are available to conduct one, the co-operation of the market research organisations in making their data available has allowed us to attempt at least a preliminary answer to some of the enduring puzzles of Irish voting behaviour.

A. SOCIAL CLASS AND PARTY CHOICE

Some popular mythology notwithstanding, Ireland has not become a classless society. The impact of class may have changed over the last thirty years or so but it has not gone away. In fact, sociologists have argued that a transformation of the class structure over this period has produced a more rather than a less rigid social system. Though Irish people may in the main be less snobbish on the one hand and less deferential on the other than their counterparts in Britain, class does matter.

A recent sociological analysis pointed out, for example, that while 38% of university entrants in 1979 came from an upper middle class background only 14% of university entrants were from the working class, and this despite the fact that those with a working class background made up 52% of people of university age.[1] The reasons for this contrast are complex and will not be discussed here; what is important however, is that such figures show that individual life chances, in this and in so many other ways, are related to class position. This raises the very obvious possibility that a person's vote is determined to a large extent by his or her class position.

For some considerable time, however, the conventional wisdom has been that Irish voting behaviour is not related to class, though this view has recently come under increasing pressure. Two possibilities have been explored: the first is that more recent trends suggest an emerging pattern of class politics where none had existed before; the second is that social class in Ireland has in the past been defined by researchers in a way that fails to show up the most important political differences between different social groups.[2] It is vitally important to maintain a clear distinction between these two possibilities; otherwise we run the risk of getting actual changes in class voting mixed up with changes in the definition of what class voting actually is. For this reason, we begin our discussion with an analysis of voting trends over time that uses the standard market research categories of social grade. These categories are the ones that have been used in the past to argue that politics in Ireland has no social bases. Following on from this, we move on to use different social categories in our exploration of the question of class voting in Ireland

Trends in class voting over time
The evidence for the 'politics without social bases' argument is quite clear if we look at voting intentions just before the 1969 election (see Table 1).[3] The outstanding feature of these figures is Fianna Fáil's remarkably even spread of support across social groups. In the other half of the electorate, patterns of support for Fine Gael and the Labour Party were mirror images of each other and were clearly class related.

Table 1: Voting intention by social grade 1969 - 1987

Percentage of social grade supporting party

Party And Year	All Classes	Upper Middle and Middle (AB)	Lower Middle (C1)	Skilled Working (C2)	Unskilled Working (DE)	Farmers >50 acres (F1)	Farmers <50 acres (F2)
Fianna Fáil							
1969	43	37	48	40	43	38	53
1977	49	45	47	54	47	48	48
1981	44	34	48	46	45	35	49
1982 (Feb)	47	35	45	45	52	35	59
1982 (Nov)	40	32	38	42	40	37	51
1987	38	26	32	45	41	30	48
Fine Gael							
1969	25	37	26	21	14	46	26
1977	28	36	27	20	22	42	38
1981	33	46	31	29	24	53	36
1982 (Feb)	35	51	38	36	25	54	28
1982 (Nov)	37	58	42	31	28	54	35
1987	25	34	24	23	15	45	35
Labour							
1969	18	10	15	27	28	2	5
1977	9	6	7	11	16	1	5
1981	10	9	10	10	16	4	2
1982 (Feb)	7	3	7	6	10	3	4
1982 (Nov)	9	4	9	11	14	6	1
1987	4	1	6	4	7	1	2
Progressive Democrats							
1987	11	18	18	9	9	10	2
Workers' Party							
1981	2	1	0	2	4	1	0
1982 (Feb)	2	0	0	3	4	0	0
1982 (Nov)	4	0	3	5	6	1	2
1987	2	1	2	3	4	0	1
Other/ Don't know/ Refused							
1969	14	17	11	12	15	14	16
1977	14	13	19	14	15	8	8
1981	11	10	11	14	15	8	8
1981	11	10	11	14	9	6	12
1982 (Feb)	7	11	10	10	10	8	9
1982 (Nov)	9	6	8	11	12	2	12
1987	19	19	18	14	24	13	14

Source: See footnote 3
Note: In the 1969 Gallup Poll survey the categories of farm size were 30 acres or more and less than 30 acres

These and other features of the 1969 figures (for example, the contrasts within the farming sector and Fianna Fáil's dip below 40% among the AB grouping) suggest, however, that for the late 1960s we need to make only minor qualifications to the 'politics without social bases' thesis.

Fianna Fáil showed some notable fluctuations in support among different social classes in subsequent elections. In 1977 it won increases, for example, among middle class and skilled working class voters and among larger farmers. It gained among the unskilled working class in the Budget election of February 1982. Prior to 1987, however, there is little to indicate the arrival of class politics on anything like the scale that can be found elsewhere in Europe. The only real straw in the wind came in November 1982, when a slight fall in the AB category and a more substantial drop among lower middle class (C1) voters combined for the first time ever to put Fianna Fáil below 40% and indeed below Fine Gael middle class voters.

The figures for February 1987 suggest that this may indeed have been a portent. Fianna Fáil, the archetype of the catch-all party, dropped to 30% among the middle class as a whole and to a mere 26% among the AB grouping. As a result, the party showed a substantial 19% gap between its lowest and highest levels of support among the non-agricultural sector of the population. This increasing class polarisation was paralleled in the farming sector, where Fianna Fáil support dropped to 30% among those farming over 50 acres.

The cross-class nature of Irish party support can also be seen in Fine Gael's recovery during the late 1970s and early 1980s, which was evident in all sectors of the population. This recovery was stronger, however, among middle class voters and especially in the upper reaches of the middle class. Among AB voters Fine Gael actually climbed to 58% support in November 1982.

Just as Fine Gael had advanced most among the middle classes so, in February 1987, it experienced its greatest losses in the same sectors. It slumped by 24 percentage points among AB voters and by 18 points among the C1s. Although Fianna Fáil also experienced losses among the middle classes, the Fine Gael drop was much larger, wiping out the party's recently won lead over Fianna Fáil in this sector. Perhaps the most striking pattern of party support revealed in Table 1 is that, in every sector of the electorate, Fine Gael in 1987 returned virtually the same levels of support it won in 1969.

The beneficiary and probable cause of these changes in middle class voting patterns was of course a new arrival on the electoral scene - the Progressive Democrats (PDs). Even on the basis of the preliminary evidence presented in Table 1, it is clear that the PDs' electoral appeal is skewed more towards the middle class than is the appeal of either of the established major parties. The PDs' support among the middle classes is twice that among either skilled or unskilled working class voters, while its support among larger farmers is five times that among small farmers.

This class bias, which is perhaps the most notable feature of Progressive Democrat support, can be seen more clearly by looking at the same data another way. Up to now we have been comparing the social classes, examining the differences in the political behaviour of each class. This will remain our main approach since we are primarily interested in the class bases of party support. A useful complementary approach, however, is to compare the parties, to examine the differences in the class composition of support for each party. The distinction between these approaches can be summarized as the difference between looking at the political distinctiveness of the classes (the approach we have been using till now) and looking at the class distinctiveness of the parties.[4] In Table 2 we present the support profiles of the main parties immediately before the February 1987 election and in 1969. These profiles of support can be compared with the profile of the entire electorate in the right-hand column of Table 2.

Table 2: Social composition of party support (social grade measure) 1987 and 1969

Social Grade	Percentage of party supporters from social grade				
	FF	FG	PD	LAB	All
1987	%	%	%	%	%
Middle Class (ABC1)	24	32	50	30	30
Working Class (C2DE)	56	36	40	63	50
Farmers 50+ acres	7	17	9	2	9
Farmers <50 acres	13	15	2	4	11
All Classes	100	100	100	100	100
1969	%	%	%	%	%
Middle Class(ABC1)	32	34	-	23	30
Working Class(C2DE)	46	30	-	73	47
Farmers 30+ acres	13	28	-	2	15
Farmers <30 acres	9	7	-	2	7
All Classes	100	100		100	100

Source: See footnote 3

Fianna Fáil emerged in 1987 with slightly less than a proportionate share of middle class voters and a slightly larger than average share of working class voters. In contrast, in 1969 the Fianna Fáil class profile mirrored that of the electorate almost exactly.

Fine Gael had a more skewed class profile than Fianna Fáil. In February 1987 the party had a less than proportionate share of working class voters (a deficiency mainly among the unskilled working class) and a more than proportionate share of farmers, especially of larger farmers.

The Progressive Democrats were also disproportionately middle class. (They were 50% middle class, while the electorate as a whole was 30% middle class). However, Table 2 cautions us against the simplistic conclusion that the Progressive Democrats are merely a middle class party. Forty percent of their support, after all, comes from the working class while only the small farmers are virtually unrepresented among PD voters.

Turning finally to the Labour Party, the point has been made elsewhere that one factor that has weakened the pattern of class voting has been the severe decline of Labour.[5] To this must now be added the point that today's smaller Labour Party is less distinctive in class terms than its 1969 predecessor and no more class distinctive than Fianna Fáil. In 1969 73% of Labour support was working class: in 1987 this had fallen to 63%.

When looking at the class distinctiveness of the parties we have found some reasons for qualifying any class-based interpretation of party support in Ireland. This should not, however, obscure the basic finding that, with the decline of Fianna Fáil middle class support and the emergence of the Progressive Democrats, the social bases of party choice in Ireland have become more pronounced.

Patterns of party support and a revised definition of social class

The social categories that we have used so far are adaptations of the scheme of social grades used by market researchers in Britain. The main change has been to treat farmers separately and to divide them into those with holdings of 50 acres and above and those with less than 50 acres. Otherwise the social grades have been adopted by market researchers in Ireland with only minor modifications. (These grades are designated by the letters A (upper middle class), B (middle class), C1 (routine non-manual), C2 (skilled manual), D (unskilled manual), and E (casual labourers, unskilled working class who are unemployed, and pensioners on state pension only). Thus the scale that we (and nearly all who have analysed Irish voting behaviour before us) have been using is essentially a grading based on income, status and lifestyle.

The use of this scheme in the analysis of voting behaviour has been extensively discussed in the British context. It has been argued that the social grades with their emphasis on life style, obscure the social and economic roots of political behaviour and should be replaced with a conception of class which emphasises the divergent economic interests of individuals. On this line of argument, the concept of class used in analyses of voting must embrace not only income but also an individual's exposure to market forces together with his or her autonomy in the work-place and the kind of experience of authority that this implies.[6]

Approaching different problems but drawing nonetheless on the same theoretical sources, Irish sociologists have advocated the need for a revised conception of social class in Ireland. Thus, in reporting on progress towards the development of a new Census-based social class scale, O'Hare emphasises that people's occupations can be classified according to whether they 'share broadly similar market and work situations'.[7]

The application of these criteria can lead to a number of different working definitions of social class. The working party developing the new Census-based social class scale agreed on an interim scale consisting of six categories. In a study of social class and inequality, on the other hand, Rottman et al. put forward a scheme consisting of thirteen 'economic groups' which can then be reduced to four 'major cleavages'; a bourgeoisie in the classic sense; a petit bourgeoisie (this, they say can be subdivided into farmers and non-farmers); a middle class of non-manual employees; and a working class.[8]

As we have never had a full scale election study in Ireland, we are able to put into practice here only a modestly revised definition of social class, though we do agree wholeheartedly that a more 'sociological' approach to the class analysis of voting patterns in Ireland is long overdue. What we have done is to combine information on occupational grade (A, B, C1, etc.) with information on whether the individual is self employed or an employee, information collected by MRBI in their election polls in the run-up to February 1987. This reclassifiction has two main effects: it takes self employed members of the upper middle and middle classes (A and B) and treats them as the bourgeoisie. Likewise, it takes the self employed from both the lower middle class (C1) and the working class (C2, D, and E) and groups them as the petit bourgeoisie. We have decided not to subdivide the remaining classes (middle and working class) on the grounds that the basis on which we could do so (the distinction between upper and lower middle class or between skilled and unskilled manual workers) does not in either case reflect those differences in the degree of autonomy in the work place that a revised conception of social class requires.

Since the distinction between large and small farmers (those farming more or less than fifty acres) has proved one of the most potent ways of distinguishing between party supporters, we have retained both of these social categories from earlier analyses. The result is a six way classification of social class into:

the bourgeoisie	(i.e. self-employed members of A and B groups)
the petit bourgeoisie	(i.e. self-employed members of C1, C2, D and E)
the middle class	(i.e. the remaining members of A and B groups)
the working class	(i.e. the remaining members of C1, C2, D and E)
large farmers	(i.e. those with 50 acres or more)
small farmers	(i.e. those with 50 acres or less)

If Irish voting behaviour is indeed more structured by class than has been assumed up to this point, and if this has been missed because of an inadequate working definition of social class, then this revised scheme should go some of the way towards solving the problem.

Table 3: Voting intention by revised social classes, February 1987

	Percentage of social class supporting party						
	Bourgeoisie	Middle Class	Petit Bourgeoisie	Working Class	Large Farmers	Small Farmers	All
Party	%	%	%	%	%	%	%
FF	20	32	44	45	31	48	39
FG	24	19	18	12	34	27	19
Lab	3	4	2	6	3	3	4
PD	28	19	11	9	14	6	13
WP	0	2	1	3	0	0	2
Oth/DK	25	24	24	25	19	16	23
All	100	100	100	100	100	100	100
N	112	584	348	889	317	268	2518

Source: MRBI/Irish Times surveys

Table 3 confirms the suspicion that the particular way in which class has been measured in studies of voting in Ireland obscures some of the differences that actually exist. Thus Fianna Fáil's claim to be a cross-class party, a claim which was anyway weakened in 1987, becomes even more tenuous when we use the more 'economic' definitions of social classes laid out above. Fianna Fáil support drops to 20% among the bourgeoisie for example. This highlights the main political distinction that seems to have been hidden by the traditional market research categories, a significant difference between the preferences of the bourgeoisie and of the salaried middle class. Just under 20% of the bourgeoisie support Fianna Fáil, compared to 32% of middle class employees, and the two groups have distinctive support profiles for each party.

This new way of looking at voting behaviour also throws most light on the support profile of the PDs. The Progressive Democrats have never seriously claimed to be a catch-all party and this is confirmed by the evidence of February 1987 polls. More than one in four of the bourgeoisie declared themselves to be Progressive Democrat voters (28%), compared to less than one in ten (9%) of the working class. Once more, it is the market research category AB that had hidden what was going on. Among the middle class, there is a considerable difference between a PD support level of 28% among the bourgeoisie, 19% among the salaried middle class and 11% among the petit bourgeoisie. Lumping the first two of these categories together fuzzes over quite a bit of the social distinctiveness of PD support. Indeed, in February 1987, the PDs led the field among the bourgeoisie.[9]

This new approach also clarifies the difference between the support bases of Fine Gael and the Progressive Democrats within the non-farming electorate. Both show very similar levels of support among the bourgeoisie and middle class. Fine Gael support, however, extends fairly substantially into the petit bourgeoisie, whereas PD support tails off rapidly in this sector.

Overall, the revised view of social class has thrown greater light on the class bases of Irish politics. Particularly among the middle class, the distinction between those on a salary (most of them paying PAYE income tax) and those working on their own account (most taxed on a self-employed basis) has a major impact on voting patterns. In February 1987, Fianna Fáil were clearly ahead among the salaried middle class, while both Fine Gael and the PDs beat Fianna Fáil among the bourgeoisie. The revised class categories also bring out the difference between the voting behaviour of the petit bourgeoisie on the one hand and that of the bourgeoisie and the middle class on the other. The essential difference is their high level of support for Fianna Fáil - as high as the level of support for that party among the working class - and their tendency to prefer Fine Gael to the PDs. They also only offer miniscule support to the Labour Party. In conclusion, we are clearly justified in saying, since each of the parties is now doing up to three times better among some social groups than among others, that Ireland is now a party system with some quite distinct social bases.

The defectors and the loyalists

Obviously, the intervention of the Progressive Democrats played a major role in bringing about a more clear-cut class-based pattern of party support in February 1987. However, it would be easy to oversimplify the effect of their intervention. This is especially so since the figures for each party's overall share of the national vote tell a deceptively simple story. Fianna Fáil went down one percentage point and the PDs' gain on their first outing almost exactly equalled Fine Gael's 12% loss. A glance at Fianna Fáil's considerable and sometimes dramatic losses in all but one of the constituencies in which former Fianna Fáil TDs stood as Progressive Democrats, however, shows just how deceptive these national figures can be.

In order to get a clearer picture of the actual movement of votes between the various parties, Table 4 compares people's reported vote in November 1982 with their voting intention in February 1987. This confirms that, while the greatest leakage of votes occurred among supporters of other parties, Fianna Fáil was not immune. Almost exactly one quarter of those claiming to have voted Fianna Fáil in 1982 did not intend to vote for the party again or were at best uncertain in February 1987. The rate of leakage from Fine Gael was 55%.

Table 4: Voting intention February 1987 by reported vote November 1982

	Percentage of those supporting party				
Voting Intention February 1987	Fianna Fail	Fine Gael	Labour	WP	Other DK
	%	%	%	%	%
Fianna Fáil	**75**	12	20	14	30
Fine Gael	2	**45**	6	2	12
PD	8	18	10	2	10
Labour	1	2	**40**	2	4
Workers' Party	1	1	9	**44**	2
Other/DK	13	22	15	35	42
All Voters	100	100	100	100	100
N	1106	989	151	43	711

Source: MRBI/Irish Times surveys

The PDs were, as might be expected, the main beneficiaries of these defections. Around 8% of former Fianna Fáil supporters switched to the PDs, compared to 18% of former Fine Gael voters. Fianna Fáil's losses were however, compensated by the defection of 12% of former Fine Gael voters and 20% of former Labour voters to Fianna Fáil. Almost nobody defected to Fine Gael or Labour, so they were the main net losers out of all of this vote switching. For obvious reasons the defectors to the Progressive Democrats from the two main parties are of particular interest. As Table 5 shows, the two main groups of Progressive Democrat voters - those who defected from Fianna Fáil and those who defected from Fine Gael - had a quite different class composition. Much more significantly, however, those who left Fianna Fáil, and those who left Fine Gael for the PDs were in each case more middle class than those who remained loyal to these parties. There were parallel but less pronounced differences in the farming sector: both Fianna Fáil and Fine Gael defectors to the PDs were much less likely to be small farmers than those who stayed loyal to their original party. Small farmers appear to have been totally impervious to the formation of the PDs.

Table 5: Class composition of defectors and loyalists: February 1987

	Party voted for Nov 1982 - Feb 1987						
Class	FF-FF %	FF-FG %	FF-PD %	FG-FF %	FG-FG %	FG-PD %	All %
Bourgeoisie	2	0	9	2	6	10	4
Petit bourgeoisie	16	15	15	15	13	11	14
Middle class	18	15	30	24	24	42	23
Working class	40	25	27	38	21	18	31
Large farmers	10	30	10	8	24	16	15
Small farmers	14	15	8	13	13	4	12
All Voters	100	100	100	100	100	100	100
N	694	20	87	98	389	151	1439

Source: MRBI/Irish Times surveys

Finally, it is worth looking at the former Fine Gael voters who defected to Fianna Fáil. These have a class profile almost identical to that of Fianna Fáil loyalists, with the exception that they are slightly more middle class. This means that they are distinctively different from 1982 Fine Gael voters who either stayed loyal or defected to the

Progressive Democrats. Quite simply, Fine Gael lost support in two different directions in 1987. Its more working class support went to Fianna Fáil and its more middle class support went to the PDs.

Class and party: a summary

We can summarize these patterns of class voting in Ireland by using our revised measure of social class in an examination of the class composition of each party's overall support. This provides an important qualification to the impression we could give by looking only at the political distinctiveness of the classes since the classes that are politically the most distinctive - the bourgeoisie and the petit bourgeoisie - are relatively small. The former is in fact extremely small (on our relatively generous definition it accounts for only 5% of the population). This means that even quite distinctive political behaviour by the bourgeoisie can make only a modest impression on the social profiles of the parties they support.

Table 6: Class composition of party support: February 1987

Percentage of party supporters from social classes

Class	Fianna Fail	Fine Gael	Labour	PD	Workers' Party	Other DK	All
	%	%	%	%	%	%	%
Bourgeoisie	2	6	3	10	2	5	4
Petit bourgeosie	16	13	6	12	9	14	14
Middle class	19	22	26	35	26	24	23
Working class	41	22	50	25	62	38	35
Large farmers	10	22	8	14	0	11	13
Small farmers	13	15	7	5	2	8	11
All Voters	100	100	100	100	100	100	100
N	987	488	98	317	47	581	2518

Source: MRBI/Irish Times surveys

This accounts for the fact, illustrated in Table 6, that although Fianna Fáil fares much worse among the bourgeoisie (a difference of 25% compared to its level of support among the working class - see Table 3), the class composition of Fianna Fáil support remains very close to the class composition of the electorate as a whole. The bourgeoisie and middle class are slightly under represented (by 2% and 4% respectively), while the working class proportion is slightly over-represented (by 4%).

Fine Gael is more distinctive, given the under-representation of the working class among its supporters. Fine Gael's share of the working class is 10% less than in the electorate as a whole and 15% less than among Fianna Fáil supporters. Fine Gael was also over-represented among large farmers, who accounted for 20% of Fine Gael support while constituting only 11% of the electorate.

The Progressive Democrats show the greatest degree of class distinctiveness; the top end of the class spectrum is over-represented (the bourgeoisie by 5% and the middle class by 12%) and this is at the expense of those at the lower end, the working class and small farmers. Only among the petit bourgeoisie and large farmers did the Progressive Democrats get its proportionate share of the votes and no more.

Turning to the two small socialist parties, Table 5 confirms the observation made at the end of our discussion of trends since 1969. Labour Party support comes from a variety of sources and, while it is disproportionately working class, the discrepancy is not very great - well over 50% of its support comes from sources other than the working class. Observations about the class composition of Workers' Party support have to be made with some caution because of the small number of Workers' Party supporters even in a sample of this size. One point is worth noting, however. While the bulk of its support is working class (more so than in the case of Labour), it also has a sizeable block of middle class support.

We can summarize the overall situation as follows. First, the class basis of Irish politics is more evident now than at any time in the previous twenty years. Second, when we refine our conception of class, the class basis of politics come into even sharper focus. This suggests that, were we to introduce further improvements into the measurement of social class (and there is obviously much room for such improvements), we would find a still clearer picture. It seems likely, however, that this would be a picture, not of a class based system, but rather of a system in which class plays a significant role.

Will this new situation last? Two factors will be crucial. The first is the outcome of the coming struggle between Fine Gael and the Progressive Democrats for what seems to be a rather volatile block of bourgeois and middle class support. The second is the effect on the party's working class base of Fianna Fáil's current policy on financial cuts in state services, balanced against the possibly opposite effect of these same cuts on at least some of Fianna Fáil's bourgeois and middle class critics. All of this depends very much upon the factors that gave rise to the patterns of support for Irish political parties that we have identified. In particular, it depends upon the role of issues and policy preferences in voting choice and to these matters we now turn.

B. ISSUES, ATTITUDES AND PARTY POLICY

Three views of the role of party policy

The precise link between party choice and policy preference remains one of the great mysteries of political science. One influential view sees each voter simply going along with the policy package put forward by the party that he or she supports. According to this version of political reality, parties sell policies to voters and, when they decide for whatever reason to change their policies, they often manage to bring the voters with them. Voters are presumed to choose the party that they support for all sorts of reasons. These reasons may have to do with personalities, scandals, the record of the Government but, above all else, they have to do with traditional and enduring party loyalties.

This view of party competition places a lot of emphasis on the selective perception of the political system by the voting public who see what they want to see in the parties they support. Voters, it is claimed, develop deep psychological attachments to parties - they become 'party identifers'. Some voters, the 'strong' identifers, support their chosen party through thick and thin and despite almost all of the short term political forces and pressures that operate during any given election campaign. These people form the bedrock of their party's long term support. Others, the 'weak' identifers, are much more easily swayed. All things being equal, they support a given party but they tend to move with the tide at election time, responding to the short term issues, the scandals, the personalities, the ebbs and the flows of a hard fought campaign.[10]

In the 1987 Irish election, for example, this 'party identification' approach would account for the fact, discussed in greater detail below, that Fianna Fáil supporters tended to regard Fianna Fáil as having the best policy on taxation, *regardless of what their preferred policy was*. The stronger the party identification, the more the voters in question are inclined to see what they want to see in party policy and, indeed, the more likely they are to see things to support in almost any policy that their chosen party puts forward. Party loyalty thereby becomes a sort of distorting lens through which the whole political world is viewed.

A quite different version of the role of party policy gives voters the whip hand. This sees parties, desperate to get elected, putting forward policies with the sole objective of getting as many votes as possible. Politicians, on this account, will say almost anything that they think that they can get away with in order to get into power. Voters, in contrast, pick a party to support precisely because it offers them the policies they want. Parties, in short, trade votes for policies, while voters buy one or other of the policy packages on offer.

Parties can't put forward any old policies, of course. People will stop taking them seriously if they keep saying different things all the time. In particular, when a party goes into government voters may take a dim view if it does quite the reverse of what it promised to do at election time. The key feature of this view of party competition, however, is that parties are keen to respond to the attitudes of voters. They look for 'gaps in the market' to exploit, groups of voters whose views are not catered for by the existing range of policies on offer. Parties compete with each other to offer the most attractive policy package to the greatest number of voters.[11]

To take another example from the 1987 election, the Labour Party rapidly shifted its policies to the left after leaving the coalition with Fine Gael. Labour clearly blamed the disastrous slump in its opinion poll support during its period in coalition on the fact that it had been forced to adopt policies that were 'too' right wing for those voters who were most likely otherwise to vote Labour. By moving policy to the left, they clearly hoped to regain this lost support by appealing once more to people wanting policies at this end of the political spectrum.

A third view of the way in which the attitudes of voters affect the outcome of an election sees parties as being more or less stuck with a particular policy package, at least in the minds of most of the electorate. On this account elections are decided by the relative importance of various issues. If a particular issue, let's say taxation, becomes more important during a particular election campaign, then this help those parties who are seen to have 'good' policies on taxation, and harms the others.

Party competition, according to this view, becomes a tussle in which party strategists attempt to massage the importance of issues, bringing to the fore issues on which they are strong, and pushing to the background issues on which they are weak. In the same way, parties try and raise the stakes by highlighting issues on which their opponents are weak and downgrading issues on which opponents are strong. This approach sees election campaigns as times when the parties spend most of their time talking past each other to the electorate, rarely engaging in real debate, whatever about all of those myths of democratic theory.

The importance of issues is of course determined in part by the 'real' social and economic world that goes on outside the political system more or less beyond the immediate control of politicians. Thus matters such as rising unemployment, balance of payments problems, international crises and so on can force issues onto the agenda whether politicians want them there or not. But the importance of issues is also determined by the way in which voters get to hear about the world. In other words it is determined to a considerable degree by the media. This view of party competition thus places quite a heavy emphasis on the skill of parties in handling the media. Election campaigns, acted out in the media, become a series of attempts by parties to increase favourable coverage of their strong policy suits and reduce coverage of their weak policy suits. It is the relative success of the parties in achieving this manipulation of the 'issue agenda', as much as anything else, that affects the course of campaigns.[12]

In the 1987 election, for example, there were a number of quite separate issues on the table. Some, such as the Anglo-Irish Agreement, favoured Fine Gael. Others, such as taxation, favoured rival parties. It was not just being ahead on an issue that counted. Rather, the key to success was to be ahead on an *important* issue. And the campaign was in large part about each party trying to increase the importance of issues which favoured it, and to understand the importance of issues which did not.

Fine Gael's commanding position on Northern Ireland policy, for example, could do it little good if people didn't think that Northern Ireland was an important issue. It was no doubt for this reason that Fine Gael, late in the campaign, tried to increase the profile of the Northern problem by raising the spectre of a Fianna Fáil renegotiation of the Anglo-Irish Agreement. It was also the reason why Haughey was keen to place the Agreement 'above' the campaign, as Peter Mair has already argued. It could even be claimed that this policy succeeded by providing a big enough banana skin for Charles Haughey, in the Great TV Debate, (see the chapters by Girvin and David Farrell above) to deny Fianna Fáil an overall majority. On the other hand, none of the attempts by Fine Gael to 'cost' the Fianna Fáil economic programme, which were attempts to raise the profile of what they saw as a weak link in the Fianna Fáil armoury, managed to capture much media attention and this ploy thus had little impact on the campaign.

In short there are three quite distinct views of the role of policy in party competition. First there is the possibility that people support the policies of 'their' party almost regardless of what those policies are; second there is the possibility that people actually choose their party on the basis of policy; third there is the possibility that parties have certain 'winning' policies, spending the election campaign attempting to convince people that these policies are indeed the important ones.

Given all of this, we set out to tap three different aspects of the impact that voter attitudes can have on party choice. The first deals with the perceived importance of the issues, the second with the personal issue positions of voters and the third with voters' views of which party had the best policies on a range of matters.

In an attempt to tap the *importance* of issues, people were asked to rate five general issue areas on a five point scale of importance running from 'very important' to 'not important at all'. The issues were:

- reducing unemployment;
- the Anglo-Irish Agreement;
- reducing taxation;
- reducing emigration and
- reducing the amount the Government is borrowing and, in turn, the national debt.

Then, in order to identify *personal issue positions* of voters directly, each respondent was asked to agree or disagree on a five point scale with the following three statements:

-'A lasting solution to the Northern Ireland Problem will require a British withdrawal from Northern Ireland.'

-'Taxation must be reduced, even if this means that the Government makes drastic reductions in its services.'

-'The Government should ensure that the policies they adopt on matters such as Divorce and Contraception are in line with the teachings of the Catholic Church.'

Finally, in order to assess *voters' views of party policies*, respondents were asked which party had the best, and which the next best, policies on the following issues:

- Northern Ireland;
- Taxation;
- Level of government spending and
- Divorce and contraception.

The relative importance of the issues

The views of voters on the relative importance of the issues are summarised in Table 7. Unemployment was overwhelmingly the most important issue of the election, with 97% seeing it as 'very important'.

What stands out from the table, however, is that voters' views of the importance of the issues did not distinguish supporters of the main parties. The only exceptions were the tendency of Progressive Democrat supporters to rate 'reducing taxation' as very important and the tendency of Fine Gael supporters not to rate emigration as very important. Overall, the importance of the economic issues overwhelmingly dominated that of Northern Ireland, a factor that gave a major advantage to parties with more popular policies on the economy, but which offered no great comfort to Fine Gael, with popular policies on Northern Ireland.

Table 7: Relative importance of main issues

Issue	% rating issue 'very important'				
	All	FF	FG	LAB	PD
Reduce unemployment	97	98	95	100	95
Anglo-Irish Agreement	15	16	16	18	17
Reduce taxation	76	74	68	74	82
Reduce emigration	46	52	38	51	52
Reduce govt. borrowing	69	65	72	69	73

N = 1000

Source: MRBI /Irish Times surveys

The personal issue positions of voters

Moving on to the actual issue positions of the voters, Tables 8-10 show the proportions of various sectors of the electorate agreeing or disagreeing with statements designed to tap attitudes on three independent and important dimensions of ideology: Northern Ireland, economic policy and church/state relations.

We see from Table 8 that Northern Ireland policy is an issue that did distinguish some social groups from others. Both white collar and blue collar employees were least likely to agree strongly that a lasting solution in the North will require British withdrawal, while small farmers and the bourgeoisie were most likely to agree strongly with this proposition. Fianna Fáil voters were markedly more likely to agree strongly with the need for British withdrawal than were supporters of the other parties. This is consistent with Fianna Fail's traditional strength among small farmers but it does show that Fianna Fail's recent blue collar gains were not based on the party's Northern policy.

We see from Table 9 that the taxation/public spending dilemma polarised voters rather more than Northern Ireland. On the one hand small farmers and the bourgeoisie were more likely to agree strongly with cutting taxes at the expense of public services. On the other hand, both white and blue collar workers were less likely to agree strongly with cutting taxes (this is, since these groups are typically assumed to pay most tax, as PAYE workers). Those who are older and those who live in rural areas also seem to be less likely to favour tax cuts.

Table 8: Attitudes on Northern Ireland

Percentages agreeing/disagreeing with the statement: 'A lasting solution to the Northern Ireland problem will require a British withdrawal from Northern Ireland.'

	Agree strongly	Agree	Neither agree nor disagree	Disagree	Disagree strongly
Total	**27**	**33**	**14**	**20**	**6**
Fianna Fáil	34	33	13	16	4
Fine Gael	20	31	16	24	9
Labour	23	44	10	21	3
Progressive Democrats	22	35	16	21	6
Bourgeoisie	35	18	22	13	11
Petit bourgeoisie	30	43	9	14	5
Middle class	24	32	10	25	9
Working class	24	36	16	20	4
Large farmers	29	36	9	19	7
Small farmers	36	28	16	13	8
Age					
18-24	24	37	13	20	4
25-34	22	40	13	20	5
35-49	31	26	16	17	10
50-64	29	30	15	21	5
65+	31	33	13	19	4
Urban	24	34	15	22	6
Rural	32	32	13	17	6

Source: MRBI /Irish Times surveys

Of party supporters, those who backed the PDs were significantly more likely to agree strongly with tax cuts at the expense of public services. This particular policy appeal cannot, however, have done the PDs much good among small farmers. While small farmers were the group most likely to favour tax cuts they were a group among which the PDs, as we have seen, were very weak. Tax policy may, however, have helped the PDs to attract votes among the bourgeoisie who favoured tax cuts strongly and who also, as we have seen above, supported the PDs more strongly than any other party.

Table 9: Attitudes on taxation vs public services

Percentages agreeing/disagreeing with the statement: 'Taxation must be reduced, even if it means that the Government makes drastic reductions in its services.'

	Agree strongly	Agree	Neither agree nor disagree	Disagree	Disagree strongly
Total	**29**	**34**	**7**	**23**	**6**
Fianna Fáil	28	37	7	22	6
Fine Gael	28	43	6	18	6
Labour	23	44	3	28	3
Progressive Democrats	37	26	7	23	7
Bourgeoisie	42	29	11	13	4
Petit bourgeoisie	31	31	11	20	7
Middle class	25	32	4	30	9
Working class	26	37	7	23	8
Large farmers	35	32	9	22	2
Small farmers	39	41	3	12	4
Age					
18-24	22	39	9	22	7
25-34	28	34	6	25	8
35-49	32	29	7	25	7
50-64	32	34	5	24	5
65+	31	37	16	15	2
Urban	25	32	8	27	8
Rural	34	37	6	19	4

Source: MRBI /Irish Times surveys

The most striking polarisation of attitudes, however, is revealed in Table 10, which deals with church/state relations. Farmers are noticeably more likely than anyone else to agree that government policy on moral issues should follow that of the church (69% of small farmers felt this). There is no real difference within non-farming sectors of the electorate, among whom around 40% agreed that the state should follow the church. There is, however, a striking age gradient on this issue. Only 12% of 18-24 year olds felt strongly that the state should follow church teaching, compared to 39% of those over 65 years old.

Table 10: Attitudes on Church/State Relations

Percentages agreeing/disagreeing with the statement: 'the Government should ensure that policies they adopt on such matters as divorce and contraception are in line with the teachings of the Catholic Church.'

	Agree strongly	Agree	Neither agree nor disagree	Disagree	Disagree strongly
Total	**22**	**26**	**11**	**28**	**13**
Fianna Fáil	27	31	9	24	9
Fine Gael	19	25	11	32	13
Labour	10	33	8	31	18
Progressive Democrats	21	21	13	28	18
Bourgeoisie	27	18	13	22	20
Petit bourgeoisie	14	23	14	35	14
Middle class	19	17	10	35	19
Working class	19	28	12	28	14
Large farmers	29	25	9	23	13
Small farmers	29	40	7	23	1
Age					
18-24	12	30	12	30	16
25-34	13	23	11	31	21
35-49	23	23	8	33	13
50-64	31	29	12	21	7
65+	39	30	12	18	1
Urban	18	21	12	33	16
Rural	26	33	9	22	10

Source: MRBI /Irish Times surveys

The 'traditional' attitude that government policy should be in line with that of the church was thus held more strongly in the traditional sectors of the more rural and the more elderly electorate. Fianna Fáil supporters were more strongly in favour of the traditional view - in contrast to those supporting Labour - while Fine Gael and PD supporters were somewhere in between.

What is clear is that the proper relationship between church and state, even if it was not on the surface an important issue for voters, was the issue that polarised the Irish electorate most strongly. It definitely produced a stronger social and political patterning of responses than either the tax vs public services dilemma, or the Northern Ireland problem.

PARTY POLICY ON THE ISSUES

So far, we have been talking about the general relationship between attitudes and party support. A range of more explicit questions was asked, however, dealing with the party that each voter felt to have the best policy on each issue. The results are reported in Tables 11-14 and provide probably the firmest evidence about the effect of attitudes on party support in Ireland.

On Northern Ireland (Table 12), and on moral issues such as divorce and contraception (Table 14), we see a clear distinction between Fianna Fáil and Fine Gael. Those who strongly agree that the British will have to withdraw before a lasting solution is found in Northern Ireland are quite a bit more likely to think that Fianna Fáil has the best policy on this issue. All others are more likely to think that Fine Gael has the best policy. The pattern on the church/state issues, however, is even more striking. Those who strongly agree that the state policies should be in line with church teaching are *much* more likely to feel that Fianna Fáil has the best policy. Those who disagree are *much* more likely to think Fine Gael has the best policy.

Table 11: Issue position and party policy; Northern Ireland

Party with best policy on N. Ireland

% Agreeing that a lasting solution to NI problem will require a British withdrawal

	All voters	Strongly agree	Agree	Disagree	Strongly disagree
Fianna Fáil	29	41	28	23	28
Fine Gael	41	31	49	46	46
Other	7	9	4	3	7
None	23	19	19	28	19
	100%	100%	100%	100%	100%
N	1000	269	325	191	57

Source: MRBI /Irish Times surveys

Table 12: Issue position and party policy; taxation

Party with best policy on taxation		% Agreeing that taxation must be reduced even if it means that the govrernment makes drastic reductions in its services			
	All voters	Strongly agree	Agree	Disagree	Strongly disagree
Fianna Fáil	34	39	34	32	34
Fine Gael	16	17	18	14	14
PD	13	19	12	12	11
Others	34	3	3	7	10
None	32	22	33	35	31
	100%	100%	100%	100%	100%
N	1000	290	340	231	64

Source: MRBI /Irish Times surveys

Table 13: Issue position and party policy; government spending

Party with best policy on government spending		% Agreeing that taxation must be reduced			
	All voters	Strongly agree	Agree	Disagree	Strongly disagree
Fianna Fáil	30	31	32	28	31
Fine Gael	30	32	31	27	31
Progressive Democrats	9	12	8	8	2
Others	4	3	4	6	8
None	28	22	25	31	28
		100%	100%	100%	100%
N		290	340	229	64

Source: MRBI /Irish Times surveys

Patterns of party support: issues, attitudes and party policy

Table 14: Issue position and party policy; divorce and contraception

Party with best policy on issues such as divorce and contraception.

% Agreeing that the Government should ensure that the policies they adopt on matters such as divorce and contraception are in line with the teachings of the Catholic church

	All voters	Strongly agree	Agree	Disagree	Strongly disagree
Fianna Fáil	32	49	38	24	16
Fine Gael	35	16	32	53	47
Others	9	8	5	5	20
None	24	27	25	18	17
N		100% 218	100% 262	100% 277	100% 131

Source: MRBI /Irish Times surveys

What is striking about both Northern Ireland and church/state relations is that views on which party had the best policy depended on people's issue positions. In contrast, views on which party had the best policy on the economic issues did not depend on issue positions. On taxation (Table 12), Fianna Fáil had a clear lead over Fine Gael across the board - among those strongly in favour of tax cuts as well as among those strongly against them. The PDs did rather better among those who favoured tax cuts, and Labour among those who opposed them, but the differences are not great.

The same pattern can be seen for attitudes to government spending. Fianna Fáil and Fine Gael were evenly matched on this issue across the board, both among those who wanted to see spending cut and among those who did not. The PDs did better among those who wanted to see spending cut and Labour among those who did not, and the patterns are rather stronger this time.

This evidence confirms that the PDs were attracting more support from those, on the right of the socio-economic spectrum, who wanted to cut taxes and spending. Labour, clearly and not surprisingly, attracted support from those on the left. *But the most remarkable finding is the way in which the balance between Fianna Fáil and Fine Gael support does not depend at all on the personal positions of the electorate on the issues taxation and spending.* Voters located on the right on these issues were as likely to support either Fine Gael or Fianna Fáil as voters on the left.

Patterns of party support: issues, attitudes and party policy

This can hardly be taken as a piece of evidence in favour of the 'rational choice' view that voters pick parties on the basis of the policies on offer. Voters with dramatically opposed views on the same issue often thought that the same party had the best policy on it, while voters with the same views often disagreed on the best party. It is a stronger piece of evidence in favour of party identification theory, suggesting as it does that people feel that 'their' party has the best policy on the issue regardless, more or less, of what that policy is.

Table 15: Party support, by party with best policy on Northern Ireland

Party with best policy on Northern Ireland

	Fianna Fáil	Fine Gael
Party Support		
Fianna Fáil	**78**	21
Fine Gael	4	**31**
Labour	2	4
Progressive Democrats	3	17
Don't know	10	25
	100%	100%

Source: MRBI /Irish Times surveys

Table 16: Party support, by party with best policy on taxation

Party with best policy on taxation

	Fianna Fáil	Fine Gael	PD
Party Support			
Fianna Fáil	**77**	13	15
Fine Gael	5	**58**	16
Progressive Democrats	3	7	**46**
Labour	4	2	2
Don't know	11	21	21
	100%	100%	100%

Source: MRBI /Irish Times surveys

Perhaps the clearest picture of the linkage between policy preferences and party choice can be seem from Tables 15-18, which show levels of party support among those who thought that a particular party had the best policy on an issue. These show clearly that Fine Gael failed to benefit from the fact that it was felt by quite a wide section of the electorate to have the best policies on a range of issues.

Quite simply, those who felt Fianna Fáil had the best policies also voted Fianna Fáil. The relationship is so stable across different issues, indeed, as to suggest that the voters' party choice was influencing their positions on the issues, rather than *vice versa*. Those who felt Fine Gael had the best policies on an issue, however, just did not vote for it to anything like the same extent. Indeed, of those who felt Fine Gael had the best policy on divorce and contraception, almost as many supported Fianna Fáil as supported Fine Gael. Only on the issue of taxation did a majority of those who felt that Fine Gael had the best policy also vote for the party.

Table 17: Party support, by party with best policy on government spending

	Party with best policy on government spending		
	Fianna Fáil	Fine Gael	PD
Party Support			
Fianna Fáil	**78**	16	22
Fine Gael	3	**42**	12
Progressive Democrats	3	15	**47**
Labour	1	3	0
Don't know	12	23	14
Total	100%	100%	100%

Source: MRBI /Irish Times surveys

Table 18: Party support, by party with best policy on divorce and contraception

	Party with best policy on divorce and contraception	
	Fianna Fáil	Fine Gael
Party Support		
Fianna Fáil	**68**	27
Fine Gael	7	**30**
Labour	2	4
Progressive Democrats	8	15
Don't know	14	23
Total	100%	100%

Source: MRBI /Irish Times surveys

Overall, the relationship between attitudes and party choice in the 1987 election was a complex one. Economic issues, and especially taxation, were clearly the most salient and clearly had the strongest effect on party fortunes. Surprisingly, however, it does not seem to have been precise *positions* on these issues that made the difference to how people voted. Voters' judgements of party policy on the issues are unrelated to their personal issue positions. Rather it seems to have been a general assessment by voters of the party under a particular issue heading that affected party preference. Thus Fianna Fáil was seen as having the 'best' policy on taxation, almost regardless of preferred policy of voters, while the two big parties tied on government spending.

The non-economic issues of Northern Ireland and church/state relations, in contrast, produced a much greater consistency between the preferred policy of voters and the party seen to have the best policy. In each case Fine Gael 'won', in crude terms, but this victory did not translate itself into party support. As we can see from the assessment of salience, Northern Ireland was not considered an important issue by many, so Fine Gael's clear lead here had little impact on the election. Though the question was not asked, it is clear that divorce and contraception policy also had little importance in the campaign - they were certainly mentioned only very rarely. Thus, once more, Fine Gael's perceived policy advantage came to naught.

To the extent that the issues affected the result of the February 1987 election, it was the economy that mattered and the debate was won by Fianna Fáil. There must remain a very strong suspicion, however, that people felt that Fianna Fáil had the best economic policies not because they had studied Fianna Fáil's economic policies but because they felt the economy was important, and because they had decided to vote for Fianna Fáil in any case.

C. THE ROLE OF PARTY LEADERSHIP IN VOTING DECISIONS

Irish party politics in the first half of the 1980s were dominated by the confrontation between two strong and prominent leaders, Charles Haughey and Garret FitzGerald. The discussion that follows examines some evidence on which to assess the importance of leaders, both potential Taoisigh and their ministerial teams, in electoral decision-making. We have just seen that the parties' precise messages on the issues were not critical in many peoples' voting decision. Much attention was given in the campaign, however, to those who articulated party messages, in particular to the party leaders but also to potential ministers in the next Government. Were the personalities of these individuals, and was the electoral assessment of their popularity, more important than what they actually said?

One of the most remarkable features of the 1987 campaign was that it was the fourth contest between the same two leaders, Charles Haughey and Garrett FitzGerald. Fine Gael had directed personal criticism at the Fianna Fáil leader at the time of his election in 1979, and one viewpoint was that he would not help his party's fortunes. The so-called 'Haughey factor' was, for some, demonstrated as Fianna Fáil failed to achieve an overall majority under Haughey at any election in the early 1980s. Furthermore, Haughey's popularity usually lagged behind that of his party.

In 1987, however, Fine Gael's leader was also under pressure, not least from the conservative wing of his own party. Public confidence in him had fallen far below what it had been in its heyday. The emergence of Des O'Malley, promoted by the PDs as an alternative Taoiseach in the event of a hung Dáil, added a new element to the old mixture, especially after his popularity in the MRBI/Irish Times polls exceeded that of his rivals.

For the three main parties in particular, then, the party leaders acted as a focus for their campaign, while the 'Great Debate' on RTE between FitzGerald and Haughey at the close of the campaign (discussed in detail above by David M. Farrell), served to emphasise this 'presidential' aspect of the election.

As television replaces the church gate as the main theatre of party competition it is natural that leaders receive more attention. Whilst their role in government may be overrated, particularly in a coalition, the Taoiseach at least tends to personify his administration and his image will be reflected in electoral assessments of his government.

In February 1987, as we have seen, few voters chose their party because of its particular economic policy, even though economic issues were central in the campaign. Arguably, most voters backed one party rather than another because they felt it would manage the economy most effectively, and assessments of each party's leadership must have played a part in their decision. Following two of the views of voting behaviour alluded to earlier, such a decision may stem either from a psychological attachment to a party or from an independent appraisal of qualities and record of the various leaders on offer. In either case, if leaders are an important element in the voting decision we will be able to see some consistency between voters' assessments of them and their choice of party.

The two IMS/Irish Independent polls commissioned during the pre-election period asked questions about the party leaders and ministers:

'Are you satisfied or dissatisfied with the way (Charles Haughey/Garret FitzGerald/Dick Spring etc.) is doing his job as Taoiseach/Leader of (Fianna Fáil/ Fine Gael/ Labour etc..) ? '

'Who do you think would make a better Taoiseach: Garret FitzGerald, Charles Haughey or Des O'Malley, if it had to be one of these three men ? '

' Which party would provide the best set of ministers ? '

Table 19: Voting intention of those satisfied with particular leaders

	% satisfied with:			
	Haughey	FitzGerald	O'Malley	Spring
	%	%	%	%
Fianna Fáil	**82**	19	37	34
Fine Gael	6	**54**	19	34
Progressive Democrat	5	17	**33**	15
Labour	3	8	6	**13**
Others	4	3	5	5
Total	100	100	100	100
N	613	742	758	588

Source: IMS/Irish Independent surveys

Table 19 shows the voting intentions of those who said they were satisfied with the performance of each leader (or of the Taoiseach, in the case of Garret FitzGerald), combining the results of the two IMS/Irish Independent polls. Haughey and O'Malley win most approval but the other two party leaders are close behind.

It is when voting intentions are also considered that more striking contrasts are seen. Those satisfied with the Fianna Fáil leader were overwhelmingly Fianna Fáil voters, whilst relatively few of those approving Spring or O'Malley voted Labour or PD. This might be taken to imply that 'the Haughey factor' helped Fianna Fáil, since Haughey's capacity to deliver his personal support to his party appears superior to that of the other leaders.

Table 20: Proportions of party supporters satisfied with leaders

% of those who intend to vote for party who feel listed leader is doing a good job

	FF	FG	PD	Labour	All Parties
	%	%	%	%	
Haughey	**69**	11	11	20	(35)
FitzGerald	14	**75**	33	41	(29)
O'Malley	32	33	**83**	39	(36)
Spring	22	46	28	**65**	(28)
Total	100	100	100	100	128

Source: IMS/Irish Independent surveys

Table 20 qualifies this conclusion, however. It shows the share of each party's supporters who were satisfied with each leader. O'Malley is most popular, approved by 83% of PD voters, with FitzGerald satisfying 75% of Fine Gael voters, Haughey 69% of Fianna Fáil voters and Spring only 65% of Labour voters. Thus, while most of those who approved of Haughey voted for Fianna Fáil it was by no means the case that all who voted for Fianna Fáil liked Haughey.

In contrast, approval of O'Malley was much greater than that of his party and hence support for him cannot be taken as *sufficient* to attract voters to the PDs. Those who voted PD liked O'Malley but by no means all those who liked O'Malley voted PD. The popularity of Garret FitzGerald and support for Fine Gael were, however, much more balanced.

Of course, some voters felt that several leaders were performing well. (Forty-four percent expressed approval of more than one leader, 38% approved only one and 18% were not satisfied with any of them). A question on the *relative* merits of the leaders as a potential Taoiseach is a better test of the link between views on party leadership and voting intentions. Tables 21 and 22 show, respectively, the party choice of those preferring each leader and the leader preferred by each parties' supporters. The analysis is confined to voters for Fianna Fáil, Fine Gael and the PDs, since only their party leaders' names were included in the list of candidates for Taoiseach.

Table 21: Voting intention by preferred Taoiseach

% of Taoiseach supporters intending to vote for party

	Haughey	FitzGerald	O'Malley
	%	%	%
Fianna Fáil	**95**	14	29
Fine Gael	3	**76**	23
Progressive Democrat	2	11	**47**
Total	100	100	100

Source: IMS/Irish Independent surveys

Broadly, the results echo those for 'satisfaction', and confirm the differences between the parties. Table 21 shows that 95% of those preferring Haughey as Taoiseach intended to vote Fianna Fáil, a remarkably high level. Comparable figures for FitzGerald are 76% and only 47% for O'Malley. A preference for Haughey as Taoiseach almost invariably went along with a vote for Fianna Fáil, whilst O'Malley's popularity vastly exceeded that of his party.

Table 22 shows that O'Malley was more popular within his own party, however, than were the other leaders in their parties; 76% of PD voters preferred O'Malley as Taoiseach, 71% of Fianna Fáil voters preferred their party leader as Taoiseach and 63 % of Fine Gael voters preferred FitzGerald. For substantial proportions of Fianna Fáil voters (17%) and Fine Gael voters (26%) O'Malley was a more attractive Taoiseach than their own party leader. But obviously this was not sufficient to induce them to vote PD and attempt to make O'Malley Taoiseach.

Leaders, then, are assessed independently of their party, at least to some degree. Approval or disapproval of a leader does not inevitably imply approval or disapproval of the leader's party. Leaders do not attract all their supporters to their party, nor do they repel all who may be dissatisfied with them. Views of the party leaders may well be an element in the elector's decision, but they do not determine it.

Table 22: Preference for Taoiseach by voting intention

	% intending to vote for:			
	FF	FG	PD	Others
	%	%	%	%
Haughey	**71**	5	4	22
FitzGerald	6	**63**	13	23
O'Malley	17	26	**76**	29
Don't know	7	6	7	26
Total	100	100	100	100
N	873	438	305	241

Source: IMS/Irish Independent surveys

The MRBI/Irish Times polls provide further information on the particular qualities that electors saw in the leaders of the contending parties. The polls asked respondents to say which leader was best in particular roles; getting things done, managing the Cabinet, getting interest groups working together, dealing with ordinary people and improving the standing of the country abroad. Each leader was seen to have different qualities. Whilst overall rankings owe much to party popularity, the perceived strengths and weaknesses of each leader are informative.

Table 23: Perceived qualities of party leaders

	% thinking leader is the best at:				
	Improving Ireland's standing abroad	Getting things done	Getting most from a cabinet team	Getting interest groups working together	Knowing/ understand problems of ordinary people
	%	%	%	%	%
Haughey	39	52	51	45	47
FitzGerald	44	17	24	19	18
O'Malley	15	27	23	30	22
Spring	3	4	3	6	13
Total	100	100	100	100	100
N	811	814	801	814	749

Source: MRBI /Irish Times surveys

Table 23 shows that Haughey's strength seems to have been in views of him in an executive role, and particularly in his ability to get things done. The same was true for O'Malley, who nevertheless was rated below Haughey on all criteria. FitzGerald, by contrast, was seen as a statesman and the Labour leader's strongest suit was seen as being in touch with ordinary people. It would be interesting to know which of these qualities were most valued by the electorate but the information is not available. There are, of course, party politicians other than the leaders who may influence the result of an election. The potential ministerial teams of each party were displayed prominently during the campaign with spokespeople and ministers confronting one another almost nightly on the TV screen. Fianna Fáil and Fine Gael, with larger teams at their disposal, could offer a broader range but all parties used several spokespeople.

Table 24 and 25 show the link between voting intentions and assessments of which party had the best ministerial talent. For Fianna Fáil, the pattern is very similar to that shown for preferences for party leadership. A total of 89% of those who felt that Fianna Fáil could provide the best ministers supported the party. Yet only 73% of Fianna Fáil voters were happy with the Fianna Fáil team.

The perception of PD ministers, however, contrasted strongly with perceptions of O'Malley, the party leader. While 72% of those who felt that the PDs had the best ministers voted PD, only 40% of PD voters thought they had the best team.

The relationship between Fine Gael voters and their assessment of Fine Gael ministers was a slight reversal of the pattern for the Fine Gael leader. Sixty-six per cent of ministerial approval was translated into votes, but 74% of Fine Gael voters felt that their ministers were best. Fine Gael ministers were more popular within the party than the Fine Gael leader and more popular amongst the electorate at large.

Labour evaluations of ministers cannot be connected with those for potential Taoiseach in the same way but it is evident that the ministerial team was not a salient feature for Labour voters. Only 19% of Labour voters thought Labour had the best team, while 24% of Labour supporters actually preferred Fine Gael's ministerial team. However, a much higher proportion of Labour voters thought there was 'no difference' between the parties on this.

Generally, more voters saw 'no difference' between teams of ministers than between alternatives for Taoiseach, but it was more unusual for voters to prefer the ministers of other parties. Moreover, the visibility of ministers or potential ministers is a function of party size. Very few Fianna Fáil or Fine Gael voters preferred (or, perhaps even knew) the look of a potential PD or Labour cabinet, although many liked the PD leader. By contrast, many PD and Labour voters preferred the ministerial teams of the other parties.

Table 24: Voting intention by perception of party with best ministers

	Party with best ministers			
% intending to vote for:	Fianna Fail	Fine Gael	PD	Labour
	%	%	%	%
Fianna Fáil	**89**	9	13	18
Fine Gael	3	**66**	9	8
Progressive Democrats	3	17	**72**	10
Labour	7	6	3	**55**
Others	4	3	2	10
Total	100	100	100	100
N	775	494	167	40

Source: IMS/Irish Independent surveys

Table 25: Perception of party with best ministers by voting intention

	Voting Intention			
% seeing party as having best ministers	Fianna Fail	Fine Gael	PD	Labour
	%	%	%	%
Fianna Fáil	**73**	5	8	11
Fine Gael	5	**74**	30	24
Progressive Democrats	3	3	**40**	4
Labour	1	1	1	**19**
Other/no difference/don't know	18	16	25	42
Total	100	100	100	100
N	881	438	305	117

Source: IMS/Irish Independent surveys

Figure 1 summarises the relationships displayed in Tables 21, 22, 24 and 25. Each party's strength is represented as a circle of standard size. In front of that circle, partly covering it, is another circle which represents the popularity of the party's leader or ministers. The degree to which the circle in the foreground covers that behind it illustrates the popularity of leaders within their party. The two areas standing out from this indicate, in the background, the degree of the leadership's unpopularity within the party and, in the foreground, their popularity outside the party. Thus, for Fianna Fáil, Charles Haughey is the preferred leader of 71% with 29% preferring someone else; only 5% of his popularity comes from those outside the party, so the leader circle in the foreground is contained almost completely with the background party circle, and fills most of that circle.

Two main points are highlighted by this figure. First, we can see the exclusiveness of the popularity of Fianna Fáil leaders in the fact that, for Fianna Fáil, the leadership circles in the foreground are almost entirely contained within the party circles in the background. Thus, in contrast to the leaders of other parties, and in particular in contrast to O'Malley personally, the Fianna Fáil leaders are not popular outside the party. There is much less difference in the attractiveness of leaders inside their parties. Second, when the relative size of leader and minister circles are compared, the marked dissimilarity in the two for the PDs is very evident. The greater popularity of the PD leader over the PD ministers actually reverses the pattern for other parties, suggesting that the PDs have a far 'narrower' leadership image than that of the other two parties.

We cannot of course decide from this figure whether people chose parties because they liked their leaders, or liked the leaders of their chosen parties. While the evidence from the perceptions of the issues was most consistent with party loyalty, the necessary evidence is not available for a judgement on the role of personnel.

We have already said that Fianna Fáil's leaders attracted a more 'exclusive' support than those of other parties. Whilst 26% of Fine Gael voters preferred O'Malley to their own leader as Taoiseach, only 5% preferred Haughey. Similarly, 13% of PD voters preferred FitzGerald to O'Malley but only 4% preferred Haughey.

The same pattern is apparent in general levels of satisfaction with the leaders. Taking Fianna Fáil, Fine Gael and PD voters only, of those satisfied with the Fianna Fáil leader, 52% were satisfied *only* with him. They were not satisfied with the performance of any other leader. Yet amongst those voters who thought that FitzGerald was doing a good job, only 14% were satisfied exclusively with him. The great majority felt at least one other leader was doing well. Much the same is true for those who approved of O'Malley's performance. Furthermore, whilst 8% were satisfied with at least FitzGerald and Haughey, and 14% with at least O'Malley and Haughey, 22% were satisifed with FitzGerald and O'Malley. The implication is that Fine Gael and PD voters were much more generous in their assessment of other party leaders than were Fianna Fáil voters. These patterns of cross party sympathy between Fine Gael and the PDs, and of Fianna Fáil exclusiveness, indicate a basis for a Fine Gael/PD alliance and reinforce a view of the Irish party system which sets Fianna Fáil apart from the rest.

However, it is evident that neither issues nor leaders played a completely decisive role in determining how people voted. Voting was not simply a matter of expressing habitual loyalties, otherwise the dramatic success of PDs and the decline of Fine Gael would not have been possible. What we do know is that voters, at least in 1987, chose parties without necessarily liking their leaders as well as without being clear about their policies.

Other factors in voting choice

A substantial proportion of voters say that it is neither leaders nor issues that sway their decision but rather the abilities of candidates to service constituency needs. In IMS polls since 1977, when asked 'which of these will be most important to you in making up your mind how to vote ?', voters more often pick the option 'choosing a candidate to look after the needs of the constituency' than any other. Alternatives offered include; 'choosing a Taoiseach', 'choosing the set of ministers who will form the Government' and 'choosing between the policies set out by the parties'. Table 26 summarises the factors that people have said influenced their vote in recent elections.

Table 26: Voting criterion by voting intention

% citing most important voting criterion as:	Voting intention 1987					1977-82 average
	Fianna Fail	Fine Gael	PD	Labour	All	
Taoiseach	19	18	8	12	15	16
Ministers	17	20	25	14	18	17
Policies	24	31	40	22	29	24
Candidate	40	32	26	53	38	41
N	428	230	149	59	1040	

Source: IMS/Irish Independent Surveys. Previous years figures from R. Sinnott, 'The voters, the issues and the Party System' in H. Penniman and B.Farrell (eds) , Ireland at the Polls, Washington: AEI/Duke (forthcoming)

Patterns of party support: leadership factors

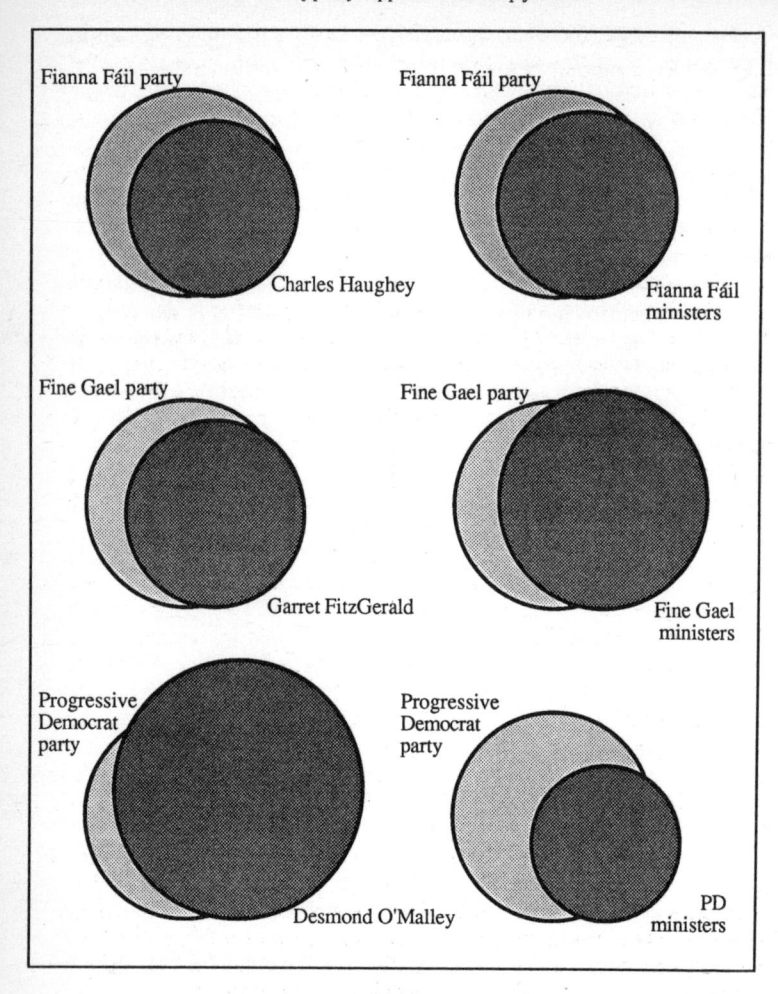

In each case the level of support for the party is represented by a light circle of fixed size in the background. The relative popularity of the party leader (or its team of ministers) is represented by the size of the dark circle in the foreground.

Figure 1: The relative popularity of parties and leaders

By and large, the overall pattern in 1987 was similar to that in previous years, with a slight increase in the effect of 'policies' at the expense of that of 'candidates'. The table suggests that 'choosing a Taoiseach' is relatively unimportant outside of the two largest parties, with only 8% of PD voters choosing this option. Generally, the biggest differences between parties occurred in the relative importance of 'policies' and 'candidates' with Labour supporters in particular, but also those of Fianna Fáil, stressing candidates, while Fine Gael and PD supporters stressed policies.

This information is ambiguous. Given the STV voting system used in Irish elections it is not certain whether the question refers only to first preference votes, to early preferences or to the overall rank ordering of parties and candidates. People who say they cast their *first preference* vote for a local candidate may in fact select the best local candidate of their first choice party. This makes it particularly difficult to find out why someone voted as they did, since an STV vote is such a sophisticated piece of information. In particular we do not yet know, on the survey evidence available, how many voters would switch parties to vote for a person they felt was the best local candidate.

If we concentrate not on the distinction between parish pump and national politics (that is, the distinction between a preference for good constituency servants and all other criteria) but on the variations within the 'national' criteria for casting a vote, then we are on safer ground. In this respect it is evident that PD voters were far more inclined to stress party policy rather than choice of Taoiseach as the main influence on their vote. It is ironic that the party with the most popular leader was most likely to be supported by people for whom that criterion was least important. Conversely, whilst many PD voters rated ministerial competence highly, the PDs' particular team of ministers was seen as a relatively weak aspect of the party's resources.

Whether voters put their faith in leaders, local candidates or policies, they will presumably only allow these factors to influence their decision if they believe what they are told about them. The extent to which voters trust parties and politicians is thus very important. As we shall now see, trust was marginally more abundant in 1987 than it had been in 1982 but remained, nonetheless, in short supply.

The IMS/Irish Independent poll of February 13 asked respondents whether or not they believed, on the whole, what was said by each party. As Table 27 shows, no party could take much heart from the responses. Only 34% trusted the PDs, 31% Fine Gael, 28% Fianna Fáil and 24% Labour. Whilst most (60%) were willing to trust at least one party, there was a marked variation in the proportion who trusted the party for which they voted. Sixty-eight per cent of Fine Gael and PD voters trusted their own party but only 55% and 54% of Fianna Fáil and Labour voters respectively trusted theirs.

Whilst it is possible that some voters see mendacity as a political asset, and others see honesty as unnecessary to effectiveness, the figures must be seen to indicate a profound scepticism and dissatisfaction with Irish political life amongst its citizens. Interestingly, those most inclined to be sceptical are also more inclined to claim parochial reasons for their vote, a total of 47% of them stressing 'candidate' as the leading factor in their decision were sceptics, compared with 35% of those citing a 'national' level criterion for casting their vote. The PDs, the newest party, are least affected by scepticism - fewer mistrusted them than any other party, although the difference between the PDs and Fine Gael is slight. There does not seen to be any clear social basis for political scepticism. Table 27 shows the percentage trusting their party in various social categories. Whilst middle class voters, older voters, rural voters and eastern (but not Dublin) voters are more trusting, differences are generally slight. The same is true of each party's voters, although young Fine Gael voters are much more sceptical than older ones.

Table 27: Proportions of voters trusting their chosen party, by demographic groups

% of social group trusting chosen party	FF	FG	PD	Labour
All voters	**54**	**68**	**68**	**55**
Social class				
Non-manual	53	72	75	65
Manual	57	68	64	63
Large farmer	54	70	59	*
Small farmer	48	52	57	*
Age				
18-24	52	47	68	54
25-34	52	65	77	56
35-40	57	71	48	58
51-65	55	78		
65+	56	77	(71)	(50)
City	55	66	64	65
Town	56	64	79	54
Rural	53	71	67	46
Dublin	53	65	62	65
Rest of Leinster	71	82	75	61
Munster	51	66	73	36
Connaught/Ulster	44	58	64	*

Source: IMS (1987)
*less than 10 cases ; () categories combined where too few cases

CONCLUSION: WHY DID PEOPLE VOTE THE WAY THEY DID?

If we had a definite answer to this question, of course, we could quit the groves of academe for the jungles of practical politics. The survey evidence assembled during the February 1987 campaign does, however, throw quite a bit of light on the matter.

In the first place, there seems to be a modest increase in class voting in Ireland. This is most clearly in evidence in the support profile of Ireland's newest party, the Progressive Democrats, and shows the Irish middle class to be the most volatile sector of the electorate. Labour's Michael D. Higgins rather contemptuously characterised early support for the PDs as a 'yuppie' vote and the survey evidence tends to bear this out. The PDs lead the field among the bourgeoisie while, if we take small farmers in Connacht as among the least yuppie of Ireland's citizens, most of them clearly view the PDs as inhabiting another political universe.

Yet Labour cannot draw much consolation from all of this as Fianna Fáil remains the party of the Irish working class, of small farmers and of the petit bourgeoisie. In 1987 at least, the critical battles of Irish politics were fought for the support of the volatile middle class, bourgeoisie and large farming sectors of the electorate, but the main contenders were Fianna Fáil, Fine Gael and the PDs. The essential task for Labour is to develop a basis in the working class at a level that would make it look more like Europe's other social democratic parties. With Fianna Fáil, the current party of the working class, in government and enacting cuts in public spending, Labour has a large target to aim at.

For the other parties, much will depend on the whims of increasingly fickle middle class voters. Having helped Fine Gael's revival in the late 1970s, these voters have gone over to the PDs in considerable numbers. Yet they now have a third alternative in a Fianna Fáil Government implementing a rigorous fiscal strategy. While reaping the tactical benefits in the Dáil of being able to play off left against right, Fianna Fáil must face up to the fact that it presents as big an electoral target for the right as it does for the left. On current survey evidence, it will find its right flank harder to protect, as middle class voters show themselves far more willing to change votes in response to changing electoral circumstances.

The second set of lessons that we can learn from the surveys concerns the effect of leaders and policies on the electorate. Choosing between different leaders, and choosing between different policies, is after all what most people like to think democracy is all about. Here the evidence strongly suggests that most people felt that the important issues had to do with the economy, yet could not see much difference between the main contenders on economic policy. Supporters of Irish parties polarise much more strongly on Northern Ireland and on church/state relations, but these were not seen as significant issues in February 1987.

This leaves us unclear about the precise role of policy. It may have been that policy had only a rather vague and erratic role in the campaign or it may be that, seeing no difference between the parties in important policy areas, voters resorted to less important policy areas to choose between them. On balance, given the clear failure of Fine Gael to cash in its chips on Northern Ireland and church/state relations, the former view seems the more plausible. Policy may have been the currency of political debate, but it does not seem to have been the deciding factor for most voters.

In the same way, leadership factors seem to have had no systematic impact. Most significantly, a very popular leader, Des O'Malley, did not produce a very popular party in the PDs. Conversely quite a few votes for Fine Gael and Fianna Fáil were cast despite the relative unpopularity of their leaders, FitzGerald and Haughey. Yet the PDs are clearly very closely identified with their leader, while a liking for Haughey seems to have been a strong inducement for voting Fianna Fáil. In this sense Charles Haughey and Des O'Malley are mirror images of one another. O'Malley was more popular outside his party but was unable to capitalise fully on his appeal. Haughey was less generally liked, but seems, given who *in particular* liked him, to have made better use of his popularity.

All of this, of course, bears out one of the fundamental rules of practical politics. This is that there is no cause for concern at being hated, just as there is no cause for rejoicing at being loved, by those who are not going to vote for you whatever happens.

7. THE ROAD FROM FEBRUARY 1987 GOVERNMENT FORMATION AND INSTITUTIONAL INERTIA

Brian Farrell

CHOOSING A TAOISEACH: THE POTENTIAL FOR STALEMATE

It was not a great result for political pundits, nor for punters. There were too many unexpected defeats, too many unanticipated victories and far too many close shaves. This election may not have shattered the moulds of Irish politics but it scattered much of the received wisdom about sitting deputies copperfastened to their secure seats, with new candidates and parties allegedly engaged in a hopeless endeavour to dislodge them. It also confirmed the signal, already registered in three elections in the 1980s, that winds of change were blowing the cobwebs off other cosy conventions. It established, for example, that government formation is no longer a neat ceremonial function following on in some clearcut and predictable liturgical sequence from the declaration of the election results.

No one could be sure, until Deputy Tony Gregory was two-thirds of the way through his speech on the opening day of the 25th Dáil, whether the House would manage to nominate any deputy as Taoiseach. Nor was it clear what options - other than an immediate, unwanted and possibly indecisive general election - were available in the event of failure. Charles Haughey was adamantly unwilling to stand aside for any alternative Fianna Fáil nominee. Speaking on the RTE radio programme 'This Week' two days before the vote, Ray Burke had spelled out the party line:

> 'Nobody will decide on the leadership of Fianna Fáil except Fianna Fáil and our leader is Charles J. Haughey. Let nobody outside Fianna Fáil have any feeling that since they've left the party they can influence our leadership. They tried that when they were on the inside and they're not going to do it from the outside . . . the only alternative to Mr. Haughey being leader and being Taoiseach is a general election.'[1]

In the event of a Dáil stalemate, was there an alternative? In procedural terms, it was doubtful whether an acting-Taoiseach could order an adjournment to facilitate political negotiation.

Constitutionally, the President might refuse a dissolution to a Taoiseach who had ceased to retain the support of a majority in Dáil Éireann but he was unlikely to do so. The dilemmas posed, including the uncertainties of another general election, illustrated how little thought had been given to issues of government formation in the past.

The reason was simple enough. Largely through historical accident, the problems had just not arisen. In his *Cabinet Government in Ireland*, Chubb could say 'the Dáil does not appoint the Government, except in a formal way' and, even in the second edition of *the Government and Politics of Ireland*, could explain 'in practice, general elections . . . usually determine which party or group of parties shall form the Government; the Dáil merely ratifies a decision already made'.[2] It was, indeed, one of the oddities of the Irish political system that, despite the operation of single transferable vote proportional representation, electoral outcomes had appeared so decisive.

Closer examination reveals some fissures in the superficially solid facade.[3] Since the foundation of the state, single-party government has been the norm; but it has not always been single-party majority government. The initial Cumann na nGaedhael administrations (1922-32) were all, in reality, minority governments. Even the historic, apparently monolithic, sixteen-year rule of de Valera had begun in 1932 as a minority government and lost its majority in two of the five subsequent elections until ousted in 1948. During the later sixteen-year rule of Fianna Fáil (1957-1973) stretching from de Valera to Lynch, Sean Lemass was a minority Taoiseach from 1961-1965.

Indeed, scanning Irish electoral history, it becomes clear that in many general elections it was not the people at the polls but the party leaders, by a combination of will, skill and luck, who determined which side won government. Frequently it was division, incompetence and lack of leadership on the opposition benches that allowed the formation and maintenance of minority administrations. There were many factors at play.

The unquestioning acceptance of the Westminster model encouraged an uncritical belief in single-party government as not merely the the norm but as morally superior. Coalitions were regarded, with a Victorian distaste for all that was unfamiliar and continental, as both alien and inherently unstable. Despite the experience of the second Sinn Féin party (an amalgam that stretched from constitutional nationalists through physical force republicans to revolutionary socialists) there was little recognition of the obvious fact that all large parties are themselves coalitions of factions.

Above all, perhaps, there was the constant performance of Fianna Fáil, sustaining its position as the leading party, always inclining towards majority support and prone to be seen (and to view itself) as the natural party of government. Its dominance over the centre of Irish politics not merely reduced the other parties but tended to marginalise them. Fianna Fáil drove them to opposite ends of an ill-defined and barely ideological spectrum. Their fragmentation offered Fianna Fáil a monopoly on government.

That was challenged in 1948. After a confusing campaign, there was at least some question of who was to form government. It says much for the strength of political habit that Fianna Fáil was so little prepared for opposition and that the parties forming the new administration should take so much care to avoid the label 'coalition'. But at least the outcome challenged received assumptions and opened up the possibilities of new modes of government formation. That watershed election inaugurated a decade in which governmental membership see-sawed. There was some alternation of parties in government but there remained no radical exploration of how representative cabinet government might be formed. Arrangements between parties rarely moved beyond an electoral pact limited to transfers; agreed programmes for government were at best headlines, rather than specific bargains on detailed policies. There were no realignments. Even in 1973, when Fianna Fáil hegemony had again lasted for an unbroken sixteen years, the 'solution' was the old pre-election combination (carefully qualified as 'national coalition') of Fine Gael and Labour. Then, as in the subsequent Fianna Fáil landslide of 1977, the complex issues of government formation were reduced to two simple questions: who would win the election and which deputies would the winner choose to bring into Cabinet?

The electoral circumstances of the 1980s reveal the inadequacies of this primitive analysis. Much has been made of the fact that in 1987, for the fourth time in a row, Fianna Fáil failed to obtain a clear cut, overall majority and this has been frequently cited as evidence of a negative 'Haughey factor'. A longer time perspective reveals that, in the nine general elections following de Valera's resignation, the party only twice gained an overall majority (under Lynch in 1969 and 1977) and won just half the Dáil seats in 1965. Equally important, of those nine occasions, there were only two elections (1973 and 1977) in which the voters were offered an unambiguous alternative to a Fianna Fáil Government in the form of the pre-election agreement on government between Fine Gael and Labour.

In short, there was always an inherent danger of stalemate in Irish electoral politics; certainly sufficient to warrant some examination of possible procedures for coping with such an outcome. Three inconclusive elections in 1981-82 were followed by hurried, unstructured and incomplete coalition agreements and by unseemly bargaining (including huckstering over the nomination of Ceann Comhairle) to secure the support of Independents or smaller parties in the effort to manufacture a parliamentary majority. The crumbling of the second FitzGerald-led Coalition again revealed the fragility of essentially ad hoc arrangements in forming government. Polls before and during the 1987 campaign pointed to the likelihood of another inconclusive result. Nothing was done.

Other countries have devised methods of handling fragmentation without any necessary instability in the government system.[4] They have institutionalised coalition arrangements without any apparent reduction in efficiency. It would have been prudent and useful in Ireland to identify in a much more exact way the potential roles, obligations and opportunities available to, for instance, the incumbent Taoiseach, Ceann Comhairle and President. Instead, ambiguities flourished and pragmatism ruled.

In 1987, some of the worst consequences of such an haphazard approach were avoided. There was no repetition of the notorious Gregory deal of 1981. The temper of the times militated against it (and was being monitored by qualitative opinion research). So did the emerging Dáil consensus on the need for financial retrenchment. An attempt to negate one Fine Gael vote by offering to retain Tom Fitzpatrick as Ceann Comhairle (reminiscent of Richard Burke's nomination to the European Commission) came to nothing but provoked some unsettling rumours. On the morning of March 10, as the new Dáil prepared to meet for the first time, Charles Haughey warned frontbench deputies and senior party officials to be ready for another election campaign.

Despite signals from Deputy Tony Gregory, whose vote was accepted as the strategic key, there was no approach. The subsequent edition of the *Sunday Tribune* captured the scene in a graphic phrase: 'It was eyeball to eyeball and Gregory blinked.' Yet, even with his abstention, it still required the casting vote of the Ceann Comhairle to secure the successful nomination of Charles Haughey as Taoiseach for the third time. It was a knife-edge parliamentary basis for a secure and durable administration.

CHOOSING A CABINET: THE END OF THE DYNASTIES?

If the 1980s have given point to critical questions about the mode of government formation, they also raise some issues regarding the selection and deployment of ministers. Significantly, it is only in this decade that there has been any serious academic effort to investigate what criteria are applied.[5] Again, the neglect is rooted in the slow pace of change in the early decades of the Irish State. Cabinets were small, there was little turnover in the ministerial ranks and little ground for analysis.

Under W.T. Cosgrave - despite four ministerial resignations and the assassination of Kevin O'Higgins - only fifteen men held office in the first decade. De Valera, more than twenty years in charge, nominated only twenty one ministers; four members of his original 1932 Cabinet continued in office into the 1960s. Two members of Costello's 1948 administration had been ministers under W.T.

Cosgrave. As new ministers were recruited under Costello (eighteen new nominations) and Lemass (nine new appointments) changes seemed minimal.

There was an obvious need to accommodate Labour and some smaller party nominees but typically there was little new blood in the tight, cosy, male world of the political elite dominated by Fianna Fáil and Fine Gael. Indeed, both on Government and Opposition front benches, many of the newer appointments were sons of former ministers and deputies. Al Cohan's study of the 'revolutionary' and 'post-revolutionary' elites revealed the extraordinary degree of personnel continuity in Irish political leadership; it also drew attention to the strong emphasis on local constituency service as a major factor in new recruitment.[6]

Even as the pool of newly-appointed ministers slowly spread under Lynch (thirteen) and Liam Cosgrave (fourteen) there was little evidence of change. When the Arms Crisis of 1970 forced a cabinet re-shuffle, it was noticeable that two of the four new ministers appointed by Lynch were family relations of former deputies; all had already served as parliamentary secretaries. The 1973 Cosgrave Cabinet included six close relatives of former deputies; two of these (Cosgrave himself and FitzGerald) were sons of former ministers, while the Attorney-General, Declan Costello, was the son of a former Attorney-General and Taoiseach.

All of this is not to suggest that the senior echelons of Irish politics are exclusively drawn from a self-perpetuating oligarchy. The system has always been sufficiently open to recruit new talent. But the narrow base and slow rate of turnover have kept it small and provided little opportunity or incentive for research and analysis. To date, there has been no serious attempt to establish the criteria for ministerial selection and deployment, beyond some general observations based on partial data. Thus, note has been taken of the restricted familial character of the political elite. It has also been assumed that politicians would typically serve an appreciable apprenticeship of some years in parliament (and usually also a period as junior minister) before gaining a place at the Cabinet table.

A popular but exaggerated observation suggests that regional electoral considerations are also significant motivation for a Taoiseach in making appointments. This latter interpretation owes much to political commentator John Healy (formerly 'Backbencher'). He translated the notion of region as a primary criterion into the colloquial language of 'distributing Mercs' (the state-supplied cars and drivers regarded as a potent symbol of ministerial power and influence). He invented the term 'half-car' as an equivalence for junior ministerial appointments. But while this point of view has an understandably populist appeal, it is in danger of being accepted as a political law. Chubb has suggested that 'with the growing rise of localism in Irish politics, it looks as though Taoisigh have paid increasing attention to geographical considerations, at least to the extent that they recognise the need to strengthen the party in a vital area by giving a post to someone from that area'.[7] But an examination of actual cabinet appointments over a long period of time suggests that there is not such a clear-cut pattern.

Against this background, it is useful to examine ministerial appointments by Haughey and FitzGerald in the period 1979-1987. How far do these reflect familial, seniority or regional criteria? What evidence do they offer of other criteria?

Family relationship has remained a significant route of entry to Dáil Éireann. In the three Dála elected in 1981-82, David M. Farrell identified 26% of deputies as having close family ties with former or sitting deputes.[8] In 1987, the *Magill Election '87* analysis reveals forty-six of the one hundred and sixty-six deputies are similarly related.[9] However, among cabinet ministers, the old dynastic tendencies have almost disappeared. Of the seven new ministers appointed by Haughey between 1979-87 four had family ties with earlier politicians; ten of the fifteen current cabinet members have no such relationships. In FitzGerald's case, the change is even more marked. While he is the son of a former minister, only four of the fifteen new ministers nominated by him between 1981-87 were related to former politicians and all were Labour nominees. It is a revealing indicator of the extent to which the character of Fine Gael changed under FitzGerald's leadership.

The value given to seniority (either extended parliamentary experience or previous appointment as junior minister) has also changed. The willingness to appoint newer deputies was already evident under Lynch and Liam Cosgrave. Six of the fifteen members of the National Coalition, 1973-77, had served only a single parliamentary term in the Dáil; only the two party leaders, Cosgrave and Corish, had previous ministerial experience. Of the five new men appointed to Lynch's last Government, only one had served two full parliamentary terms and one (O'Donoghue) was nominated on his first day in the Dáil; none had previous ministerial experience at any level.

The two most recent Taoisigh have shown a similar willingness to promote newer deputies over longer serving backbenchers. Two of the five new ministers named by Haughey in 1979 were serving their first Dáil term; two of the three new men nominated in March 1982 also belonged to the 'class of 1977'. Three of the new Fine Gael ministers chosen by FitzGerald in 1981 had only served a single parliamentary term, Alan Dukes was named to Agriculture on his first day in the Dáil and James Dooge nominated to Foreign Affairs from the Seanad. Again, in December 1982, one of the three new Fine Gael appointments (M. Noonan) was first elected in June 1981 and another (Hussey) in March 1982. On the other hand, in forming his latest administration, Haughey's four new ministers included two with ten years Dáil service (Aherne, O'Hanlon) and one (M.J. Noonan) first elected in 1969.

All of this suggests that seniority has been less compelling than other considerations in the ministerial selections of FitzGerald and Haughey. Although Haughey's freedom of action was severely restricted by internal party tensions and FitzGerald's by coalition requirements, they both determinedly pruned their governmental inheritance. In 1979, Haughey had to negotiate George Colley's agreement to serve but he dropped four ministers from Lynch's last Government. Closeness to the leader, rather than seniority in the Dáil and continuity in government, could be seen as the new criterion. The five new ministers nominated in forming the first Haughey administration were all identified as loyal supporters in his bid for leadership.

In 1981, FitzGerald exhibited a similar tendency to favour colleagues who shared his own enthusiasm for the 'new' Fine Gael and dropped three party members of the Cosgrave Coalition (Ryan, Burke, O'Donnell). In March 1982, Haughey replaced Colley with Ray MacSharry as Tanaiste and promoted three other loyal lieutenants, initially nominated by him as ministers of state, to full cabinet rank. In his second administration, FitzGerald chose two of his three new ministers from 'new' Fine Gael. In 1987, Haughey's four new nominations appeared, again, to be influenced by considerations of political reliability.

These 1987 appointments did nothing, however, to correct the regional and age imbalance in the Haughey Cabinet. Despite repeated rhetorical emphasis on Ireland's young population three of the new ministers were in their fifties and only one was in his mid-thirties. This contrasts with an average age in the mid-forties for new recruits to the four governments in the period 1979-82. Moreover, the third Haughey administration illustrates in a marked way the low priority given to any carefully calibrated selection based on purely regional considerations: three of the four newcomers are from constituencies already represented at the cabinet table. Mary O'Rourke shares four-seat Longford-Westmeath with Albert Reynolds; Rory O'Hanlon is with John Wilson in the Cavan-Monaghan five seater and Michael F. Noonan joins Gerry Collins in the safest Fianna Fáil three-seat constituency in the country. It scarcely adds up to a strategy for maximising new votes and seats. How does it compare with other ministerial selections in the 1980s?

In Haughey's first two administrations there was some effort to redress the Munster bias developed under Lynch and to give symbolic recognition to the old Fianna Fáil heartlands in the West. Notably, on two occasions (1979, 1982) when dropping western-based ministers Haughey was careful to nominate deputies from the same

The aftermath: forming a government

constituencies. Despite the large population increases in Dublin and Leinster - both critical areas for Fianna Fáil electoral strategists - neither were unduly favoured. Moreover, the challenge of 'independent Fianna Fáil' Neil Blaney was not matched by any Haughey Cabinet appointment in Donegal.

FitzGerald's selections were even more a challenge to the received wisdom. In both his administrations there was a preponderance of members from the Dublin and Leinster regions, giving some support to popular charges that FitzGerald had surrounded himself with a 'Donnybrook set'. A more telling criticism might be that, in his total of five years in government, in forming two administrations and changing so many ministers in a major re-shuffle in February 1986, he gave relatively inexperienced politicians little opportunity to master their departmental briefs.

Charles Haughey's third administration suggests a more cautious managerial approach, with a major emphasis on appointing experienced politicians to the most senior posts in government; Finance, Foreign Affairs and Justice are all held by previous incumbents in these departments and Agriculture, Industry and Commerce, Energy and Environment entrusted to ministers with previous experience.

Haughey has also made some institutional changes. At cabinet level, responsibility for the public service has again been returned to Finance and, in accordance with the party manifesto, a new Minister for Marine has been appointed. At junior level, a new higher tier of ministers of state with special responsibilities for specific areas (science and technology, food, horticulture and marketing) was announced. But, within days of taking office, the new Government announced that the financial situation did not permit any funding for these new areas. Moreover, existing cabinet procedures and the provisions of the Ministers and Secretaries Act has frustrated past efforts (notably under Lemass) to develop the authority and responsibility for junior ministers. Unless there are significant structural changes in the Irish governmental system, it seems likely that most ministers of state, like their parliamentary secretary predecessors, will be appointed for electoral reasons and ceremonial duties.

INSTITUTIONAL INERTIA AND THE ROLE OF TAOISEACH

The failure to restructure the system is one of the most remarkable features of modern Irish government. The Whitehall model, so readily adopted nearly seventy years ago, has been much modified in Britain. An elaborate system of cabinet committees, a three or four tiered ministerial hierarchy and an elaboration of the Cabinet Office, have all contributed to a major re-shaping.[10] In the process, the central

The aftermath: forming a government

relationship of prime minister and cabinet has been changed. It is these institutional arrangements, as much as the powerful personality of Mrs. Thatcher, which have given a certain presidential character to executive leadership in Britain. She presides over some one hundred and sixty groups in the cabinet committee network, and holds about forty five two hour cabinet meetings annually that process sixty to seventy cabinet papers.[11]

In Ireland, there has been little institutional innovation. There are few cabinet committees to relieve the pressure of business on government. The complex, the controversial and the insoluble continue to compete with the current, the commonplace and the critical for scarce time and attention on the Government agenda. Without any formalised committee system, the full cabinet meets about seventy five times a year, frequently for several hours in the course of a day and handles as many as eight hundred cabinet papers.

Whatever the differences between Irish and British Cabinet processes and circumstances, it is clear that the head of Government is in a powerful position. Analysing that position with any degree of precision is difficult. The Taoiseach is required to play multiple roles - chief executive, party leader, national spokesman, principal legislator, critical negotiator, main ideologue, media target, available scapegoat - and to do many of these things simultaneously.[12] While it is possible to distinguish between 'chairman' and 'chief' models of leadership in Ireland, it is also important to recognise that these ideal types should not be confused with the real world of politics in which the same leaders may switch from one role to the other.

In the past, a combination of factors suggested the utility of the 'chairman' model. The Constitution and the legal system, the processes of cabinet government and civil service procedures, the pressures of party colleagues, rivals and supporters, the familiar and ambiguous attitudes towards public authority, the patterns and precedents established by predecessors, all tended to limit the exercise of executive leadership.

Newer circumstances have nudged most recent incumbents to the other end of the spectrum. Increasingly competitive elections and sophisticated campaigning methods based on mass marketing techniques have concentrated attention on the party leader; within an overcrowded cabinet system, the Taoiseach is the final arbiter in inter-departmental and political wrangles; internationally, the Taoiseach is spokesman of the nation at European and Anglo-Irish summits; regular public opinion polling and media attention have accepted and abetted these emphases. There is constant pressure to play the role of chief.

Both Haughey and FitzGerald - despite obvious dissimilarities in personality - have contributed to the modern elevation of the Taoiseach's role. Each has had a marked impact on the texture and personnel of their parties; each has encouraged an expansion in the size and influence of the Taoiseach's department within the public service; each has been alert to, and provided for, the central function of effective media relations in modern government; each has exercised - though in markedly different styles - the Taoiseach's right to form and re-form governments, and has done so with less caution than their predecessors. The contrast and conflict between Haughey and FitzGerald has been central to Irish party politics in the 1980s; the similarities and comparisons, however, are perhaps more revealing indicators of how Irish government works.

AN EMERGING CONSENSUS?

The public antipathy between the two major party leaders, coupled with the overheated and highly competitive round of elections, obscured a developing consensus in national politics in the 1980s. Disagreements on the precise formulation of the Hillsborough package, on the Single European Act, even on the constitutional referenda, provided the opportunity for continuing partisan squabbling between Fianna Fáil and Fine Gael. These were, in some sense, the games that professional politicians play. But the unreality and futility of so much of adversarial politics was exposed as, for four elections in a row, the citizens refused to give either side an unambiguous mandate to govern. And the extraordinary degree of acquiescence (if not support) secured for the unpopular policies of retrenchment being pursued by the third Haughey administration illustrate the reality of a broad underlying consensus on national economic management. Such a development might seem ironic, set against the background of recent Irish politics. Yet, out of contradictory and opposing forces, a new pattern has emerged. It owes much to the major party leaders.

The decision of Desmond O'Malley to form the Progressive Democrats may have deprived Fianna Fáil of an over-all majority; the refusal of a deal on transfers denied any prospect of coalition to Fine Gael. The PDs have not broken the mould of the Irish party system, however, they have helped to force some reconsideration of strategy on the two main parties. Dick Spring's refusal to perpetuate existing coalition arrangements also helped to stimulate some new Dáil approaches. Haughey's careful refusal to give any specific commitments under the pressure of campaigning reduced Fianna Fáil's potential vote but has given it greater freedom in government. Garret FitzGerald's determination to fight an election on the 'Bruton budget' and to resign the party leadership helped to create the basis and atmosphere for the consensus.

FitzGerald's sudden announcement did more than remove a possible irritant to the harmonious working of the new Dáil.[13] It pre-empted a

The aftermath: forming a government

potentially acrimonious post-mortem on Fine Gael's performance in government and in the election. The capacity to field three strong candidates, conduct a vigorous leadership contest and manage a smooth transition in the leadership was a boost to party morale. It presented a neat and pointed contrast to the internal leadership challenges in Fianna Fáil. The emergence of Alan Dukes, with experience as minister in three departments (including Finance) suggested that FitzGerald had taken some care to provide for a succession likely to maintain his own preferred view of Fine Gael as a social democratic party. To date, Dukes has been willing to allow the underlying consensus on the management of the public finances to take precedence over any partisan temptation to bring down the minority Haughey administration. At the end of the first Dáil session, for example, he pulled back from an imprudently judged parliamentary pretence of opposition to Fianna Fáil's proposals for health cuts, as Fine Gael abstained in a vote that could, if it had been lost, have brought down the Government.

Indeed, it is internal Fianna Fáil dissatisfaction on the backbenches and in the grass-roots which has posed the greatest threat so far to the party's insecure hold on government. However, early indications suggest that the tough line is being held. The collapse of a threatened three day power strike in May, in the face of an unyielding Government, was one signal. Perhaps more important, a threatened revolt by local party politicians on health cuts has been resisted. Apart from one softening of policy (apparently at the behest of the Minister for the Environment) on home improvement grants, the third Haughey administration is fulfilling the tasks identified by the Taoiseach in his television address at the outset of his leadership in 1979. Yet, the fragile parliamentary support for the Government must cast serious doubts over its capacity to endure in office. This has given rise to new speculation that another effort might be made to adjust the operation of the electoral system (perhaps by again increasing the number of three-seat constituencies) so as to maximise the probability of a decisive outcome in subsequent elections.

This seems a classic case of fussing over symptoms instead of addressing causes. The reality is that, at many different levels, the Irish political, administrative and governmental system is exhibiting signs of strain.[14] The system so easily and unthinkingly adopted from the British has never been thoroughly overhauled. Incremental changes, partial adaptations, pragmatic adjustments have been made, but there has been no fundamental examination and no signficant and coherent structural reform. As already indicated, there has been no attempt to consider the inherent problems likely to arise in government formation, no development of cabinet procedure, and parliamentary reforms have largely been cosmetic (in the form of a weak committee system and some adjustments in the chaos of parliamentary question-time).

Simple tinkering with the electoral machinery will not, of itself, resolve the frustrations of deputies nor satisfy their constituents. Applying the axe of retrenchment to the public service is not a substitute for reform. Contemplating yet more referenda - whether on the conduct of foreign policy or the provisions for bail - is an inadequate response to the obvious need for comprehensive constitutional change. Irish society has changed in the half-century since de Valera revised the old Free State Constitution and called it Bunreacht na hÉireann. It is changing still, and there is a growing unrest and unease with a set of governmental arrangements which are seen to be weak on competence and increasingly deficient in securing acquiescence.

To date, the Irish system has weathered many storms: an uncertain beginning in civil war, a disappointing economic performance, a demographic revolution from decline through growth and back to emigration, the buffeting of transition to a post-industrial phase after the old crises. But there are too many signs of a drift towards ungovernability; one need only instance the politically embarrassing failure to cope with tax equity and collection. There is too much evidence of a crisis-management mentality in Irish government. The very fragility of the 25th Dáil might provide the opportunity for a more radical reappraisal of how modern Ireland might better organise its affairs.

9. THE GENERAL ELECTION IN CONTEXT

HISTORICAL AND EUROPEAN PERSPECTIVES

John Coakley

INTRODUCTION

Several superlatives spring immediately to mind in relation to the Irish general election of February 1987. It has been described enigmatically as 'both the longest and the shortest of elections'.[1] The three traditional parties each won their lowest share of the poll for many years. Fianna Fáil recorded its lowest percentage of the first preference vote since 1961, Fine Gael its lowest since 1957 and the Labour Party its lowest since 1933.[2] The electorate was more volatile than at any election since 1943, while the Progressive Democrats made 'the most dramatic electoral debut of any party for nearly 40 years'.[3] As a new 'fourth' party, the Progressive Democrats won a larger share of the first preference vote than any fourth party since 1948. The number of candidates was much greater than ever before; and the victory margin of the Taoiseach-designate when the Dáil first met after the general election was the smallest ever.

The 1987 general election may be analysed both from the perspective of voting behaviour and from the perspective of its implications for Irish political institutions. Within each of these points of view, a further distinction can be made: the February election may be compared over time with earlier Irish general elections, or compared cross-nationally with other liberal democracies.

IRISH ELECTORAL BEHAVIOUR 1922-1987

Although more people were eligible to vote in the February 1987 election than ever before, voting turnout, at 73%, was rather lower than the post-war average of 75%. This represented a drop from the pattern in the 1965-81 period, when turnout varied between 75% and 77%. There is little likelihood that the dramatic peak (82%) in electoral turnout reached in 1933 will be matched in the near future.

The changing fortunes of the parties for which Irish electors have voted since 1922 are illustrated in Figure 1. While this brings out vividly the continuing, slow decline in Labour support since 1969 and the sharp reversal in the steady growth in Fine Gael support that had been taking place since 1977, it also helps to place in context the sudden upsurge in support for the Progressive Democrats. They were not the first 'fourth party' to attempt to break the mould of three-party dominance; indeed, it is clear that the combined dominance of Fianna Fáil, Fine Gael and the Labour Party had been more seriously challenged in the 1920s (and especially in June 1927) and in the 1940s (and especially in 1948) than it was in 1987.

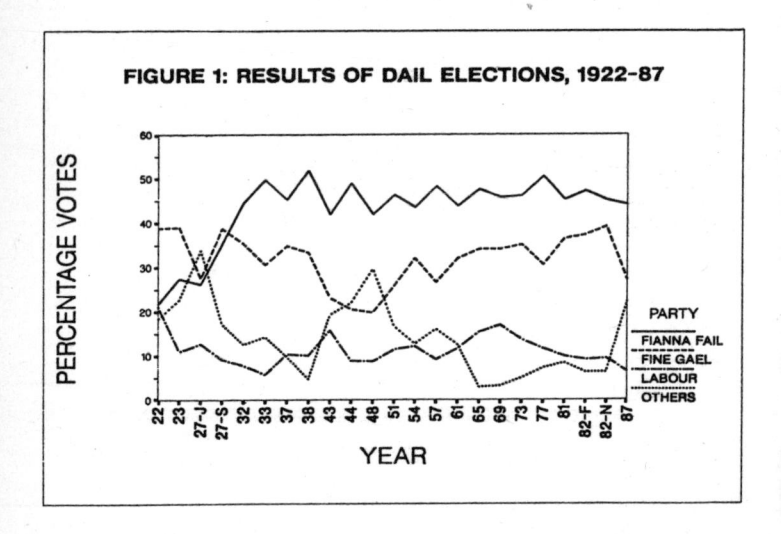

FIGURE 1: RESULTS OF DAIL ELECTIONS, 1922-87

For Fianna Fáil the election represented an upset of the electoral see-saw. Ever since 1933 the party has alternately gained and dropped at the polls in successive elections, with two exceptions: in 1977 its share of the poll increased when the momentum of the see-saw suggested that it should have dropped, and ten years later it dropped when precedent would have suggested an increase. On both occasions, commentators attributed the result to the personality of the party leader. Despite short-term fluctuations, however, Fianna Fáil's support since 1932 has remained within a relatively narrow band: it has never dropped below 42% nor risen above 52%.

The pattern of electoral support for Fine Gael over the long term (if we include its predecessor, Cumann na nGaedhael, in the reckoning) resembles an elongated but rather bumpy U-curve. Its share of the poll dropped at every election from September 1927 to 1948, with the exception of 1937, the first election contested by the newly-formed Fine Gael party. From then on, however, it gained support at each election until November 1982, apart from two setbacks in 1957 and 1977. By 1948, then, Fine Gael's share of the vote (20%) had dropped to half of its predecessor's strength in September 1927 (just under

39%); but by November 1982 this lost ground had been won back, Fine Gael winning its highest-ever total of just over 39%. In this context the 1987 result, which represented a decline to the Fine Gael support level of the 1950s, was a serious blow indeed.

If Fianna Fáil's electoral cycle is a short one and Fine Gael's is long then the Labour vote fluctuates over the medium term. For Labour, the peaks took place in 1922, 1943, 1954 and 1969, the troughs in 1933, 1948, 1957 and (as the party no doubt hopes) in 1987. A remarkable accompaniment of Labour decline since 1969 has been the rise of the Workers' Party. This has been most spectacular in the Dublin area, where in 1987 the Workers' Party built on its success in the 1985 local elections by going on to exceed the Labour share of the first preference vote. The Labour Party, of course, had traditionally been weak in Dublin, where it became a significant force only in the 1940s, and it was not until 1969 that its share of the vote in Dublin first exceeded that in the rest of (predominantly rural) Leinster.

The relationship between Labour Party and Workers' Party support is illustrated in Figure 2. This highlights the fact that the overall drop in support for the left has not been nearly as catastrophic as the decline in the Labour vote suggests. (The addition of other splinter parties of the left, such as the Socialist Labour Party and the Democratic Socialist Party, would strengthen this conclusion even further.) It appears, however, that a significant realignment is taking place on the left, and especially in Dublin, with a movement of support from the Labour Party to the Workers' Party.

The rise of the Progressive Democrats can also be placed in context by looking at the long-term patterns revealed in Figure 1. In terms of its ideology and its support base, the party has been described as 'a right-wing equivalent to the Workers' Party'.[4] This may be the result of an increasing urbanisation of Irish society. Twelve of the 14 Progressive Democrat deputies elected in 1987 came from urban or substantially urban constituencies, as did three of the four Workers' Party deputies.

It is less clear, however, whether the Progressive Democrats will be able to build on their success in the next election. Figure 1 shows that new fourth parties (such as the Farmers' Party in 1922, the National League in 1927, Clann na Talmhan in 1944 and Clann na Poblachta in 1948) tend to be ephemeral phenomena, normally beginning their decline in the second election they contest and always declining in subsequent elections.

FIGURE 2: LABOUR PARTY AND WORKERS' PARTY AT GENERAL ELECTIONS, 1969-1987

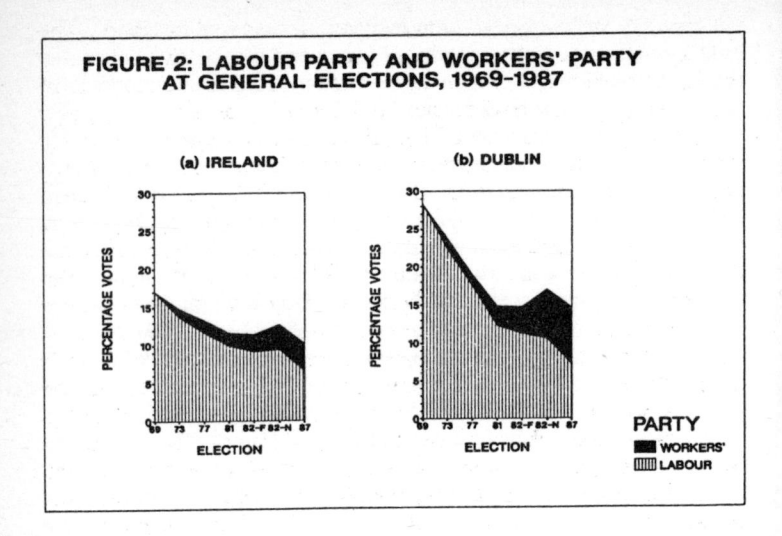

IRELAND AND THE EUROPEAN ELECTORAL EXPERIENCE

The distinctive features of Irish party politics are best highlighted in a broader European context, by making comparisons with a group of West European countries that have a tradition of liberal democracy. This group consists of nine of the 12 member-states of the European Community (this excludes Greece, Spain and Portugal, where contemporary democratic practices have more recent roots). It also includes the four Nordic countries which are outside the European Community and the small states of Austria and Switzerland, making a total of 15 countries.

In terms of **electoral turnout,** Ireland lies rather close to the bottom of this group of countries. In the first position lie the Benelux countries, Austria, Iceland and Italy, where turnout is almost always greater than 90% (though this may be encouraged by compulsory voting). Next comes a group of countries where turnout is normally in the 80-90% band: Norway, Sweden, Denmark and the Federal Republic of Germany. The next band consists, at the top, of Finland and France, where turnout is close to but usually below 80%, together with Ireland and the United Kingdom, where it is usually at the mid-70% level. Finally comes the peculiar case of Switzerland, where turnout has dropped at each general election from 1947 (72%) to 1979 (48%), recovering only slightly to 49% at the most recent election, in 1983.

In terms of **party choice,** it is important to emphasise that the Irish experience resembles the typical West European experience in form but contrasts strikingly with it in content. In terms of its 'shape' - the number of parties, their relative size and the stability of the configuration of parties over time - the Irish party system is typical of that in other western democracies. Furthermore, the issues that have given birth to the dominant Irish parties of today are not demonstrably more irrelevant to contemporary political life than the issues which generated dominant parties in many other western political systems. Neither is the success with which one generation bequeaths its partisan preferences to another a peculiarly Irish phenomenon. In most European states with a tradition of parliamentary democracy the contemporary party system has been 'fossilised' since the introduction of universal suffrage in the earlier part of the present century .[5]

Not alone do many contemporary European parties find their raison d'etre in conflicts which are now no longer relevant, but the electoral strength of these parties has not changed greatly over the years, and Figure 1 above is typical of the position in other countries as well. Once having won the allegiance of a portion of the newly-enfranchised electorate, parties have tended to retain their support over time and across generations. They thus still tend to find their ideological justification in the issues of yesterday rather than in the concerns of today.

This generalisation must, of course, be qualified. In the first place, even such self-perpetuating organisations as political parties are capable of adapting and of taking positions on issues far removed from their ideological roots. Parties frequently fight elections on platforms that bear no relationship to (or are even incompatible with) their 'fundamental aims', as defined in the party statutes or constitution.

Second, some of the issues of the early twentieth century continue to be relevant today. The perception by workers of a conflict between their interests and those of capital, which generated Europe's socialist, social democratic and labour parties, is an obvious example. A perception by farmers of a conflict of interest with the consumers of agricultural produce, reflected in the appearance of 'centre' (farmers') parties in Northern Europe, is another example.

Third, voters have not always remained faithful to traditional parties: there have been several mutations among parties of the right in France, for example, while the Danish and Dutch party systems have undergone considerable change in recent years.

The Irish electorate is, then, not unusual in its faithfulness to traditional parties and in typically western forms of voter loyalty. Its distinctiveness lies instead in the ideological divisions that have separated Irish parties and in particular in the fact that the two dominant parties share a common ideological position and similar policy stances on most issues. The February 1987 general election confirmed this tendency, pointing to the continued presence of two distinctive features of the Irish party system: the modest degree of support for parties of the left and the existence of an unusually powerful cross-class party of the centre-right.

It is neither possible nor appropriate to examine here the vexed question of the weakness of the Labour Party. It may, however, be useful to place the electoral position of the Labour Party in comparative perspective. Table 1 summarises the average strength of Western Europe's 'weak' labour or mainstream socialist parties, defined as those affiliated to the Socialist International but winning on average less than one third of the vote in post-war elections.

Table 1: The electoral strength of the traditional left in countries with 'weak' socialist parties, c. 1945-1987

GROUP	PERIOD	NO. OF ELECTIONS	MEAN VOTE FOR TWO MAIN PARTIES OF LEFT		
			Socialists	Communists	Total
Countries with a strong Communist Party					
Finland	1948-87	12	25	19	43
France	1945-86	13	21	22	43
Iceland	1946-87	14	15	17	33
Italy	1946-87	11	13	27	40
Countries with a weak Communist Party					
Belgium	1946-85	14	30	4	34
Netherlands	1946-86	13	29	4	33
Switzerland	1947-83	10	25	3	28
Ireland:	1948-87	13	11	0	11

Source: calculated from Tom Mackie and Richard Rose, The international almanac of electoral history 2nd ed (London: Macmillan, 1982) and Keesing's contemporary archives.

The countries fall into three groups. In the first lie Finland, France, Iceland and Italy, where socialist weakness is largely accounted for by the strength of the communist challenge. In the second lie Belgium, the Netherlands and Switzerland, where alternative sources of partisan cleavage (such as religious or linguistic divisions) have cut across class-based conflict. In the third category lies Ireland, the weakness of whose Labour Party has never been adequately explained. It should, however, be noted that other left-wing parties (corresponding to the Workers' Party in Ireland, for instance) serve further to fragment the left-wing vote and may contribute to an underestimation of the real strength of the left. Nevertheless, the fact that only a little more than

10% of voters on average support the traditional parties of the left makes Ireland a deviant case among the liberal democracies of Western Europe.

A further remarkable feature of Irish party politics viewed from a comparative perspective is the Fianna Fáil phenomenon. In absolute terms the really big European parties are, of course, the big parties in the big countries. The 'big five' (those which won at least 10 million votes in the most recent election, each of which coincidentally took place in 1987) are the German Christian Democrats (17 million voters), the German Social Democrats (14 million), the Italian Christian Democrats (14 million), the British Conservatives (14 million) and the British Labour Party (10 million). In relative terms, however, when size is measured in terms of share of the vote, Fianna Fáil emerges as Europe's second most popular party, being beaten narrowly for first position by the Swedish Social Democrats. This may be seen from Table 2, which ranks European parties which won at least 45% of the popular vote in at least one election since 1945. Surprisingly, only 11 parties from the 15 countries fall into this category. In terms of average share of parliamentary seats won, indeed, Fianna Fáil was the most successful party in Europe for much of the period in question; it was beaten into second position by the British Conservatives only in 1983.

Table 2: European parties winning at least 45% of the popular vote in at least one election, c. 1945-1987, in order of average share of votes

Party	Period	No. of elections	Share of votes		Share of seats	
			Mean %	Rank	Mean %	Rank
Social Democrats (Sweden)	1948-85	13	46	1	47	4
Fianna Fáil (Ireland)	1948-87	13	46	2	49	2
Socialist Party (Austria)	1945-86	13	45	3	47	5
Christian Democrats (FRG)	1948-87	11	45	4	46	7
People's Party (Austria)	1945-86	13	44	5	46	8
Conservative Party (UK)	1945-87	13	43	6	50	1
Labour Party (Norway)	1945-85	11	43	7	48	3
Labour Party (UK)	1945-87	13	42	8	47	6
Christian Democrats (Italy)	1946-87	11	39	9	42	9
Social Democrats (FRG)	1949-87	11	38	10	39	11
Christian Socials (Belgium)	1946-85	14	37	11	40	10

Source: calculated from Tom Mackie and Richard Rose, The international almanac of electoral history 2nd ed (London: Macmillan, 1982) and Keesing's contemporary archives.

The recent impact of new parties should not be seen as setting Ireland apart from other western countries. In this respect, Ireland resembles Scandinavian countries such as Denmark and Norway. In these countries a strong alternative socialist left developed in the 1960s and 1970s, in a manner similar to the Workers' Party in Ireland. Activists and supporters of these parties consisted largely of disaffected former supporters of the traditional left-wing parties, who found the socialist parties too pragmatic and the rigidities of orthodox, Moscow-oriented communism too restrictive. Furthermore, the Irish Progressive Democrats resemble in a number of ways the Progress parties of Denmark and Norway, both of which appeared in the 1970s. The ideological orientation of the Norwegian party is summarised in its original name, which incorporated a reference to its founder: 'Anders Lange's Party for a Strong Reduction in Taxation and Public Intervention'. Though characterised by certain eccentric features, these parties clearly share positions on several ideological issues with the Irish Progressive Democrats.

THE 1987 ELECTION AND IRISH POLITICAL INSTITUTIONS

Two institutional issues raised by the results of the February 1987 election are worth taking up here. The first is the capacity of the voters, through the electoral system, to produce a parliament that meets certain criteria of adequacy, efficiency and justice. The second is the capacity of the parliament to produce a government that meets the same criteria.

What, precisely, these criteria should be in practice is a question to which only a political answer may be given. The principles of representation and efficiency tend often to be appealed to at the same time, but it is difficult to achieve both. Constitutions in Europe typically aim to produce a parliament that represents the major political divisions in society and a government that is efficient in dealing with them. The former is normally achieved by means of a proportional representation system of election, the latter by the majoritarian principle that allows considerable discretion to governments which control a parliamentary majority.

Ireland's electoral system has recently been criticised severely on the grounds that it produces a parliament that is *too* representative. The almost unique single transferable vote system of proportional representation (shared with only one other sovereign state, the Republic of Malta, for general elections) tends to encourage multi-dimensional proportional representation. Voters may use criteria such as place of residence, gender or age, as well as party affiliation, when filling in their ballot papers. The extent to which the system encourages personal voting has been blamed for encouraging the election of deputies who engage in clientelist practices and allegedly ignore their responsibilities as legislators. While the view that deputies tend to undertake a heavy load of casework is plausible, Michael Gallagher has argued convincingly that it can not be demonstrated that this is due to the electoral system.[6]

In setting the 1987 election in context a second aspect of the electoral system needs to be examined. This is the effectiveness of the Irish system in translating votes into seats - the extent to which the proportion of Dáil seats won by a party matches its electoral strength as measured by its share of the first preference vote. Although activists within the dominant parties complained that the electoral system had allowed the Progressive Democrats to break into parliament too easily, in fact the new party was seriously discriminated against. This may be seen from Table 3, which reports the 'bonus' seats won by each party in the election. This is calculated by subtracting the percentage of votes won by each party from the percentage of seats that it won. Table 3 also reports the minimum, maximum and average bonus won by each party between 1948 and 1982.

Table 3: 'Bonus' seats won by parties at Irish general elections*

PARTY	GENERAL ELECTION 1987			GENERAL ELECTIONS 1948-82		
	Votes %	Seats %	Bonus %	Min Bonus %	Max Bonus %	Av Bonus %
Fianna Fáil	44	49	5	0	7	3
Fine Gael	27	30	3	-1	3	1
Labour Party	6	7	1	-4	1	-
Progressive Democrats	12	9	-3	-	-	-
Others	11	5	-6	6	-1	4

Sources: for 1948-82 data, Michael Gallagher, 'The political consequences of the electoral system in the Republic of Ireland'. Electoral Studies 5 (3) 1986, pp. 253-275; for 1987, Michael Gallagher, 'The outcome' in this volume.
* Excluding seat of outgoing Ceann Comhairle

Fianna Fáil and Fine Gael did rather well in 1987, winning respectively 5% and 3% more seats than their share of the poll entitled them to. Not only did this permit Fianna Fáil to go on to form a Government despite the drop in its share of the poll since November

1982; it also cushioned Fine Gael's sharp decline in its share of the vote by awarding the party a disproportionate number of seats. Even the Labour Party gained slightly from the system, but the clear losers were the Progressive Democrats, whose share of the seats was 3% below their share of the first preference vote.

Turning to the manner in which a new Taoiseach and Government are selected, (see also the discussion by Brian Farrell, above) the central issue is the alignment of political forces on the occasion of the first meeting of a new Dáil. This typically sets the tone for Government - Opposition relationships for the rest of the Dáil session. In placing the 1987 experience in context, we can identify four types of situation that have arisen since 1922. In the first and most obvious type, the Dáil simply registers the result of the preceding general election by nominating the party leader who 'won' that election. On eight occasions (1933, 1937, 1938, 1944, 1957, 1965, 1969 and 1977) a single party, Fianna Fáil, has won an overall majority. On one other occasion (in 1973) a Fine Gael - Labour 'National Coalition', formed before the election, did so. To this category may be added the three instances in which Fianna Fáil changed its leader while retaining a Dáil majority (in 1959, 1966 and 1979).

In the second type of situation the outcome is predictable even though no party or coalition has won an overall majority. This was the case on four occasions. In 1922 and 1923 the pro-treaty/Cumann na nGaedhael party, though lacking an overall majority, had a working Dáil majority because of the abstentionist policy of the anti-treaty group. Although this majority disappeared as a consequence of Fianna Fáil's entry into the Dáil two months after the June 1927 election, the well-known preference of Farmer and independent deputies for Cumann na nGaedhael over any possible rival secured the easy renomination of Cosgrave. In 1954 no party had an overall majority, but it was known that Fine Gael, Labour and Clann na Talmhan (who between them had a bare majority) intended to form a coalition after the election.

In the third type of situation, the Dáil constitutes a forum in which negotiations can take place after an indecisive general election result, but the outcome is fairly predictable. The most intense discussions take place privately, of course, before the new Dáil meets, but it is on the crucial Dáil vote that these focus. Six instances may be cited. Following Fianna Fáil's decision to abandon its abstentionist policy and its good showing in the September 1927 election, Cumann na nGaedhael was forced to rely more heavily on independent support and it even entered on a post-election coalition with the Farmers' Party in October 1927. (The award of only one Government post to the Farmers, however - a parliamentary secretaryship - bears out the view that they were in a weak bargaining position, having little option other than support for Cumann na nGaedhael.) Fianna Fail's accession to

The general election in context

power in 1932 was similarly dependent on support from outside the party; for this it could rely on the Labour Party, but Cumann na nGaedhael was in any case reconciled to the inevitability of a transfer of power. In 1943 and 1961 a Fianna Fáil Taoiseach was returned with some independent support (and, in the former case, with the aid of the neutrality of the Labour Party and of Clann na Talmhan). More recently, in December 1982 the Labour Party fairly predictably decided to join a Fine Gael-led coalition following a general election in which no party secured an overall majority. The final example dates from 1930, when Cosgrave resigned as prime minister but, following the refusal of the Dáil to nominate either the Fianna Fáil or the Labour leader in his place, was renominated to the post.

The final type of situation resembles the third except that the outcome remains uncertain until the Dáil vote actually takes place. There are five examples. In 1948 a five-party 'Inter-Party Government', whose policies were agreed after the general election, was able to oust Fianna Fáil with the support of independents. Three years later, in 1951, Fianna Fáil returned to office with the narrowest of margins, again with independent support. More recently, the defeat of Charles Haughey and selection of Garret FitzGerald in 1981 followed hard post-election bargaining between Fine Gael and Labour and extensive negotiation with non-aligned deputies. The return of Charles Haughey in March 1982 was the culmination of a similar round of negotiations. The victory margin of the Taoiseach-designate was lowest of all in 1987, when a tied vote on the nomination of Charles Haughey was broken only by the casting vote of the Ceann Comhairle.

Of the 27 cases since 1922 in which a new Government was formally appointed to office, the outcome has been in serious doubt on only five occasions. On none of these occasions, however, was the uncertainty prolonged, the Taoiseach being elected almost immediately on the first meeting of the new Dáil. In the five 'critical' cases identified above, the issue was typically decided within two hours; the exceptions were in 1951, when four hours elapsed before the new Dáil nominated a Taoiseach, and, at the opposite extreme, in March 1982, when the whole process took about an hour. The fact that three of these five occasions were in the 1980s may be a pointer to future cabinet instability but it may also reflect a temporary electoral rebellion against established parties, a temporary deterioration in inter-party relations, or both. The speed with which the issue was formally resolved, despite long agonising between the time at which the outcome of the election became known and the date set for the first meeting of the new Dáil, should, however, be underlined.

A EUROPEAN PERSPECTIVE ON ELECTIONS AND POLITICAL INSTITUTIONS

Although the Irish electoral system is fundamentally different from the European list systems, its overall effect on the party composition of parliament is similar. In terms of proportionality, the Irish electoral system's performance is average - not perfectly proportional, but not excessively disproportional even by the standards of list systems. The most distinctive consequence of Ireland's version of proportional representation is the presence in parliament of a large number of independent or non-aligned deputies, a phenomenon relatively unknown in the rest of Western Europe.

It has been suggested above that the Irish party system, far from being fragmented and unstable, has been dominated by a relatively small number of parties (one of them the second strongest in Europe) with stable support bases. Although this might be expected to facilitate the process of government formation and coalition building, dissatisfaction with current procedures for electing the Dáil and selecting the Government has recently been expressed with increasing frequency. An extraordinary instance of this was the speculation that, in the event of the Dáil's failing to elect a Taoiseach-designate on March 10, an immediate general election would have to be called.[7] It is difficult to reconcile this view with the traditions of liberal democracy, of which a fundamental feature is acceptance of the supremacy of the ballot-box. For political leaders to call for a second election so soon, in circumstances where the parties had not shifted from the stances adopted in the first election and no other significant factors had intervened, could be construed as little more than an attempt at a moral bludgeoning of the electorate.

So great is the gap which separates the Irish political tradition from that of continental Europe that it may be worth identifying the principal respects in which Ireland differs from the European norm. In many of these respects it is not merely Ireland which is different; the English-speaking liberal democracies, whose political systems are typically based on the Westminster model, also tend to deviate from European norms. The Irish perspective may be seen as deviating from the European one in five respects; the views that a constitution is to be interpreted literally, that elections are a device for facilitating stable government, that election of parliament and selection of Government are inseparable processes, that the bare-majority cabinet is the ideal Government, and that an adversarial relationship between Government and Opposition is normal and proper.

The Constitution

In general, constitutions of western democracies are old (the oldest include, for example, that of the United States dating from 1787,

Norway from 1814, Belgium from 1831) and were drawn up in the context of a socio-economic environment and a political cultural climate radically different from contemporary ones. The meaning of such constitutions has changed fundamentally, to the point where many of their original basic principles are in sharp conflict with contemporary norms. Yet constitutions tend to be amended rather infrequently, and there may be cases (such as that of the Norwegian Constitution) where alteration of fundamental principles is not permitted at all. The response of most liberal democracies to constitutions which define and legitimise institutions of state in the language and spirit of another era has been to reinterpret the text in the light of current custom and usage. Thus the legal systems of European states generally recognise a substantial 'unwritten' component of the constitution; the actual text is not taken as a document which is binding in a literal sense.

The inadequacy of a constitution as a guide to political reality is clear from provisions that relate to the selection of prime-ministers. Constitutions of western democracies typically vest responsibility for the selection of a prime minister in the head of state, subject to the condition that the prime minister must have the confidence of parliament (the latter is implicit in the United Kingdom, but is explicit in most other cases, such as France, Italy, Spain and the slightly more complex case of the Federal Republic of Germany). No further guidance on the factors which the head of state should take into consideration is normally given. The bald statement in the Belgian Constitution to the effect that 'the King appoints and dismisses his ministers', for instance, gives little idea of the very complex extra-constitutional procedures that have evolved to govern the process of prime-ministerial selection. Giving a head of state merely nominal power to appoint a prime minister in a country with a multi-party system is little more than window-dressing.

The constitution is typically silent on the subject of the factors that actually determine who becomes prime minister (of which election results and inter-party bargaining are the most common). By contrast, the Constitutions of Ireland, Sweden and Switzerland are unusually explicit in placing responsibility for the selection of a prime minister firmly within parliament.

From a continental European perspective, then, there is little point in blaming the Constitution for contemporary woes. Within reason, the Constitution means whatever the political elite (and especially the Supreme Court) wishes it to mean. It could be argued in these terms, for example, that divorce continues to be legally prohibited not because of the wording of article 41.3 but because of the absence of elite consensus in reinterpreting the text of an article framed fifty years ago with a morally conservative intention. The feeble powers exercised by the President of Ireland may, similarly, be attributed not merely to the wording or to the spirit of the Constitution but also to the limited extent to which incumbents have asserted themselves in three areas:

(1) Areas in which the President is specifically authorised to act independently of political advice, such as deciding whether or not to grant a parliamentary dissolution when the initiative has been passed to him by a Taoiseach who has lost the confidence of the Dáil but requested a dissolution;

(2) Areas in which the President is specifically prohibited from acting independently of political advice, such as the issuing of personal political statements or speeches which have not been approved by the Government; and

(3) Areas in which the Constitution is silent, such as the undertaking of private soundings by the President among party leaders and others.[8]

The weakness of the Irish Presidency and its unassertive role in the aftermath of indecisive elections, then, is a function not merely of constitutional stipulations but also of elite political culture.

The role of elections

In general, the continental European view of elections is that they are mechanisms for ensuring that parliament continues to be representative of the people. To secure this, provision is made for periodic polls at which parliamentary representatives are elected by direct, secret, equal and universal suffrage on the principle of proportional representation. Except in such cases as Germany and Italy in the 1930s and contemporary Eastern Europe, where elections have been used to legitimate one-party regimes, and France for much of the Fifth Republic, where a deliberately biased electoral system was used, elections are not seen as devices to procure or perpetuate stable government. Indeed, it is obvious that stable government does not depend on elections at all and may perform better without them, as the experience of many dictatorships has shown.

In Ireland, as in other English-speaking countries, many of the democratic assumptions of continental Europe are not fully accepted. First, a strong body of opinion questions whether parliament should be representative of the people. The notion of proportional representation as a prerequisite to democracy is by no means universally accepted, as the extent of support within the two major parties for a non-proportional electoral system indicates.

A degree of confusion within the political elite regarding the nature of proportional representation is suggested by a number of factors: provision for the filling of casual vacancies in the Dáil by means of by-elections (which are incompatible with the notion of proportional representation); description of the alternative vote system as 'proportional representation in single-member constituencies', a contradiction in terms; and the peculiar provision in article 12.2.3 of the Constitution that the President be elected 'on the system of proportional representation', a provision that would require President Hillery to be approximately 50% Fianna Fáil, 40% Fine Gael and 10% Labour.

Second, the political elite appears to regard a parliamentary dissolution and the calling of a general election as a legitimate device by which the Government may attempt to increase its parliamentary support by catching the Opposition unawares and presenting itself to the electorate at the most favourable time. In continental Europe, by contrast, a general election is normally seen as a device to renew a parliament whose mandate has lapsed, to break a political deadlock or to permit voters to pass judgement on a significant change of political or constitutional course. In some countries, such as Norway and Switzerland, premature dissolution of parliament is prohibited, and elections take place every four years with entirely predictable regularity; in the others, 'snap' elections that are politically motivated are very much the exception. In Ireland, however, the Dáil has been allowed to run its full course on only one occasion (the Dáil of 1938-43).

General elections and the process of government formation

The Irish Constitution requires a new Government to be formed after each general election. As with every other liberal democratic constitution, it does not require a general election to take place every time there is a change of Government. The point to be underlined is the sharp distinction between the selection of parliamentarians by electors, and the selection of Governments by parliamentarians. In almost all European states, the constitution allows voters only an indirect say in the choice of their rulers. Constitutionally, the function of a general election is to renew the mandate of parliament, not necessarily to select a new Government. Yet in Ireland the collapse of a Government is almost always followed, in practice, by a new general election (the exceptions were in 1930, a politically unimportant example, and 1959, 1966 and 1979, when Fianna Fáil changed leaders while in office).

By contrast, in continental Europe Governments frequently collapse and are replaced by other Governments without any general election. Most changes of Government in Italy and Finland have taken place in this manner, and the practice in Belgium and the Netherlands has become similar. In France and Germany there are also recent instances of such transfers of power without a parliamentary dissolution. It is parliamentary rather than electoral rebellion that brings down most Governments in some countries and brings down some Governments in most countries. The corollary is that, since parliament has dismissed a Government, it is up to parliamentarians (and not necessarily up to the electorate) to replace it.

The bare-majority cabinet

While the predominant view in liberal democracies is that parliament should represent the major groups in society, this view is not carried forward to the notion that the cabinet should in turn represent the major groups in parliament. Instead there are broadly speaking two types of approach to the business of cabinet formation: the Westminster model, of which the so-called 'bare-majority' cabinet is the characteristic feature, and the consensus model, which is characterised by various forms of executive power-sharing.[9]

The distinction between these two models may be illustrated by considering Table 4. This presents a notional (but not politically unrealistic) parliamentary balance between three parties, none of which has an overall majority. Logically, eight types of cabinet are possible - one type each of three-party and no-party cabinets, and three types each of two-party and one-party cabinets. Examples of all of these types may be drawn from the continental European experience.

Table 4: Two models of government formation

Assumption: three parties with the following relative parliamentary support:

Party A: 45%   Party B: 35%   Party C: 20%

I. 'Logical' model: 8 possible cabinet types:		II. 'Arithmetical' bare-majority model: 1 possible cabinet type:	
1. A + B + C	100%	-	
2. A + B	80%	-	
3. A + C	65%	-	
4. B + C	55%	1. B + C	55%
5. A	45%	-	
6. B	35%	-	
7. C	20%	-	
8. No party	0%	-	

Type 1, an all-party cabinet, might appear to be one of the most unusual, but it does occur in practice. The best example is Switzerland, a country regarded by many as the home of democracy, where all four major parties (but not the minor parties) have been represented in all Governments since 1959 in proportion to their strength in parliament . (Since the Swiss electorate is as stable as its counterpart elsewhere, this means that for the past three decades there have been two Radical Democrats, two Christian Democrats, two Socialists and one member of the Swiss People's Party in the seven-member cabinet.) In Finland, 'grand coalitions' of up to five of the six traditional parties are common.

Finland also offers many examples of types 2 and 3. Small parties supported by fewer than 5% of voters are frequently to be found in Governments which enjoy very large parliamentary majorities, even though they may not be necessary for the securing of a parliamentary majority and serve only to take up offices that could be awarded to supporters of bigger parties. In countries such as Germany and Belgium, with a 'two-and-a-half party' balance of political forces similar to that of Ireland, the strong Socialist and Christian Democratic parties have on occasion coalesced with each other rather than using the small Liberal Party to gain a majority.[10] Although such Governments (especially in Germany) are more the exception than the rule, they do represent an attempt to reconcile conflicting demands in society rather than an attempt by one 'moral community' to secure a victory over its rivals. Many other examples of these two types, and of type 4, may be obtained from the experience of European states.

In countries where grand coalitions are common, minority governments of types 5, 6 and 7 are also frequently to be found. The persistence of governments of these types reflects the extent to which parties are disposed to support cabinets in which they do not themselves participate, an attitude that is not commonly to be found in the English-speaking world.

At the end of the scale is type 8. Examples will be found in the non-party governments that are frequently formed in Finland. Though admittedly caretaker cabinets, these may remain in office for many months.

The alternative model to this relatively unrestrictive one is that of the bare-majority. This rests on the assumption that parties give priority to their own self-interests and that they find large majorities objectionable for two reasons. The first is that the more parliamentary supporters a Government has, the more difficult is the task of satisfying demands for patronage from a fixed pork barrel and the more demanding the task of maintaining parliamentary discipline. Second, if this majority has been obtained by coalition with another party or parties, policies may be compromised and constraints are imposed on the allocation of offices. Each party's objective in such situations, therefore, is to participate in a Government which has an overall majority and contains as few members of other parties as possible. This means that cabinet types 5 to 8 are excluded since they are not majority cabinets. It also means that types 1 to 3 are excluded since they include redundant supporters. This leaves type 4 as the most likely outcome on these assumptions.

A study of government formation patterns in Europe over the period 1945-83 shows a sharp contrast between the continental European and the the Westminster patterns. On average, bare-majority cabinets held office in continental European states for 20% of the time (ranging from 0% in Denmark and Switzerland to 56% of the time in Norway). In the United Kingdom this figure rose to 98% and the Irish figure was 70%.[11] It could indeed be argued that this approach underestimates Ireland's adherence to the bare-majority pattern, since it does not take account of the many minority governments which were supported by independent deputies but which should, given the realities of politics, be regarded as bare-majority cabinets.

The deviant Irish-British approach is underlined by the provision that only parliamentarians can be included in Government. In practice it is politically difficult in Ireland to include in a cabinet anyone who is not a Dáil deputy. In continental Europe it is normally possible to include non-parliamentarians, and in cases such as France, Norway and the Netherlands, there is a specific prohibition of dual membership of parliament and the Government; parliamentarians who are appointed to the cabinet are required to resign their seats. In the Irish tradition, the alleged ill-effects of the electoral system in procuring the election of deputies who are more concerned with brokerage than with the business of government are compounded by the de facto requirement that cabinet ministers be selected from the very small pool of 80 to 90 Dáil deputies who are acceptable in terms of party affiliation.

Government-Opposition Relations

A final point of contrast between the Irish and the continental European traditions arises from the notion that any party which is not represented in the Government is necessarily in Opposition. This assumption is deeply ingrained in Ireland and in other countries which follow the Westminster model, giving parliamentary relations an adversarial character that is different from that which is normal on the continent, where parties not included in the Government nevertheless frequently see themselves as forming part of a governing 'majority'. In Ireland, parties not included in the Government criticise the Government's actions not merely on ideological or even policy grounds, but because 'it is the Opposition's duty to oppose'.

Although the outcome of the 1987 general election produced no sign that Irish political leaders were thinking along the lines of formal grand coalitions of the kind that are common in Europe, a significant movement away from adversarial politics did take place. This is to be seen in a commitment by the main opposition party, Fine Gael, not to engage in opposition merely for its own sake but actually to support the government, even in areas where its policies were unpopular, in major areas of economic policy. It remains to be seen, however, how long this position can be sustained in the context of an elite political culture that accepts the adversarial assumptions of the Westminster model.

CONCLUSION

The principal novelty of the February 1987 election was undoubtedly the rise of the Progressive Democrats. The appearance of this new force in the Dáil did not, however, represent an intrusion by a radically new political perspective; the factors accounting for its rise had more to do with personality and organisational factors than with ideology. The new party does, however, represent (in a manner parallel to the Workers' Party at the opposite end of the political spectrum) at least a hint of movement towards a redefinition of Irish politics along left-right lines. The Progressive Democrats are more unambiguously conservative than either Fianna Fáil or Fine Gael. Otherwise, the general election results resembled earlier Irish and contemporary European elections in the predictable survival of traditional parties more or less unscathed, notwithstanding the losses suffered by the Labour Party and Fine Gael.

In terms of its implications for Irish political institutions, the election may have more far-reaching consequences; there is a dangerous tendency for politicians who do not like the results of elections to attempt to change the rules rather than to modify their own behaviour. The proposal that the electoral system be altered to make the Dáil less representative of political currents among the electorate is one example of this: the proposal that the Constitution be amended to allow the President to play a more active role in resolving government formation 'crises' is another. The danger of any move away from proportional representation has been emphasised above, and Ireland's cabinet formation 'crises' need to be seen in context. On the basis of the measure used above, the longest 'crisis' (in 1951) lasted for four hours; in continental Europe the corresponding period may be as long as nine months. The case for amendment of the Constitution is less convincing than the case for a change in attitude by party elites, a change which would entail acceptance of the notion of a multi-party Dáil without any clear majority bloc and of the propriety of more vigorous political intervention by the President.

The tyranny of the Westminster model is likely to be used by the two large parties, and to be acquiesced in by the Progressive Democrats and the Labour Party, in justifying the maintenance of the present system of government formation in Ireland. This is clearly in the interests of both Fianna Fáil and Fine Gael, each of which would stand to lose by aligning itself alongside the other. Paradoxically, the very similarity of these two parties - the fact that, aside from dynastic and historical considerations, each appear to find its raison d'etre in attacking the other - is the major obstacle to coalition between the two. The identity of both would be threatened in such an alliance.

Neither is it clear that this system is best calculated to resolve difficult economic problems. In circumstances where the message from each side is gloomy, each is likely to lose supporters to the other and thus retain a relatively healthy position.

Albert Hirschman, discussing the dangers that face business organisations in analogous circumstances, warns of the 'ineffective flitting back and forth of groups of consumers from one deteriorating firm to another without any firm getting a signal that something has gone awry'.[12] While the formation of an all-party coalition to remedy such a situation might be unnecessarily drastic in Ireland, a less radical move towards co-operation between the big parties might serve both the short-term interests of the right and the long-term interests of the left.

NOTES TO CHAPTERS

NOTES TO CHAPTER 1

1. See MRBI election questionnaires for the 1981 and two 1982 elections.
2. Surveys reported in *Irish Times*, 27 November 1986.
3. This speech is reported in the *Irish Times*, 13 October 1986.
4. This speech is reported in the *Irish Times*, 19 January 1987.
5. *Irish Press*, 21 January 1987.
6. Report of press conference can be found in the *Irish Press*, 21 January 1987.
7. Fine Gael manifesto as reported, in summary version, in *Irish Times*, 22 January 1987.
8. On the Progressive Democrats see Lyne, T. 1987. 'The Progressive Democrats 1985-87', *Irish Political Studies*, 2 , (1987) 107-14. *Irish Times*, 29 January 1987 for report on PDs press conference.
9. Progressive Democrats 1987. *A Nation that Works* Dublin: Progressive Democrats.
10. Fianna Fáil, 1987. *The Programme for National Recovery* . Dublin: Fianna Fáil.
11. Haughey's speech reported in the *Irish Times*, 30 January 1987.
12. A summary of the Workers' Party manifesto is reported in the *Irish Times* , 28 January 1987. The Labour Party, 1987. *A Programme for Economic Recovery,* Dublin: The Labour Party.
13. The reports of this exchange are contained in the *Irish Press* and the *Irish Times*, 5 and 6 February 1987.
14. These two paragraphs are based on reports appearing in the *Irish Press*, 9 and 13 February 1987.
15. *Irish Times*, 11 February 1987.
16. *Irish Times*, 16 February 1987.

OTHER SOURCES

Kenny, Shane and Feargal Keane. 1987. *Irish Politics Now: 'This Week' guide to the 25th Dáil*. Dingle, Brandon.

Sinnott, Richard, 1987. 'The General Election in the Republic; 17 February 1987' *Irish Political Studies*, 2, (1987), 115-24.

Trench, Brian (ed.) *Magill Book of Irish Politics: Election February 87*, Dublin, Magill.

The *Irish Independent*, *Irish Press* , and *Irish Times* were consulted for the duration of the campaign. The *Irish Times* is normally used for quotations.

NOTES TO CHAPTER 3

1. For a detailed analysis, see Peter Mair, 1987. *The Changing Irish Party System: Organisation, Ideology and Electoral Competition*. London: Frances Pinter, 138-206.
2. Peter Mair, 1987. *The Changing Irish Party System: Organisation, Ideology a and Electoral Competition*, 189.
3. In an interview with Gene MacKenna, *Irish Times*, 26 May 1976.
4. *Irish Times*, 30 March 1981.
5. See the discussion of the Lemass Strategy, Paul Bew and Henry Patterson, 1982. *Sean Lemass and the Making of Modern Ireland, 1945-66*. Dublin: Gill & Macmillan, 957.
6. Walsh, Dick, 1982. *The Party: Inside Fianna Fáil*. Dublin: Gill & Macmillan, 957.
7. *Irish Times*, 5 February 1979.
8. Peter Mair, 1987. *The Changing Irish Party System: Organisation, Ideology a and Electoral Competition*, 41.
9. January 1978, 14.
10. Fine Gael, 1987. *Breaking Out of the Vicious Circle*. Dublin: Fine Gael, 11.
11. Fine Gael, 1987. *Breaking Out of the Vicious Circle*, 47.
12. The Progessive Democrats, 1987. *A Message to the Irish People*. Dublin: The Progressive Democrats, 7.
13. The Progessive Democrats, 1987. *A Message to the Irish People*, 6.
14. The Progessive Democrats, 1987. *A Message to the Irish People*, 4.
15. The Progessive Democrats, 1987. *A Message to the Irish People*, 6-7.
16. *Irish Press*, 3 May 1954.
17. Press statement, 30 January 1987.
18. The Labour Party, 1987. *People Matter Most*. Dublin: The Labour Party, 1, 7.
19. The Labour Party, 1987. *People Matter Most*, 16.
20. The Workers' Party, 1987. *Manifesto: General Election*. Dublin: The Workers' Party, 3.
21. Press statement, 27 January 1987.
22. Dáil Debates 361:2600, 19 November 1985.
23. 16 November 1985.
24. Fianna Fáil, 1987. *The Programme for National Recovery*. Dublin: Fianna Fáil, 69.
25. Noted by the author, Fianna Fáil press conference, 29 January 1987.
26. See *The Programme for National Recovery*.
27. See Bew and Patterson, 1982. *Sean Lemass and the Making of Modern Ireland, 1945-66*.
28. See *The Programme for National Recovery*, 38.
29. Fine Gael, 1987. *Breaking Out of the Vicious Circle*. Dublin: Fine Gael, 69.
30. The Progressive Democrats, 1987. *A Nation that Works*. Dublin: The Progressive Democrats, 15.
31. The Progressive Democrats, 1987. *Justice for All*. Dublin: The Progressive Democrats, 33.
32. *People Matter Most.*, 22.
33. *Manifesto*, 6-7.
34. See *The Changing Irish Party System*, 21.

NOTES TO CHAPTER 4

* What follows is based on a series of unstructured interviews in April-May 1987 with 14 strategists from all five political parties and on some access to party documents, much of which is non-attributable. As some strategists prefer not to be identified the decision has been taken to preserve anonymity for all. Some parties are more open than others and this undoubtedly effects the balance and quality of the accounts in this chapter.

1. David M. Farrell and Martin Wortmann, 'Party Strategies in the Electoral Market', *European Journal of Political Research*, 15 (3), 1987.
2. David M. Farrell, 'The Strategy to Market Fine Gael in 1981', *Irish Political Studies*, 1, (1986), 1-14.
3. Vote-management is where a party chooses candidates carefully distributed throughout the constituency so as to maximise its chances of winning seats. This was first applied on a grand scale by Fine Gael in 1981, see Stephen O'Byrnes, *Hiding Behind a Face*, Dublin: Gill and Macmillan, 1986. For a discussion of vote management in 1987 see the chapter by Michael Gallagher.
4. In the past Fianna Fáil and Fine Gael have each used three advertising agencies. Both parties now only use one.
5. See Shane Kenny and Fergal Keane, *Irish Politics Now*.
6. Considerable media attention had been addressed to the supposed 'vital' role of strategists in pulling FitzGerald's 'puppet strings'. This did not please the party's hierarchy, see O'Byrnes, *Hiding Behind a Face*, 277.
7. A second qualitative survey was carried out during the campaign. The party also commissioned a national opinion poll during the election. There was a gap between some of the published polls and party strategists were anxious for information on whether Fine Gael's vote was rising. The party made great use of constituency polls, generally organised on a 'scientific' basis by local activists. A 'large proportion' of the party's twenty five marginals were polled. One constituency was polled four times.
8. Denis Coghlan, 'Fitzpatrick keeps FG in fighting trim', *Irish Times*, 26 September, 1986.
9. This 'constituency audit' had been intiated prior to the setting up of the strategy committee.
10. Respondents associated party's TDs with the party in the following proportions: Desmond O'Malley 85 percent; Mary Harney 49 %, Bobby Molloy 32 %, Pearse Wyse 23 %, Michael Keating 23 %.
11. The panel formats on 'Today Tonight' were varied. In the eleven panel discussions during the campaign the combinations were as follows: Fianna Fáil and Fine Gael (three programmes); Fianna Fáil, Fine Gael and Labour (one); all five parties (three); Progressive Democrats and Labour (one); Progressive Democrats, Labour and Workers' Party (three). In all cases the presenters attempted to achieve some form of proportionality in the discussion.
12. The PPB television schedule ended up as follows: Fianna Fáil five of five minutes; Fine Gael four of six minutes; Labour, two of two and a half minutes; Progressive Democrats one of four minutes; Workers' Party one of three minutes; the others were bunched together in one two minute broadcast.
13. Windmill Lane is the leading production and recording studio in the country used by many top pop groups.

NOTES TO CHAPTER 5

1. Peter Mair, 'More central power in the parties',14-16 in Brian Trench (ed.), *Magill: Election February 1987*.
2. M. A. Marsh, 'Ireland', 173-201 in Ivor Crewe and David Denver (eds.), *Electoral Change in Western Democracies*, London: Croom Helm, 1985.
3. Mogens N. Pedersen, 'The dynamics of European party systems: changing patterns of electoral volatility', *European Journal of Political Research*, 7:1 1979,1-26. For discussion of the concept, see Ivor Crewe, 'Introduction: electoral change in western democracies: a framework for analysis',1-22 Crewe and Denver (eds.), *Electoral Change*.
4. Brendan Walsh, 'The distribution of votes',77-79 in Shane Kenny and Fergal Keane, *Irish Politics Now*. There is no evidence that Fianna Fáil was hit by the intervention of Sinn Féin; in fact, it did better where there was a Sinn Féin candidate (an average gain of 0.1%) than where there was not (an average loss of 1.5%).
5. The figure referred to is Pearson's coefficient (r). A value of zero would denote that the two factors were not related at all; a value of 1 would denote that the two match perfectly.
6. A breakdown of each party's strength in each region of the country since 1922 is given in Michael Gallagher, 1985, *Political Parties in the Republic of Ireland*, Manchester: Manchester University Press and Dublin: Gill and Macmillan, 1985, 156-60.
7. Walsh, 'The distribution of votes', 79.
8. Thomas Lyne, 'The Progressive Democrats 1985-87',113; Richard Sinnott, 'The general election in the Republic', 122.
9. This section draws heavily on Michael Gallagher, 'The transfer pattern', 10-13 in Trench (ed.), *Magill: Election February 1987*.
10. Robert A. Newland, 1982. *Comparative Electoral Systems*, London: Arthur McDougall Fund, 71-3. Another element of chance permitted under British's STV laws is the selection by random sampling of the votes to be transferred from a surplus (see Michael Gallagher and A. R. Unwin, 'Electoral distortion under STV random sampling procedures', *British Journal of Political Science*, 16:2 (1986), 243-53). Antony Unwin has calculated that the probability of Tom McEllistrim rather than Dick Spring being elected in Kerry North at this election if a different selection of papers had been taken from Deenihan's votes could be as high as 0.45.
11. These issues are discussed in Michael Gallagher, 'Does Ireland need a new electoral system?', *Irish Political Studies*, 2, (1987), 27-48, and 'The political consequences of the electoral system in the Republic of Ireland', *Electoral Studies*, 5:3 (1986), 253-75.
12. STV's performance on this criterion is assessed unfavourably by Richard Katz in 'The single transferable vote and proportional representation', 135-45 in Arend Lijphart and Bernard Grofman, 1984,*Choosing an Electoral System*, New York: Praeger.
13. John Loosemore and Victor J. Hanby, 'The theoretical limits of maximum distortion: some analytic expressions for electoral systems', *British Journal of Political Science*, 1:4 (1971), 467-77.
14. The classification scheme used is as follows. Under 'commercial' are included business people, mainly small businessmen such as shopkeepers, publicans, auctioneers, contractors and so on. In Table 11, 'lower professionals' are mainly schoolteachers, while 'higher professionals' include doctors, lawyers,

lecturers, architects, accountants and economists. The main sources for data on the pre-1987 deputies are earlier editions of Ted Nealon's *Guides* to the Dáil and of the *Magill* series; for full details, see the first article cited in note 15. For the newly elected TDs, Trench (ed.), *Magill: Election February 87* and Kenny and Keane, *Irish Politics Now*.

15. For an analysis of the November 1982 Dáil, see Michael Gallagher, '166 who rule: the Dáil deputies of November 1982', *Economic and Social Review*, 15:4 (1984), 241-64, which gives figures on occupations for each Dáil back to 1961, and David Farrell, 'Age, education and occupational backgrounds of TDs and 'routes' to the Dáil: the effects of localism in the 1980s', *Administration*, 32:3 (1984), 323-41, which gives figures for selected Dala back to 1922. For a comparison between the November 1982 Dáil and other parliaments, see Michael Gallagher, 'Social backgrounds and local orientations of members of the Irish Dáil', *Legislative Studies Quarterly*, 10:3 (1985), 373-94.

16. J. L. McCracken, 1958. *Representative government in Ireland: a study of Dáil Eireann 1919-1948*, London: Oxford University Press; John Whyte, *Dáil deputies: their work, its difficulties, possible remedies*, Dublin: Tuairim pamphlet No 15, (1966).

17. Des Dinan, 'Constitution and parliament', 71-86 in Brian Girvin and Roland Sturm (eds.), 1986, *Politics and Society in Contemporary Ireland*, Aldershot: Gower.

18. 'Local authority' here refers to one of the 27 county councils or the five major city corporations (Cork, Dublin, Galway, Limerick and Waterford), so the term 'local authority member' in this chapter denotes a member of any of these bodies.

19. Brian Farrell, 'Dáil deputies: 'The 1969 generation", *Economic and Social Review* 2:3 (1971), 318; David Farrell, 'Age, education and occupational backgrounds', 329.

20. Of course, some seats are marginal as between other parties, but these are less important in terms of the formation of the next government.

NOTES TO CHAPTER 6

1. David B. Rottman and Philip J. O'Connell, 'The Changing Social Structure', in Frank Litton (ed.), 1982. *Unequal Achievement: The Irish Experience 1957-1982*, Dublin: Institute of Public Administration, 74-75.

2. The original 'politics without social bases' thesis was developed by John Whyte in J.H. Whyte, Ireland: Politics Without Social Bases' in Richard Rose, (ed.) 1974. *Electoral Behaviour: A Comparative Handbook*, New York: The Free Press, 619-652. The suggestion that recent evidence indicates a trend towards a more clear cut class pattern is examined in Michael Laver, 'Ireland: Politics with Some Social Bases: An Interpretation Based on Survey Data', *Economic and Social Review*, 17,(3), (1986), 193-213.

3. The 1969 data differs from that for the other years in one important respect; the poll was taken some time prior to the election campaign, in April 1969. The election took place on 18 June. The sources of the data are : 1969: Whyte,'Ireland: Politics Without Social Bases' Tables 2 and 3, 631-632; 1977: *Irish Times*/NOP Election Surveys, May-June 1977 (figures based on amalgamated results of all three surveys, n=1788); 1981: *Irish Times*/ IMS Political Opinion Poll, 7-8 June 1981(n=1050); February 1982: *Irish Times*/

IMS Poll: Election '82, 13-14 February 1982 (n=1051); November 1982: *Irish Independent-Sunday Independent* /IMS Poll 9-10 November 1982 (n=1049); 1987: *Sunday Independent*/ IMS Poll, 14 February 1987 (n=1051)
4. The terms are borrowed from Anthony Heath, Roger Jowell and John Curtice, 1985. *How Britain Votes,* Oxford: Pergammon Press, 21.
5. Michael Laver, 'Ireland: Politics with Some Social Bases', 210.
6. Much of the impetus for the revision of the concept of social class has come from the work of the Oxford Social Mobility Research Group. For application in a political science context see Heath, Jowell and Curtice, *How Britain Votes,* 13-27 and David Robertson, 1984, *Class and the British Electorate,* Oxford: Blackwell, 107-125.
7. Aileen O'Hare, 'An outline of work to-date and in-progress, on the development of An Irish Census-Based Social Class Scale', Unpublished Paper prepared in collaboration with the *Working Party for the Development of an Irish Social Class Scale,* Dublin: The Health Research Board, (1984),4.
8. D.B. Rottman, D.F. Hannon, N. Hardiman and M.M. Wiley, 1982. *The Distribution of Income in the Republic of Ireland: A Study in Social Class and Family-Cycle Inequalities*, Dublin: The Economic and Social Research Institute, 24-25.
9. The PD lead among the younger (under 35 years)bourgeoisie was quite pronounced - PD 35%, FG 25%, FF 15%. While caution should be exercised because the number of respondents is quite small (40), it could be argued that in this sense the Progressive Democrats are a 'yuppie' party.
10. This is the view put forward by the influential 'Michigan School' of voting theory, best summed up in the work of Campbell A., P. Converse, W.Mills and D.Stokes, 1960. *The American Voter,* NewYork: Wiley
11. This is the view put forward by the 'economic' theories of the 'rational choice' school of party competition, based on the seminal work of Downs, A., 1957. *An Economic Theory of Democracy,* New York: Harper and Row.
12. A recent example of a 'saliency' theory of party competition can be found in Budge I. and D. Farlie, 1983. *Explaining and Predicting Elections,* London: George Allen&Unwin

NOTES TO CHAPTER 7

1. Quoted in Shane Kenny and Fergal Keane, *Irish Politics Now,* 59.
2. Basil Chubb, 1974. *Cabinet Government in Ireland.* Dublin: Institute of Public Administration, 54 and 1982. *The Government and Politics of Ireland,* London: Longman, 143.
3. For a fuller account, see Brian Farrell, 'Government Formation and Ministerial Selection', in Howard Penniman and Brian Farrell, (eds.), 1987. *Ireland at the Polls: Four general elections 1981-1987,* Chapel Hill, N.C.: Duke University Press, forthcoming.
4. See Vernon Bogdanor, (ed.), 1983. *Coalition Government in Western Europe,* London: Heinemann for Policy Studies Institute.
5. See John Coakley and Brian Farrell, 'The Selection of Cabinet Ministers in Ireland, 1922-1982', in Mattei Dogan and Dwane Marvick (eds.), *Gateways to Power: Leadership Selection in Pluralist Democracies,* Berlin, New York: Walter de Gruyter, forthcoming.
6. Alvin S. Cohan, 1972. *The Irish Political Elite,* Dublin:Gill and Macmillan.
7. Chubb, *Cabinet Government,* 86.

8. David M. Farrell, 'Age, Education and occupational backgrounds of TDs and routes to the Dáil: the effects of localism in the 1980s'. *Administration*, 32, 3, 1984.
9. Brian Trench (ed.) *Magill Book of Irish Politics: Election February '87.*
10. See Peter Hennessy, 1986. *Cabinet*, Oxford : Basil Blackwell.
11. For a full account of the Thatcher Cabinet see chap. 3 of Hennessey, *Cabinet*, .
12. The point was registered in Brian Farrell, 1977. *Chairman or Chief? the role of Taoiseach in Irish Government*, Dublin: Gill and Macmillan, p.x. but tended to be lost in a subsequent concentration on the chairman/chief models.
13. The career, resignation and consequences of FitzGerald's leadership are discussed in Shane Kenny and Fergal Keane, *Irish Politics Now*, 62-73.
14. For a discussion of these points, see, e.g., T.J. Barrington, 'Whatever happened to Irish Government?' in F. Litton, (eds.)*Unequal Achievement,* Basil Chubb, 'Prospects for democratic politics in Ireland', in Penniman and Farrell, Brian Farrell, 'Politics and Change' in Kieran A. Kennedy, (ed.), 1986, *Ireland in Transition: economic and social change since 1960*, Dublin: Mercier in association with RTE.

NOTES TO CHAPTER 8

1. Richard Sinnott, 'The general election in the Republic', 17 February 1987, *Irish Political Studies* , 2, (1987), 115-124.
2. Brendan M Walsh, 'How the nation voted: The distribution of votes', in Shane Kenny, Fergal Keane, *Irish Politics Now:* 77-89; Walsh identifies 1951 rather than 1957 as the most recent date at which Fine Gael won a lower share of the poll than in 1987.
3. Michael Gallagher, 'The outcome', in this book.
4. Thomas Lyne, The Progressive Democrats 1985-87, *Irish Political Studies,* 2, (1987),107-114.
5. See Stein Rokkan, 1970.*Citizens, elections, parties,* Oslo: Universitetsforlaget.
6. Michael Gallagher, 'The political consequences of the electoral system in the Republic of Ireland', *Electoral Studies* 5 (3) 1986, 253-275 and 'Does Ireland need a new electoral system?', *Irish Political Studies* , 2, 1987, 27-48.
7. Shane Kenny, Fergal Keane, *Irish Politics Now*, 58-59.
8. This point is, of course, being made from a behavioural rather than from a legal-constitutional point of view. The most notable instances in which state presidents have exercised powers specifically withheld from them, or bestowed on other political institutions, are the cases of the United States and of the Fifth Republic in France.
9. See Arend Lijphart, 1984. *Democracies: Patterns of majoritarian and consensus government in twenty-one countries,* New Haven: Yale University Press, 1-45.
10. This is an oversimplification of the Belgian position, where the three traditional parties have each split into entirely separate Dutch- and French-speaking sections.
11. Calculated from Jan-Erik Lane and Svante O. Ersson, 1987. *Politics and society in Western Europe* , London: Sage, 225
12. Albert O. Hirschman, 1970. *Exit, voice, and loyalty: Responses to decline in firms, organisations, and states* , Cambridge, Ma: Harvard University Press, 26.

APPENDIX

NOMINATIONS, RESULTS AND MAPS, BY CONSTITUENCY

Appendix: Results and maps

Table A1: Candidates nominated, by constituency

Constituency	No. of seats	Fianna Fáil	Fine Gael	PDs	Labour	Workers Party	Others
Carlow-Kilkenny	5	3	3	2	1	1	-
Cavan-Monaghan	5	3	2	-	-	1	3
Clare	4	4	2	2	1	-	2
Cork East	4	2	2	2	1	1	1
Cork North-Central	5	4	2	2	2	1	6
Cork North-West	3	2	2	1	-	-	-
Cork South-Central	5	4	2	2	1	1	6
Cork South-West	3	2	2	1	-	-	1
Donegal North-East	3	2	2	-	1	-	3
Donegal South-West	3	2	2	-	-	1	1
Dublin Central	5	3	3	1	2	1	4
Dublin North	3	3	2	1	2	-	2
Dublin North-Central	4	3	2	1	1	1	5
Dublin North-East	4	4	2	2	1	1	3
Dublin North-West	4	3	2	-	1	2	6
Dublin South	5	3	3	1	1	1	6
Dublin South-Central	5	3	2	1	1	1	5
Dublin South-East	4	4	3	1	1	2	5
Dublin South-West	4	2	3	1	2	1	6
Dublin West	5	3	3	2	1	1	10
Dun Laoghaire	5	3	3	3	1	1	4
Galway East	3	3	2	1	-	-	-
Galway West	5	4	3	2	1	1	6
Kerry North	3	3	1	-	1	-	2
Kerry South	3	3	2	1	1	1	2
Kildare	5	4	2	2	1	1	2
Laoighis-Offaly	5	4	4	1	1	-	3
Limerick East	5	3	2	2	1	1	6
Limerick West	3	2	3	1	1	-	-
Longford-Westmeath	4	3	3	2	1	-	1
Louth	4	3	3	1	1	1	5
Mayo East	3	3	2	-	-	-	1
Mayo West	3	3	2	-	-	-	-
Meath	5	4	3	2	2	1	4
Roscommon	3	2	2	-	-	-	1
Sligo-Leitrim	4	3	3	1	-	-	3
Tipperary North	3	2	2	1	1	-	3
Tipperary South	4	3	2	2	1	1	4
Waterford	4	3	2	1	1	2	3
Wexford	5	3	3	2	1	1	2
Wicklow	4	2	2	3	1	1	3
Totals	**166**	**122**	**97**	**51**	**37**	**29**	**130**

Source: Department of Environment; Franchise Section

Appendix: Results and maps

Table A2: Totals of first preference votes

Constituency	Fianna Fáil	Fine Gael	PDs	Labour	Workers Party	Others
Carlow-Kilkenny	25,527	14,873	8,063	7,358	1,664	-
Cavan-Monaghan	31,747	18,927	-	-	577	6,561
Clare	25,022	13,274	5,603	600	-	2,874
Cork East	16,347	12,739	4,276	888	6,986	543
Cork North-Central	16,127	11,372	7,245	3,720	2,628	2,251
Cork North-West	15,120	14,488	3,796	-	-	-
Cork South-Central	18,460	12,254	14,047	4,862	2,349	4,287
Cork South-West	15,132	14,566	3,570	-	-	134
Donegal North-East	9,512	8,734	-	393	-	10,781
Donegal South-West	18,384	9,403	-	-	2,512	1,276
Dublin Central	19,993	5,973	6,361	1,399	1,463	12,267
Dublin North	16,542	8,878	4,008	3,433	-	1,157
Dublin North-Central	21,344	10,397	3,582	2,973	1,643	2,985
Dublin North-East	19,663	7,243	4,655	2,227	3,297	1,194
Dublin North-West	16,737	6,493	-	1,370	7,480	2,541
Dublin South	20,496	17,704	11,957	2,684	1,308	3,182
Dublin South-Central	21,149	14,267	5,212	4,701	3,946	2,417
Dublin South-East	12,522	12,251	5,961	3,480	1,910	2,146
Dublin South-West	16,004	5,250	8,169	5,065	5,086	1,880
Dublin West	20,920	11,456	6,014	1,185	6,651	5,486
Dun Laoghaire	14,576	17,077	11,023	6,484	4,054	2,488
Galway East	17,056	10,419	5,463	-	-	-
Galway West	19,979	9,600	11,360	3,878	1,567	6,378
Kerry North	16,711	10,087	-	6,737	-	1,227
Kerry South	17,926	5,946	3,215	4,559	735	830
Kildare	22,913	14,124	6,320	7,567	1,238	1,543
Laoighis-Offaly	30,204	17,479	5,353	818	-	2,268
Limerick East	12,633	8,881	18,427	2,201	246	7,225
Limerick West	17,443	9,464	6,580	519	-	-
Longford-Westmeath	26,017	12,416	5,401	1,038	-	280
Louth	18,470	10,820	5,219	6,205	570	5,525
Mayo East	17,224	13,028	-	-	-	668
Mayo West	17,197	13,093	-	-	-	-
Meath	27,694	14,172	4,831	3,631	790	4,077
Roscommon	16,201	12,093	-	-	-	4,067
Sligo-Leitrim	23,574	14,160	2,521	-	-	5,451
Tipperary North	17,099	7,859	2,444	4,558	-	1,331
Tipperary South	17,661	8,480	4,402	3,820	407	6,731
Waterford	19,000	12,420	5,347	3,358	3,407	1,062
Wexford	23,233	16,783	4,708	5,086	1,250	1,862
Wicklow	14,988	12,184	5,450	7,754	3,509	2,118
Totals	**784,547**	**481,127**	**210,583**	**114,551**	**67,273**	**119,084**

Source: Department of Environment; Franchise Section

Table A3: Vote share and seats won

Constituency	Percentage of first preferences				No. of Seats Gained				
	Fianna Fáil	Fine Gael	PD	Labour	Fianna Fáil	Fine Gael	PD	Labour	Total
Carlow-Kilkenny	44	26	14	13	2	1	1	1	5
Cavan-Monaghan	55	33	-	-	3	2	-	-	5
Clare	53	28	12	1	2	2	-	-	4
Cork East	39	31	10	2	2	1	-	-	3
Cork North-Central	37	26	17	9	2	2	1	-	5
Cork North-West	45	43	11	-	1	2	-	-	3
Cork South-Central	33	22	25	9	2	1	1	1	5
Cork South-West	45	44	11	-	1	2	-	-	3
Donegal North-East	32	30	-	1	1	1	-	-	2
Donegal South-West	58	30	-	-	2	1	-	-	3
Dublin Central	42	13	13	3	3	-	1	-	4
Dublin North	49	26	12	10	2	1	-	-	3
Dublin North-Central	50	24	8	7	2	2	-	-	4
Dublin North-East	51	19	12	6	2	1	-	-	3
Dublin North-West	48	19	-	4	2	1	-	-	3
Dublin South	36	31	21	5	2	2	1	-	5
Dublin South-Central	41	28	10	9	2	2	-	1	5
Dublin South-East	33	32	16	9	1	1	1	1	4
Dublin South-West	39	13	20	12	2	-	1	1	4
Dublin West	40	22	12	2	2	1	1	-	4
Dun Laoghaire	26	31	20	12	1	2	1	1	5
Galway East	52	32	17	-	2	1	-	-	3
Galway West	38	18	22	7	2	1	1	1	5
Kerry North	48	29	-	19	1	1	-	1	3
Kerry South	54	18	10	14	2	1	-	-	3
Kildare	43	26	12	14	2	2	-	1	5
Laoighis-Offaly	54	31	10	1	3	2	-	-	5
Limerick East	25	18	37	4	1	1	2	-	4
Limerick West	51	28	19	2	2	-	1	-	3
Longford-Westmeath	58	28	12	2	3	1	-	-	4
Louth	39	23	11	13	2	1	-	1	4
Mayo East	56	42	-	-	2	1	-	-	3
Mayo West	57	43	-	-	2	1	-	-	3
Meath	50	26	9	7	3	2	-	-	5
Roscommon	50	37	-	-	2	1	-	-	3
Sligo-Leitrim	52	31	6	-	3	1	-	-	4
Tipperary North	51	24	7	14	2	1	-	-	3
Tipperary South	43	20	11	9	2	1	-	-	3
Waterford	43	28	12	8	2	1	1	-	4
Wexford	44	32	9	10	2	2	-	1	5
Wicklow	33	26	12	17	2	1	-	1	4
Totals	**44**	**27**	**12**	**6**	**81**	**51**	**14**	**12**	**166**

Appendix: Results and maps

Table A3: Vote share and seats won (continued)

Constituency	Percentage of first preferences		No. of seats gained	
	Workers Party	Others	Workers Party	Other
Carlow-Kilkenny	3	-	-	-
Cavan-Monaghan	1	11	-	-
Clare	-	6	-	-
Cork East	17	1	1	-
Cork North-Central	6	5	-	-
Cork North-West	-	-	-	-
Cork South-Central	4	8	-	-
Cork South West	-	-	-	-
Donegal North-East	-	37	-	1
Donegal South-West	8	4	-	-
Dublin Central	3	26	-	1
Dublin North	-	3	-	-
Dublin North-Central	4	7	-	-
Dublin North-East	9	3	1	-
Dublin North-West	22	7	1	-
Dublin South	2	6	-	-
Dublin South-Central	8	5	-	-
Dublin South-East	5	6	-	-
Dublin South-West	12	5	-	-
Dublin West	13	11	1	-
Dun Laoghaire	7	4	-	-
Galway East	-	-	-	-
Galway West	3	12	-	-
Kerry North	-	4	-	-
Kerry South	2	3	-	-
Kildare	2	3	-	-
Laoighis-Offaly	-	-	-	-
Limerick East	1	15	-	1
Limerick West	-	-	-	-
Longford-Westmeath	-	1	-	-
Louth	1	12	-	-
Mayo East	-	2	-	-
Mayo West	-	-	-	-
Meath	1	7	-	-
Roscommon	-	13	-	-
Sligo-Leitrim	-	12	-	-
Tipperary North	-	4	-	-
Tipperary South	1	16	-	1
Waterford	8	2	-	-
Wexford	2	4	-	-
Wicklow	8	5	-	-
Totals	**4**	**7**	**4**	**4**

Appendix: Results and maps

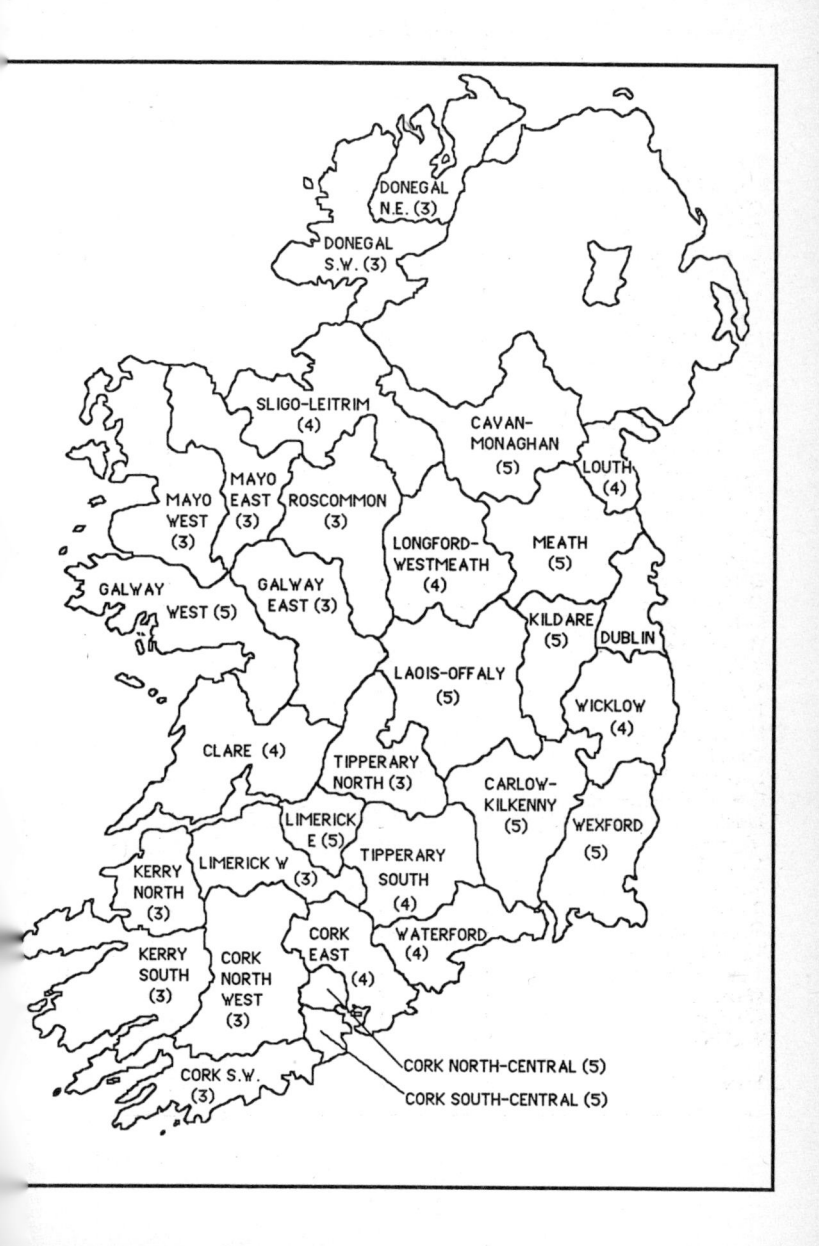

Figure A1: Constituency boundaries, (number of TDs): Ireland

Appendix: Results and maps

Figure A2: Constituency boundaries, (number of TDs): Dublin

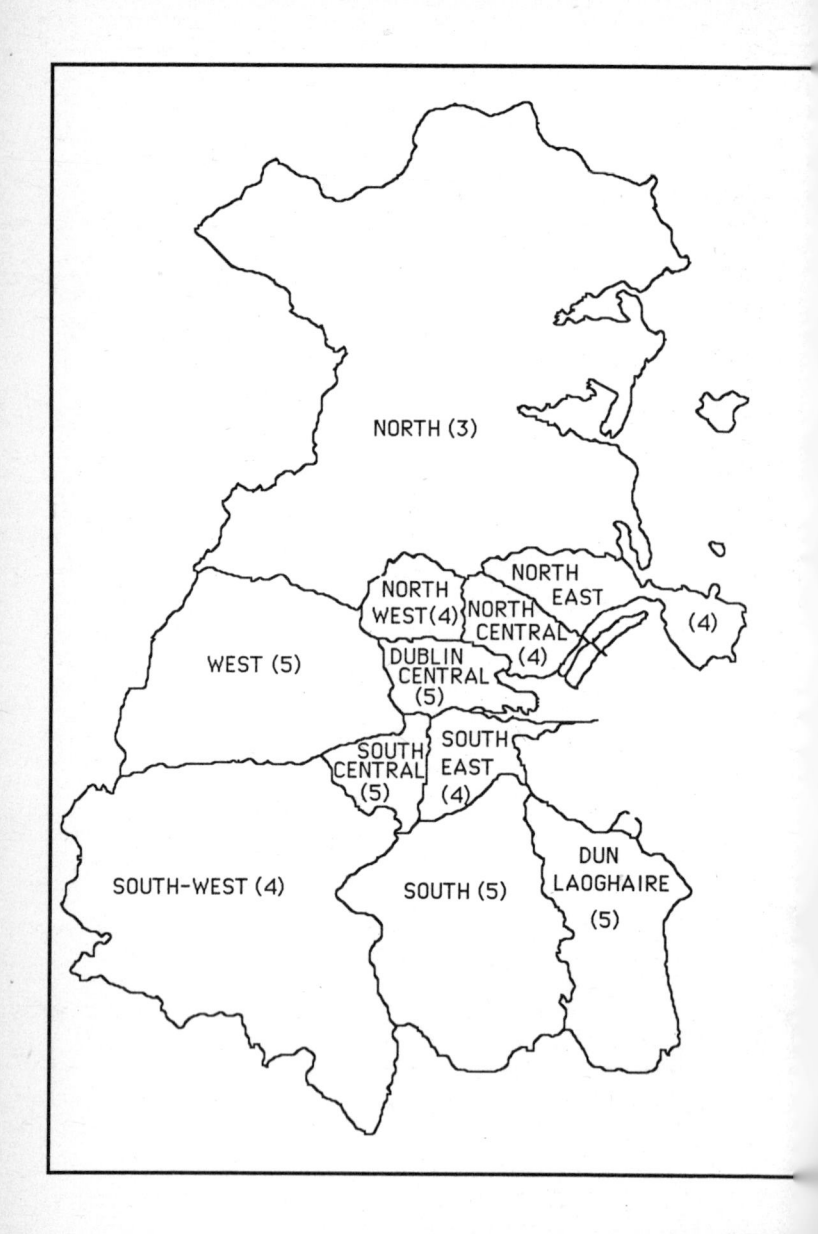

Appendix: Results and maps

Figure A3: Fianna Fáil vote share: Ireland

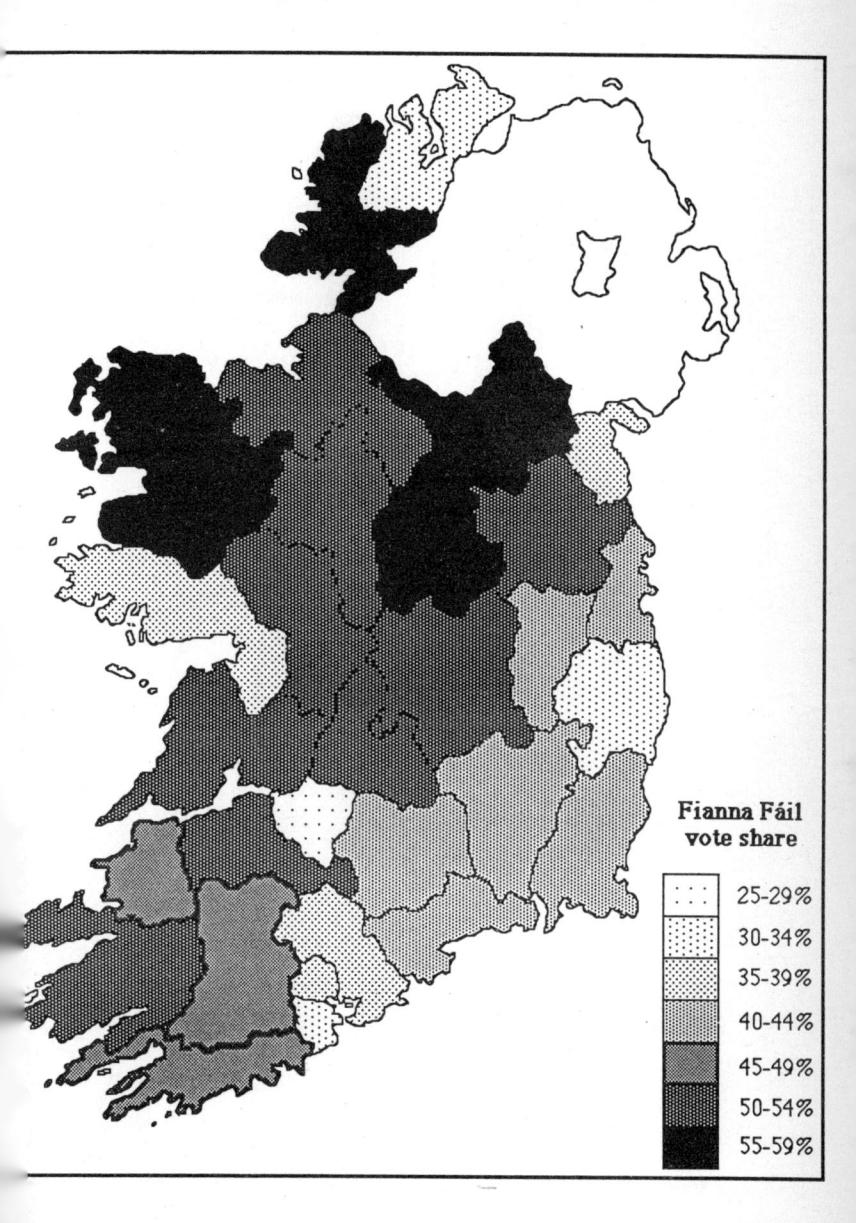

Fianna Fáil vote share

- 25-29%
- 30-34%
- 35-39%
- 40-44%
- 45-49%
- 50-54%
- 55-59%

Appendix: Results and maps

Figure A4: Fianna Fáil vote share: Dublin

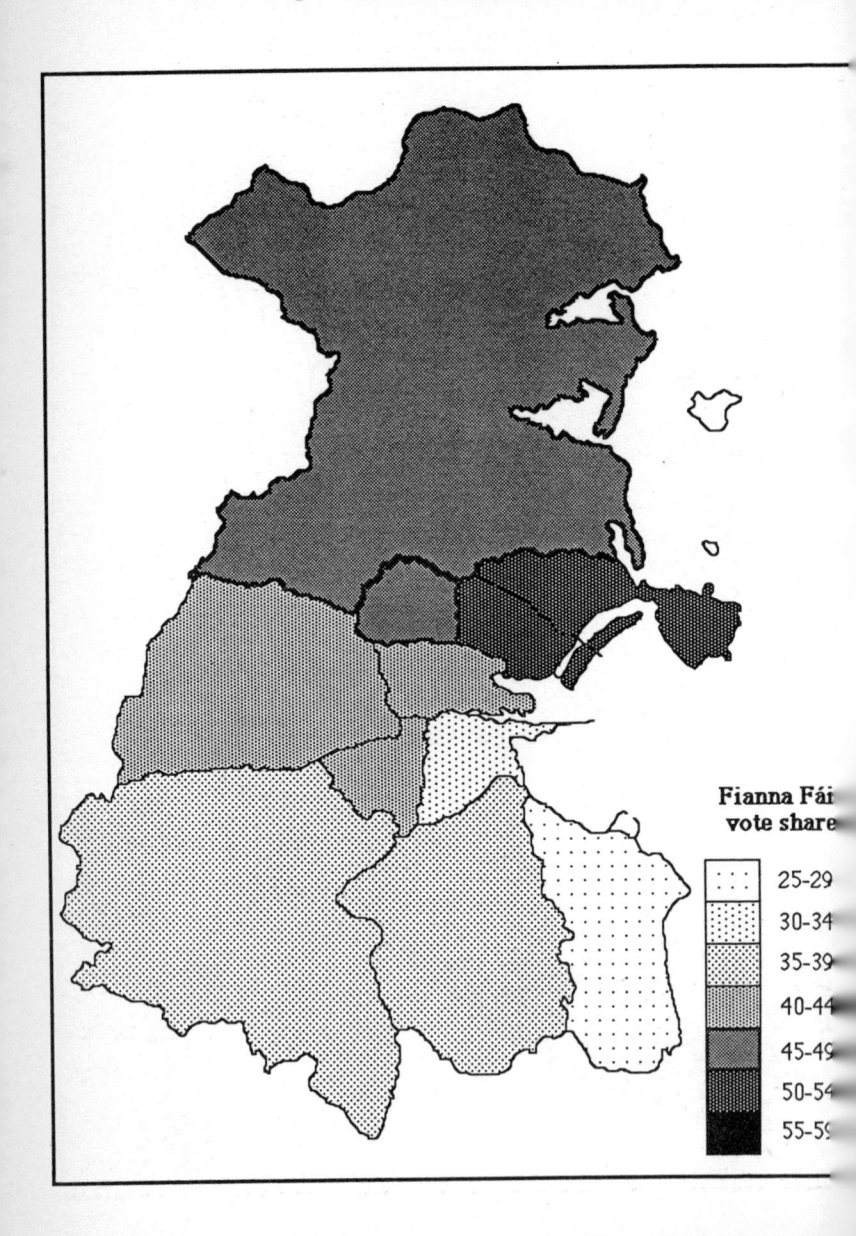

Fianna Fáil vote share

- 25-29
- 30-34
- 35-39
- 40-44
- 45-49
- 50-54
- 55-59

Appendix: Results and maps

Figure A5: Fine Gael vote share: Ireland

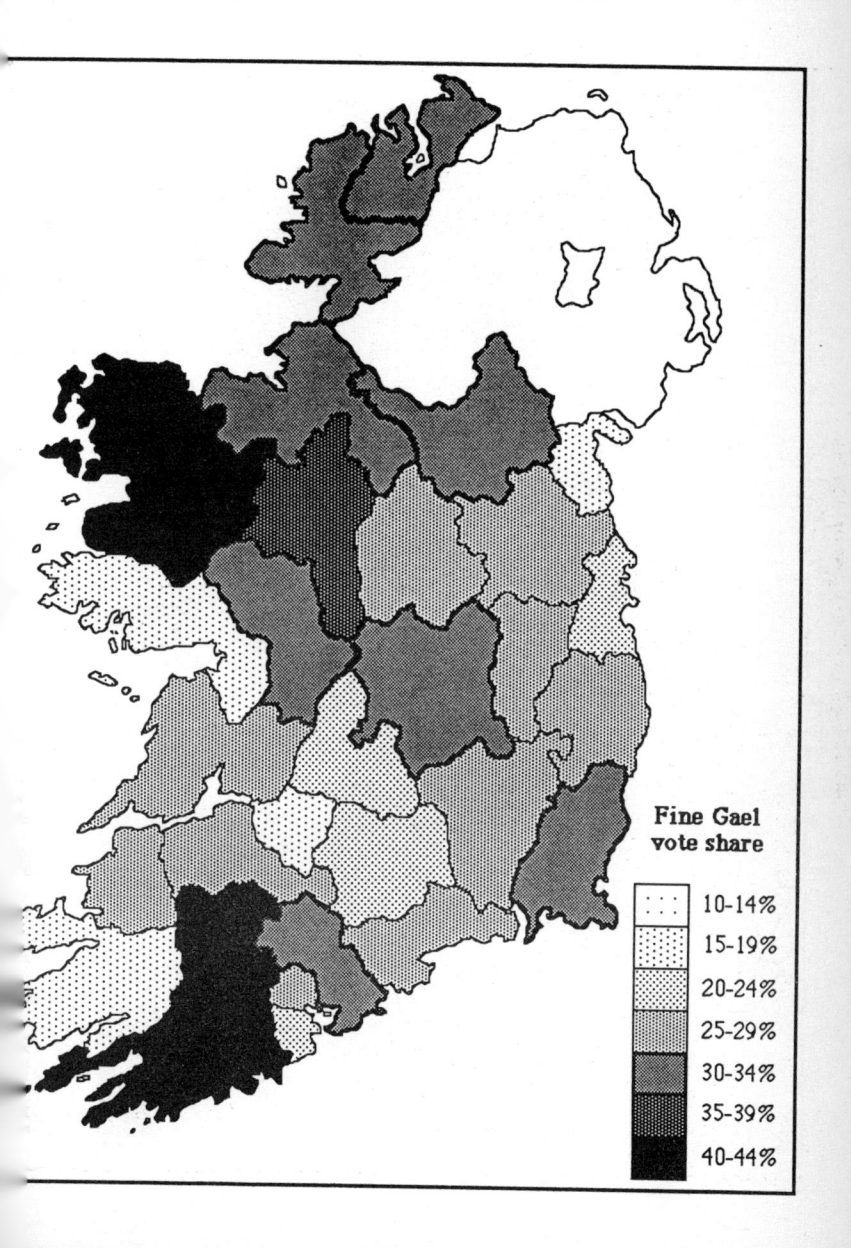

Fine Gael vote share

- 10-14%
- 15-19%
- 20-24%
- 25-29%
- 30-34%
- 35-39%
- 40-44%

Appendix: Results and maps

Figure A6: Fine Gael vote share: Dublin

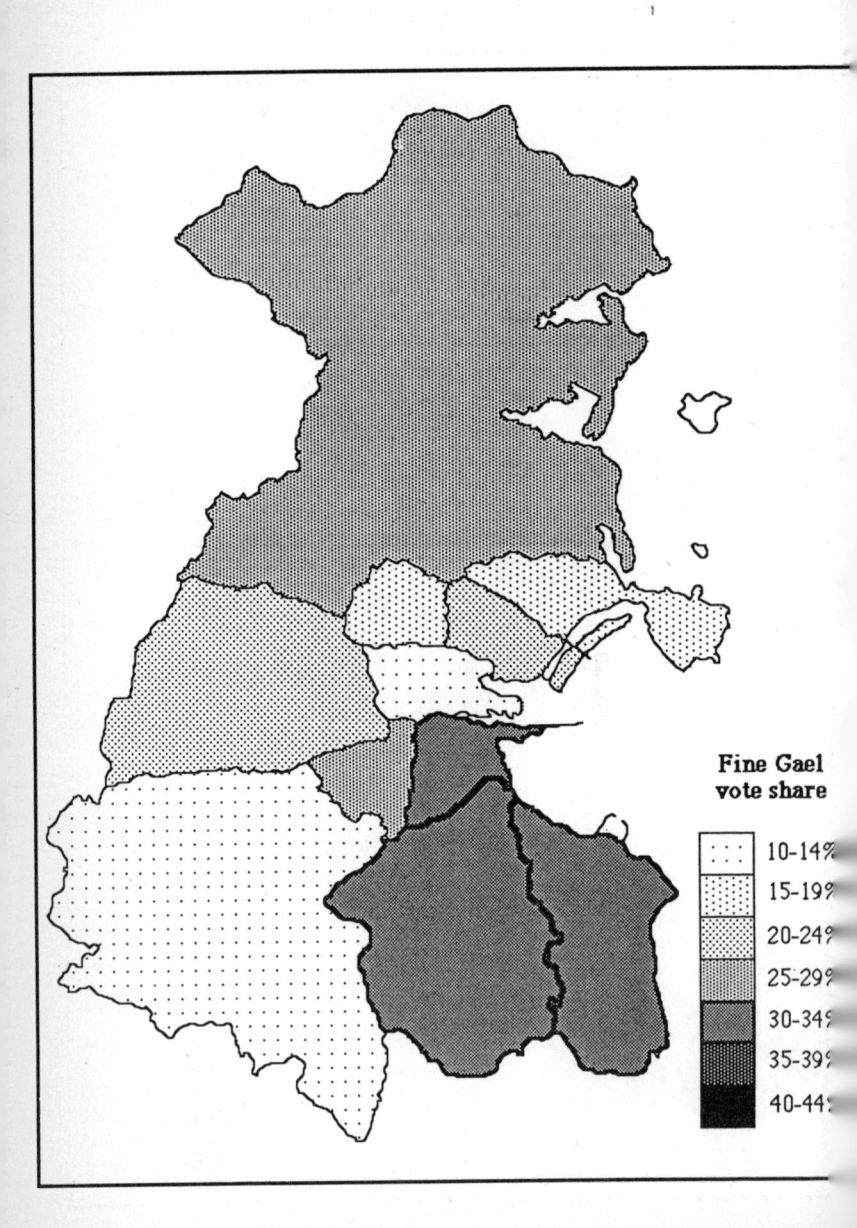

Fine Gael vote share

- 10-14%
- 15-19%
- 20-24%
- 25-29%
- 30-34%
- 35-39%
- 40-44%

Appendix: Results and maps

Figure A7: Progressive Democrat vote share: Ireland

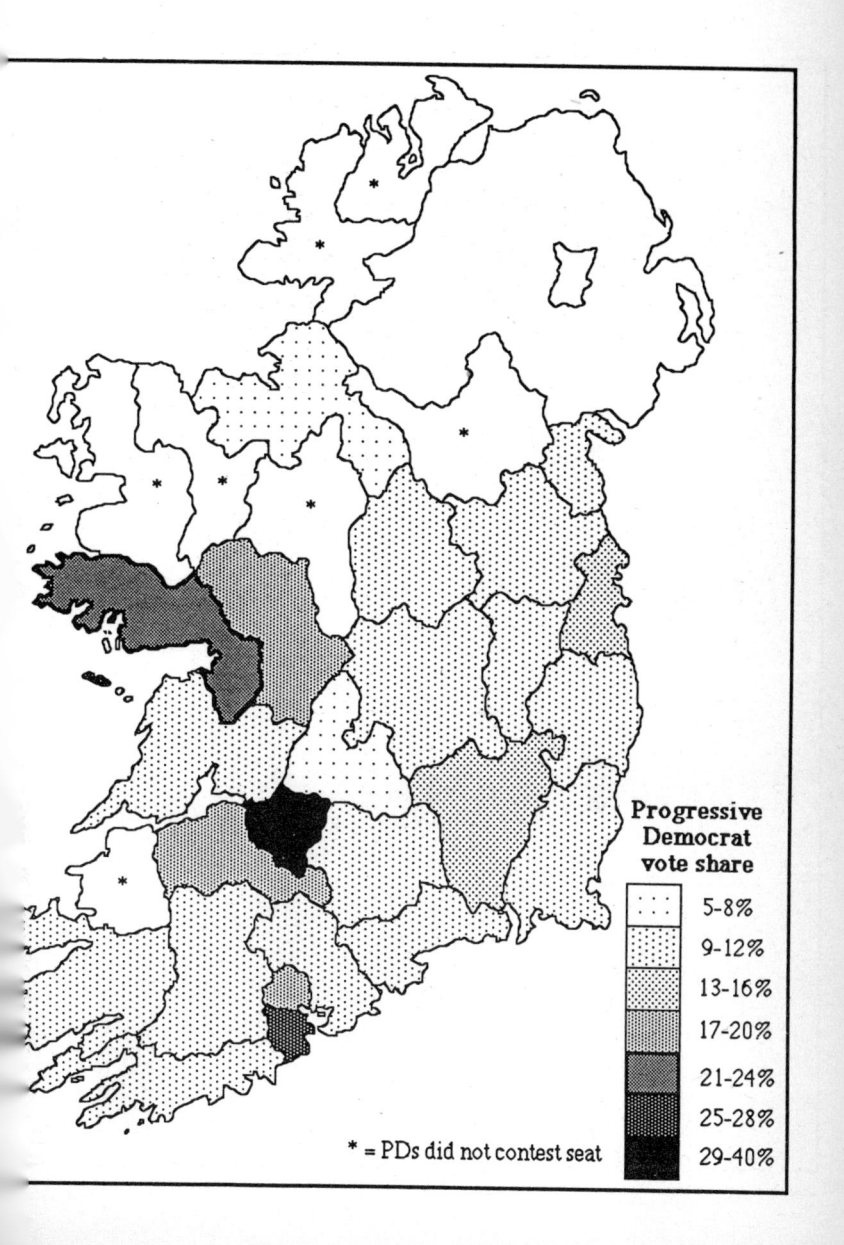

Progressive Democrat vote share

- ⋯ 5-8%
- 9-12%
- 13-16%
- 17-20%
- 21-24%
- 25-28%
- 29-40%

* = PDs did not contest seat

Appendix: Results and maps

Figure A8: Progressive Democrat vote share: Dublin

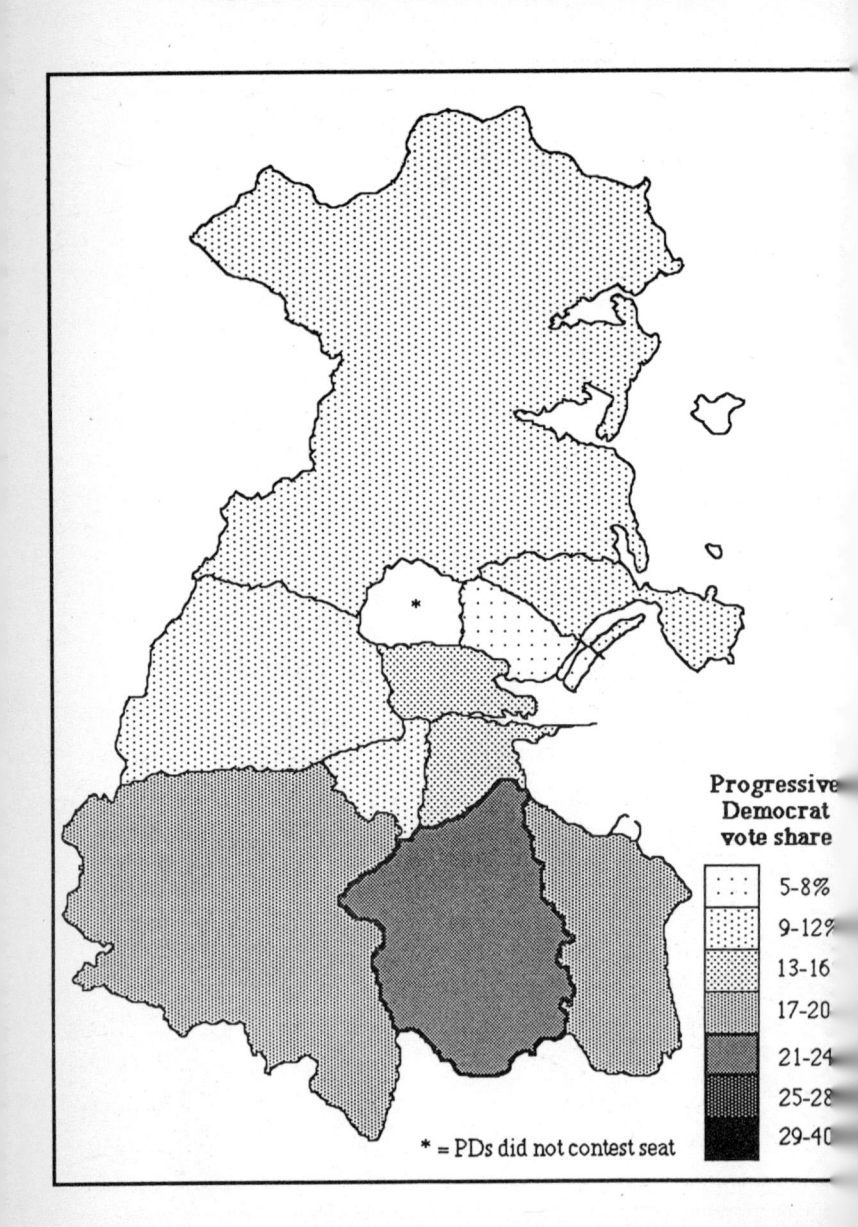

Progressive Democrat vote share

- ⋯ 5-8%
- 9-12%
- 13-16%
- 17-20%
- 21-24%
- 25-28%
- 29-40%

* = PDs did not contest seat

Appendix: Results and maps

Figure A9: Labour vote share: Ireland

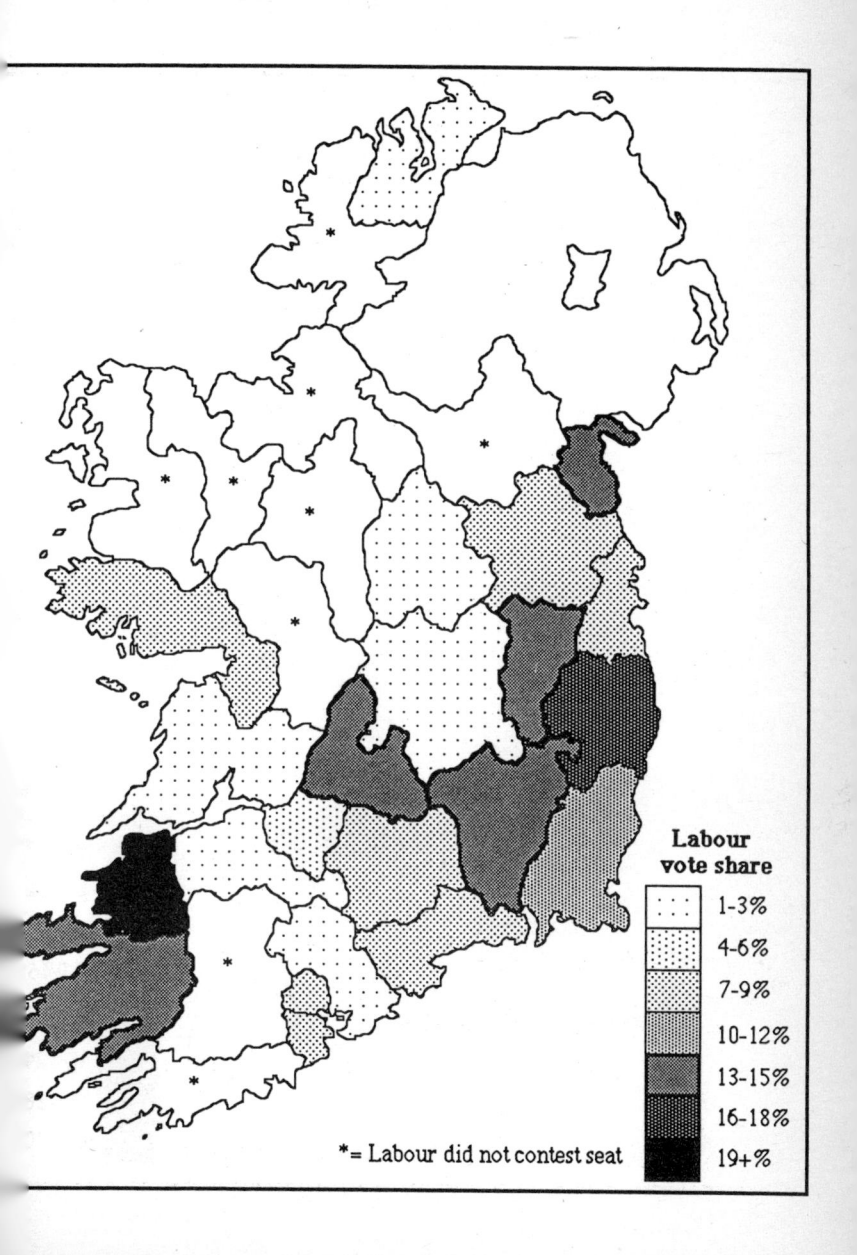

Labour vote share
- 1-3%
- 4-6%
- 7-9%
- 10-12%
- 13-15%
- 16-18%
- 19+%

*= Labour did not contest seat

Appendix: Results and maps

Figure A10: Labour vote share: Dublin

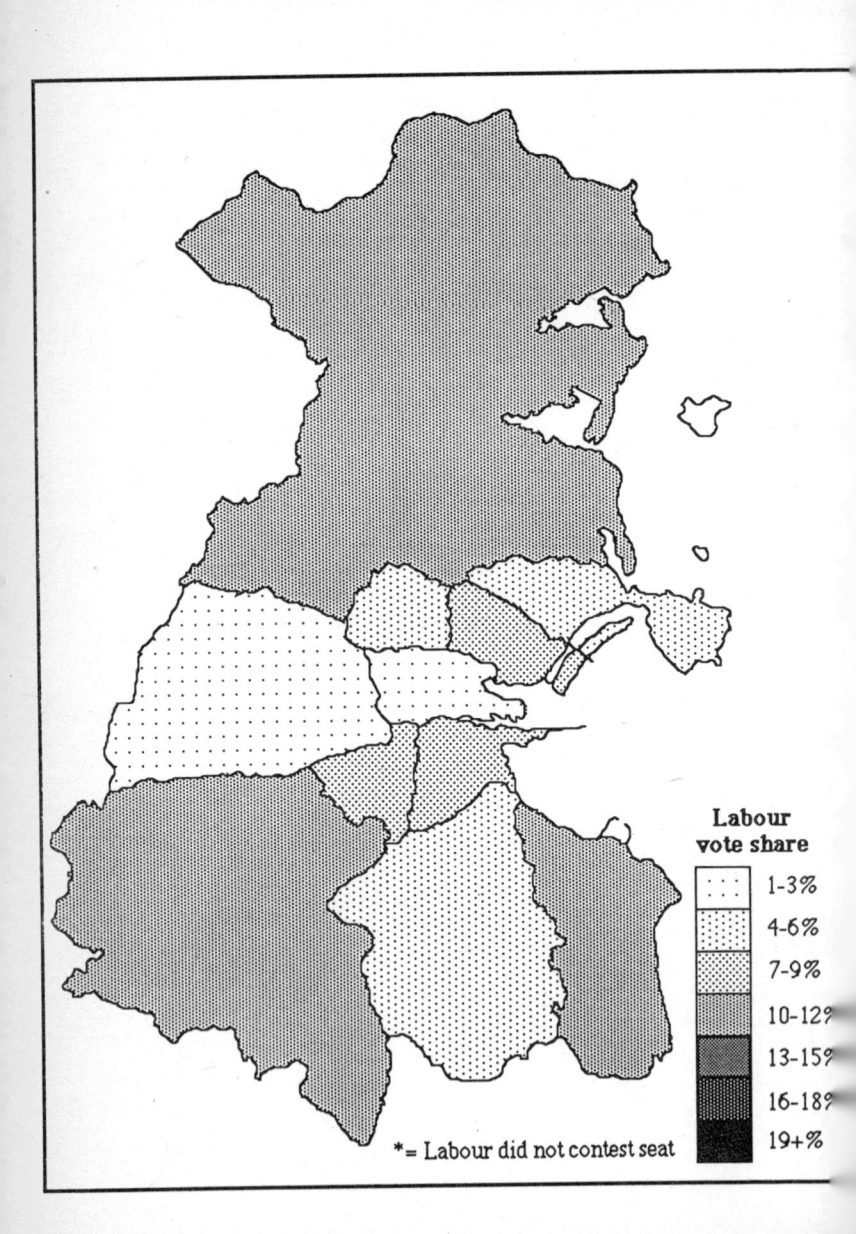

Labour vote share

- 1-3%
- 4-6%
- 7-9%
- 10-12%
- 13-15%
- 16-18%
- 19+%

* = Labour did not contest seat

THE CONTRIBUTORS

John Coakley is Lecturer in Politics in the National Institute for Higher Education in Limerick, and is currently completing a major comparative study of the new nations of Europe.

David M. Farrell is Lecturer in Sociology in the College of Commerce in Rathmines and is currently completing a doctoral thesis on the marketing of Irish parties.

Brian Farrell is Professor of Politics in University College Dublin, and is the author of *Chairman or Chief? The Role of the Taoiseach in Irish Government.* (Gill & Macmillan 1971) and *Sean Lemass* (Gill and Macmillan 1984).

Michael Gallagher is Lecturer in Politics in Trinity College Dublin, and is the author of *The Irish Labour Party in Transition* (Manchester University Press 1982) and *Political Parties in the Irish Republic* (Manchester University Press 1985).

Tom Garvin is Lecturer in Politics in University College Dublin, author of *The Evolution of Irish Nationalist Politics* (Gill and Macmillan 1981) and of a forthcoming study of the Irish nationalist revolution.

Brian Girvin is Lecturer in Politics in University College Cork, is co-editor of *Politics and Society in Contemporary Ireland* (Gower 1986) and editor of *The Transformation of Contemporary Conservatism* (Sage 1988).

Michael Laver, Professor of Political Science and Sociology in University College Galway, is the author of *Playing Politics* (Penguin 1979), *The Politics of Private Desires* (Penguin 1981), *The Crime Game* (Martin Robertson 1982), *Invitiation to Politics* (Blackwell 1983), and *Social Choice and Public Policy* (Blackwell 1986).

Peter Mair is Lecturer in Government in the University of Manchester, co-editor of *Western European Party Systems* (Sage 1983) and author of *The Changing Irish Party System* (Frances Pinter 1987).

Michael Marsh is Lecturer in Politics at Trinity College Dublin and author of a number of articles and book chapters on party politics in Ireland.

Richard Sinnott is Lecturer in Politics in University College Dublin and an expert in Irish political behaviour, on which he is currently completing a major study.